MOUNT RAINIER

A CLIMBING GUIDE

MOUNT RAINIER

A CLIMBING GUIDE

Second Edition

FOREWORD BY BRUCE BARCOTT

MIKE GAUTHIER

THE MOUNTAINEERS BOOKS

3 1257 01622 4429

M THE MOUNTAINEERS BOOKS

*is the nonprofit publishing arm of The Mountaineers Club,
an organization founded in 1906 and dedicated to the exploration,
preservation, and enjoyment of outdoor and wilderness areas.*

1001 SW Klickitat Way, Suite 201, Seattle, WA 98134

© 2005 by Mike Gauthier
All Rights Reserved

Second edition: First printing 2005

No part of this book may be reproduced in any form, or by any electronic, mechanical, or other means,
without permission in writing from the publisher.

Published simultaneously in Great Britain by Cordee, 3a DeMontfort Street, Leicester, England, LE1 7HD

Manufactured in the United States of America

Project Editor: Mary Metz
Editor: Cynthia Newman Bohn
Maps and photo correction: Ani Rucki
Cover design: The Mountaineers Books
Book layout and design: Ani Rucki
All photographs by the author unless otherwise noted
Cover photograph: *David Gottlieb, Winthrop Glacier*
Frontispiece: *Joe Puryear climbs the Emmons Glacier, 13,500 feet.*
Dedication page: *Mount Rainier, Winter Sunset*

Library of Congress Cataloging-in-Publication Data
Gauthier, Mike, 1969-
  Mount Rainier : a climbing guide / Mike Gauthier ; foreword by Bruce Barcott.— 2nd ed.
    p. cm.
  Includes index.
  ISBN 0-89886-956-0
  1. Mountaineering—Washington (State)—Rainier, Mount—Guidebooks. 2. Rainier, Mount (Wash.)—
Guidebooks. I. Title.
  GV199.42.W22R344 2005
  796.52'2'09797782—dc22
                           2004031024

Editor's Note: The authors of sidebar texts are identified by their initials.
   S.C.   Skip Card
   M.G.   Mike Gauthier
   P.K.   Paul Kennard
   E.S.   Eric Simonson

DEDICATION

In memory of JIM BROWN, PHIL OTIS, & SEAN RYAN

CONTENTS

Part I

THE MOUNTAIN

Part II

THE ROUTES

Rangers at Camp Schurman, discussing route conditions with climbers

INTRODUCTION TO THE SECOND EDITION

The second edition builds upon the foundation I established in 1999. Now there are more images, stories, and information from Mount Rainier's experts and aficionados. In this edition, you'll find

- **More photography.** There are 63 new aerial and climbing images. The photo collection has been updated and expanded. Now it's even easier to pick your climbing line, understand the objectives, and visualize the route.
- **More biographies and history.** Climbers come home from Mount Rainier with stories to share. Here you'll learn interesting tales of success and woe—stories that illuminate the routes and locations around the mountain through biographical accounts.
- **More on the glaciers.** Mount Rainier is an arctic island in a temperate sea. Glaciers dominate the mountainous landscape and climbers must contend with them. Now you'll learn more about the ice, glaciers, and geography on the lower 48's most glaciated peak.
- **More on training and guiding.** Many climbers (and almost every Northwest climber) come to Mount Rainier to improve their skills and prepare for other mountains. A third of the climbers attempting the summit go with a guide service. Why is Mount Rainier such a training destination? Because it *is* North America's mountaineering destination. Whether you're learning the ropes, practicing on the glacier, or leading a trip, this guidebook will help you train better and get the most from your Mount Rainier experience.
- **More routes.** New route descriptions and photos of Little Tahoma, Washington State's third highest peak. An airy summit with dramatically steep faces, Little Tahoma is the beautiful satellite peak of Mount Rainier.

Mike Gauthier
January 2005

INTRODUCTION TO THE FIRST EDITION

We were just below Pebble Creek, about to slog up the vanilla plain of the Muir snowfield, when Mike greeted a bandana'd hiker and his friend grubbing some cashews.

"How you guys doing today?" he asked.

"We're doing great, man," said Bandana Boy, wiping the late July sweat from his cheek. "How could we not? We're on Rainier!"

He said it as if we had all rounded a corner and stumbled upon the spot where God had stashed Eden all these years. And in a way, we had. At our feet the heathers, all pinks and whites, were beginning to reclaim the Paradise Valley from the winter's eight-month freeze. To our left the Nisqually Glacier's crevasses split open like creamy wounds in snow unsoiled by the summer's rockfall. Behind us not a single cloud obscured the view of the Tatoosh and southern Cascades. And before us stood Rainier, big and fat and available, blocking out half the postcard sky. This is what makes this place so damn wonderful and so damn dangerous, makes people around here behold this mountain like a god and love it like a grandmother. Mike put it in technical terms: Ripper day.

It's a day like this that makes people take Rainier too lightly, makes them plan a two-day summit run, makes them turn tail and run in shock when a front moves in from the Pacific and spanks every living thing above 6,000 feet. Because the truth of the matter is, this is one hell of a deceptive mountain. On the right day a fit climber may zigzag up the cleaver with no hassle from the gods of wind, rain, and snow. Thing is, we don't get too many right days around here. Most are wrong ten ways from Tuesday. The altitude you may plan for, the endurance you can train for, the will you must summon, but the weather can only be gambled with. There are plenty of other fourteen-thousanders on the continent, but none that will give you the wild ride of Rainier.

One bit of advice: Take your rewards along the way. Take them on the White River trail in to Glacier Basin, at midnight under the stars at Camp Muir, at dawn on Disappointment Cleaver, at midmorning astride an Emmons Glacier crevasse. Emulate John Muir, who lounged in Rainier's mountain meadows on his way to the top, gazing at the mountain "in silent admiration, buried in tall daisies and anemones by the side of a snowbank." The summit may hold some personal triumph, but it does not promise splendors for the eye. You may see nothing but the hazy outline of your climbing partners, or you may catch a glimpse of the tableau that struck Hazard Stevens, the first recorded climber to reach the summit, with awe. "The wind," he wrote, "was now a perfect tempest, and bitterly cold; smoke and mist were flying about the base of the mountain, half hiding, half revealing its gigantic outlines; and the whole scene was sublimely awful."

The American alpinist Alex Lowe once said there were two kinds of climbers: "Those who climb because their heart sings when they're in the mountains, and all the rest." Your guide up Rainier's many faces is one whose heart sings arias. Mike Gauthier is an old-school climber in a young man's body, a mountaineer who's spent one third of his life on Rainier. He has been to the top of this mountain more than 150 times, and in one punishing summer season recorded thirty-six summits—if you do the math, that works out to a run to Columbia Crest every 60 hours or so. Like the bandana'd fellow that day on the trail, when he's on Rainier, Mike's doing great, man. He picks up his mail in the mountain lowlands, but his true home is 10,000 feet high, at Camp Muir and Camp Schurman, where he plies his trade as a national park climbing ranger. If the mountain's glaciers contain the story of every climber who's crossed them, Mike Gauthier has left volumes of joy and sorrow on the faces of Rainier. From him I've learned to distrust the mountain while loving every minute I spend upon it, to use wisdom and prudence and boldness when traveling its flanks, and to have the best time possible under the worst conditions imaginable. Some days I see the summit from Seattle and wonder if he's up there hunkered down against the tempest in the sublimely awful scene. Most days he is.

Bruce Barcott
Seattle, Washington
August, 1999

Climbing teams making their way up the lower Emmons Glacier

ACKNOWLEDGMENTS
FOR THE SECOND EDITION

Mount Rainier attracts, fascinates, and charms a wide variety of enthusiasts: naturalists, sightseers, athletes, public servants, scientists, and some who just come up and say "*Awe*." Spending time with these unique personalities while on the mountain has been a remarkable gift.

The talent and energy of the contributors enrich the value and depth of this guide. They are true experts; I thank them for their advice, voice, and assistance. Skip Card, a long time news reporter covering Mount Rainier, highlights various routes with personal stories and short biographies. Paul Kennard, an ardent skier, National Parks Service (NPS) scientist and Rainier aficionado, shares specific information about Mount Rainier's ice and glacial systems. Eric Simonson has made more than 250 Mount Rainier ascents in the course of thirty years of guiding. He offers sage advice on instruction, client, and guiding success.

While working for the NPS, I have been fortunate to climb, rescue, and ponder the mountain with: Asha Anderson, Charlie Borgh, Aaron Brillhart, Mike Carney, Paul Charlton, Barton Churchill, Cori Conner, Ted Cox, Erik Dodd, Sean Halling, Rebecca Doyle, Sheri Forbes, Nick Giguere, David Gottlieb, Jill Hawk, Matt Hendrickson, Jon Jarvis, Chris Jones, Ty Kellett, Glenn Kessler, John Leonard, Bree Loewen, Stefan Lofgren, Terry O'Connor, Chris Olson, David Orsatti, Dee Patterson, Stoney Richards, Jeremy Shank, Adrienne Sherred, Jill Testerman, Dave Uberuaga, Mark Westman, and Steve Winslow.

Many people have taken the time to write and share their thoughts about the book and the mountain. I greatly appreciate them and welcome more. I salute the professionalism and patience of everyone at The Mountaineers Books. They have again supported my effort to produce a comprehensive Mount Rainier guide and are a pleasure to work with.

To those friends who hang out in Longmire and provide inspiration—Mimi Allin, Fletcher Brinkerhof, Bruce Barcott, Jeff Moran, and Bruce Rushton—my thanks. I am especially grateful to Ed Hrivnak, a climber, rescuer, and pilot. His hands guided the plane behind many of the aerial images.

If you're not climbing alone, then the most important decision you make is with whom you are climbing. My climbing partners are awesome; it's wonderful to be with them in the mountains.

ACKNOWLEDGMENTS
FOR THE FIRST EDITION

This guide would be incomplete without the input and assistance of many kind people, all of whom care very much about Mount Rainier. I would like to recognize the contributions from those who live, work, and study on the mountain for the National Park Service. Your Mount Rainier experience and advice were irreplaceable to this guide: Mike Carney, Rick Kirschner, Uwe Nehring, Garry Olson, Regina Rochefort, Barbara Samora, Darin Swinney, John Wilcox, Steve Winslow, and the Mount Rainier Climbing Rangers. A special thanks to Sheri Forbes for her backstop review.

To those who aided me in a variety of ways: answering questions, offering suggestions, flying me around, reviewing text, and going the extra mile, thank you very much: Rachel Bishop, Skip Card, Jess Jagerman, Scott Hacker, John Kissell, Bob Krimmel, Jack Leicester, Donald Ross, Josh Silverstein, Roger Ternes, and Doug Uttecht. Similarly, I praise the entire staff of The Mountaineers Books for their skilled assistance in producing this guide. It was a pleasure to work with Cindy Bohn, Helen Cherullo, Kathleen Cubley, Margaret Foster, Don Graydon, Alison Koop, Ani Rucki, and Margaret Sullivan.

Many climbers have shared their thoughts, feelings, and stories about Mount Rainier with me. Their personal insights were a highlight during this project and I look forward to seeing them again on the mountain: Alex Bertulis, Eddie Boulton, Dan Davis, Dawes Eddy, Jon Olson, Allen Sanderson, Eric Simonson, Peter Whittaker, and Jim Wickwire.

Very big thanks are in order to Jim Litch and Mark Moore. Their specialized expertise added professional voice and gives climbers insightful information about safely ascending Mount Rainier. And to Bruce Barcott, your encouragement and assistance were very much appreciated.

Finally, my deepest gratitude goes to the friends and climbing partners who have shared time on Mount Rainier with me. Our adventures were invaluable and your personalities have indelibly marked my work. Thank you for your patience, understanding, support, and inspiration: George Beilstein, Lara Bitenieks, David Gottlieb, Chad Kellog, Stefan Lofgren, Tom Mallard, Dee Patterson, Joe Puryear, and Mark Westman.

Part 1

THE MOUNTAIN

Mount Rainier is by far the most coveted summit in the Cascade Range. At 14,410 feet (4,392 meters), just 84 feet lower than highest-in-the-lower-48 Mount Whitney, this glacier-clad volcano towers above Seattle and much of the Pacific Northwest countryside. With the largest system of glaciers in the United States outside Alaska, the giant hulk of a mountain carries thirty-five square miles of ice. Mount Rainier's familiar shape and looming presence is a virtual symbol of the Cascades and the Northwest, and its far-reaching visibility and accessibility make it North America's premiere mountaineering destination. Mount Rainier is a tremendous resource for climbers, offering great mountaineering experiences of many different kinds.

Experienced mountaineers and novice climbers alike test their mettle on Mount Rainier. Steep glacial ice and huge crevasses challenge routefinding and technical skills. The thin air of high altitude strains every climber's constitution. Storms from the Pacific bring heavy snowfall, whiteouts, and fierce winds.

While such demanding conditions provide climbers with a challenging experience, it's the chance for success and the pleasures of mountaineering that are the lures. Limitless views, spectacular sunrises, expansive glaciers, mysterious crevasses, and the possibility of standing on the summit are some of the joys that attract climbers.

Spectacular beauty coupled with rigorous mountaineering conditions also makes Rainier an excellent training ground. Whether you're preparing to climb an even more challenging peak or just want to practice mountaineering skills,

Mount Rainier from Paradise Washington

Rainier has it all. Within a day's hike from your car, you can experience technical climbing on snow and ice, high altitude, and glaciers. A panorama that includes Mount Hood in Oregon plus Mount St. Helens and Mount Adams in Washington is an hour's walk from the Paradise Ranger Station.

This massive volcano dwarfs nearby mountains and can be viewed from Canada to central Oregon. Swollen rivers fed by glaciers divide its flanks. Its lower hills are forested with old-growth Douglas-fir, cedar, and hemlock. Summer meadows attract botanists, photographers, and those seeking an escape from urban life. "The mountain," as local residents refer to Rainier, is a Pacific Northwest icon, and a weather forecast can be obtained by simply asking if "the mountain" is out. With its raw beauty, easy access, and high challenge, it's no wonder that thousands of climbers each year attempt to reach the summit.

A HISTORY OF ASCENTS

Climbers have been attracted to Mount Rainier since at least the mid-nineteenth century, with recorded climbing attempts beginning in 1852. Two surveyors, whose names are not known, ascended via the Emmons and Winthrop Glaciers, probably in 1855. Their accurate description of the summit crater and its steam caves makes their ascent believable, though little else is known of the climb. In July 1857, a party led by Lieutenant August Valentine Kautz reached the high slopes of the upper mountain.

General Hazard Stevens and Philemon Beecher Van Trump are credited with the first documented ascent. Climbing for 11 hours from their timberline camp on August 17, 1870, the pair reached the summit. Arriving late in the day, they were forced to spend the night inside one of the summit crater ice caves, next to the warmth of a steam vent.

Other notable ascents include John Muir's climb in 1888, when A. C. Warner

Near the Beehive on the upper Cowlitz Glacier, a climber ascends towards Gibraltar Ledges.

took the first photographs of the summit and its crater. In 1890, Fay Fuller became the first woman to climb Mount Rainier. By the turn of the century, about 160 mountaineers had reached the top.

Summit attempts became more and more popular, with the number totaling more than a thousand in 1961—about six hundred of them successful ascents. During the late 1950s, '60s, and '70s, climbing fever took hold. Many of Rainier's more difficult routes, like the Willis Wall, Curtis Ridge, and Tahoma Cleaver, saw first ascents. Competition among climbers to complete new ascent lines and variations was fierce. By 1979, nearly eight thousand climbers were attempting the peak each year. By then virtually every climbing line had been ascended, many during the winter.

Mount Rainier attracts climbers now more than ever, with top athletes pushing new limits. Unfinished winter routes, speed climbs, and ski and snowboard descents challenge today's adventurer. On August 9, 2004, former climbing ranger Chad Kellogg went from the Paradise trailhead at an elevation of 5,420 feet to the 14,410-foot summit and back in 4 hours and 59 minutes—a trip that takes the average climber a good 2 days. Backcountry snowboarders carve turns on steep headwalls and glaciers, while ski mountaineers circumnavigate the mammoth peak in less than 3 days. There is always something new to strive toward on Mount Rainier.

More than ten thousand climbers a year now attempt the mountain, with a success rate of about 50 percent. Summit climbs that took weeks in the late nineteenth century are now routinely completed in 2 or 3 days. Times have changed and so has the way we play on Mount Rainier. High-tech gear, sophisticated climbing techniques, instant weather information, route reports, and extensive knowledge of the terrain and geology make the dream of climbing Mount Rainier a possibility for many.

THE NATIONAL PARK

Mount Rainier is managed and protected by the National Park Service. The 235,625 acres of Mount Rainier National Park provide recreational opportunities for the million-plus people of the neighboring Puget Sound metropolitan area and for visitors from around the world.

RANGER STATIONS AND INFORMATION CENTERS

Several ranger stations and other facilities provide services and information useful to climbers.

Climbing Information Center. Located in the historic Guide House, across from the Paradise Inn at the upper end of the upper parking lot at Paradise; 360-569-2211, Ext. 2314; open daily in summer. Climbing rangers staff the station in the mornings, providing permits and route and weather information. This is the best place to call for current reports on climbing conditions. During periods when the station is not staffed, phone callers can listen to recorded information.

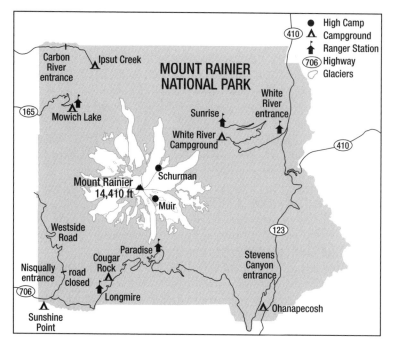

Henry M. Jackson Visitor Center. The large, round building at Paradise; 360-569-2211, Ext. 2328; open daily from early May to mid-October; weekends and holidays the rest of the year. This is the main visitor and information center for the park. National Park interpretive rangers provide a wide variety of information for all visitors, and the center houses interpretive displays about the park's cultural and natural history. You can get a climbing permit here when the Climbing Information Center is closed. The Jackson Visitor Center has the only public shower facilities in the entire park. The showers are on the lower level. Bring quarters; it's worth it.

Longmire Museum and Longmire Wilderness Information Center. These two facilities are near each other at the upper end of Longmire; 360-569-4453 or 360-569-2211, Ext. 3317, April through September, and Ext. 3314, October through March; open daily year-round. Rangers provide permits and information to climbers and other backcountry users on the south and west sides of the park. Go to the museum during periods when the information center is closed.

White River Ranger Station. One mile west of State Route 410, on the White River–Sunrise road on the east side of the park; 360-569-2211, Ext. 6030; open daily from late May to mid-October. Rangers provide permits and climbing and backcountry information for the north and east sides of the park.

Wilkeson Ranger Station. In the town of Wilkeson, on State Route 165, 13 miles before the Carbon River entrance at the northwest corner of the park; 360-569-2211, Ext. 2358; open daily in summer. Rangers provide permits and climbing and backcountry information for the north and west sides of the park.

Mailing address for park headquarters is Mount Rainier National Park, Tahoma Woods, Star Route, Ashford, WA 98304-9751. A call to the main number, 360-569-2211, provides an automated voice menu that gives access to basic recorded information or to the extension numbers of other park offices. The main switchboard extension is 2334.

Internet site for information on climbing at Mount Rainier is *www.nps.gov/mora/climb/climb.htm*. The email address for Mount Rainier National Park is *morainfo@nps.gov*.

GETTING TO THE PARK

Mount Rainier National Park has excellent road access from all directions in summer. Many roads are closed in winter. An entrance fee of $10 pays for a single-vehicle pass valid for 7 days. A Mount Rainier pass good for one year from month of purchase is available for $20. A $50 Naitonal Parks pass is valid at all national parks for one year from month of purchase. Prices are as of 2005.

Following are directions to the park from the metropolitan areas of Seattle, Portland, and Yakima.

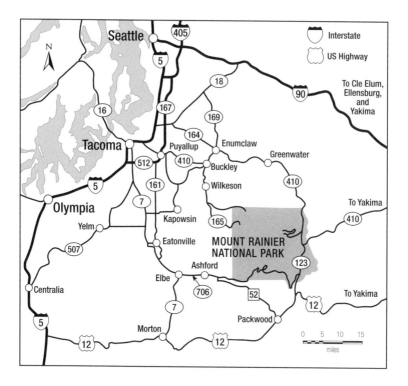

Paradise, Longmire, and Westside Road Climbing Access

Routes on the south and west sides of the mountain are accessed from Seattle or Portland through the Nisqually entrance in the southwest corner of the park—the only entrance open year-round. Access to the routes from Yakima in eastern Washington is through the Stevens Canyon entrance in the park's southeast corner, closed in winter.

From Seattle: Take I-5 south to I-405. Go east 3 miles on I-405 and then take State Route 167 south 21 miles to State Route 512. Drive on State Route 512 for 3 miles, exiting right onto State Route 161 south. Drive south on State Route 161 through Puyallup and Graham to Eatonville. Turn left at the stop sign in Eatonville (look for the Mount Rainier signs) and follow the two-lane country road to its end at a T. From the T, turn left on State Route 7 and continue to Elbe. Stay left on State Route 706 in Elbe and drive 13 miles east through Ashford to the Nisqually entrance of Mount Rainier National Park. The park road from here to Longmire and Paradise is kept open year-round.

From Portland: Take I-5 north to U.S. Hwy. 12. Head east for 30 miles to Morton, then north 17 miles on State Route 7 to Elbe. Connect with State Route 706 in Elbe and travel east for 13 miles to the Nisqually entrance.

From Yakima: Take State Route 410 from Yakima for 18 miles, and turn left on U.S. Hwy. 12. Follow U.S. 12 for 47 miles to State Route 123. Turn right on State Route 123, heading north for 6 miles to the Stevens Canyon entrance. Turn left here onto State Route 706 (Stevens Canyon Road) and follow the signs to Paradise or Longmire. (Routes 410 and 123 and Stevens Canyon Road are closed in winter due to heavy snowfall.)

Mowich Lake and Carbon River Climbing Access

Routes on the northwest side of Mount Rainier should be accessed from Mowich Lake.

From Seattle: Take I-5 south to I-405. Go east 3 miles on I-405 and then take State Route 167 south, following it 11 miles to State Route 18 and the Auburn exit. Follow Route 18 for 1 mile to State Route 164, getting off at the Auburn-Enumclaw exit. Take a left at the stoplight onto State Route 164 heading east to Enumclaw, where the highway will T against State Route 410. Turn right (west) at the stoplight and go 4 miles to Buckley, where you'll go left on State Route 165. Follow Route 165 through Wilkeson and Carbonado and beyond to a one-lane bridge crossing followed by a fork in the road. Stay to the right, continuing 17 miles on the unpaved road to Mowich Lake. (If you are going to Ipsut Creek Campground, stay left at the fork and continue 16 miles up the Carbon River road.)

From Portland: Take I-5 north to exit 127, State Route 512. Stay in the right-hand lane on Route 512 as it becomes State Route 167 north. Continue in the right lane for 1 mile and then exit onto State Route 410. Follow Route 410 east for 11 miles to Buckley, there turning right onto State Route 165. Follow Route 165 through Wilkeson and Carbonado and beyond to a one-lane bridge crossing followed by a fork in the road. Stay to the right, continuing 17 miles on the unpaved road to Mowich Lake. (If you are going to Ipsut Creek Campground, stay left at the fork and continue 16 miles up the Carbon River road.)

From Yakima: Take State Route 410 from Yakima for 69 miles to the east park entrance, at Chinook Pass. Continue on Route 410 for 46 miles around the north end of the park to Buckley, where you'll turn left on State Route 165. Follow Route 165 through Wilkeson and Carbonado and beyond to a one-lane bridge crossing followed by a fork in the road. Stay to the right, continuing 17 miles on the unpaved road to Mowich Lake. (If you are going to Ipsut Creek Campground, stay left at the fork and continue 16 miles up the Carbon River road.)

White River Climbing Access

The White River area provides the best entry and exit (descent) for routes on the north and northeast sides of the mountain.

From Seattle and Portland: Get onto State Route 410 (see driving directions above for Mowich Lake). Stay on Route 410 to the park boundary and arch, 31 miles east of Enumclaw. Continue 5 miles to the White River–Sunrise turnoff, where you'll go right. The White River Ranger Station and entrance booth is 1 mile down the road.

From Yakima: Take State Route 410 from Yakima for 69 miles to the east park entrance, at Chinook Pass. Continue 7 miles along State Route 410 and turn left (west) at the White River–Sunrise turnoff. The White River Ranger Station and entrance booth is 1 mile down the road.

Most of the park's climbing access roads are closed in winter. These include State Routes 410 and 123 within the park, Stevens Canyon Road (State Route 706 between Narada Falls and State Route 123), and the Mowich Lake road. The only road access to the park during late fall, winter, and spring is through the Nisqually entrance. If you intend to climb a route on the east, north, or west side at these times, you'll have to ski or snowshoe along the closed road.

Three vendors provide transportation services from the Seattle area. Grayline bus service offers regular tour schedules to the park from downtown Seattle. For information, call 1-800-426-7532 or 206-626-5208. Rainier Overland operates a shuttle between Seattle-Tacoma International Airport and the town of Ashford and locations within the park. Call 360-569-2604. Rainier Shuttle operates scheduled runs between the airport and Paradise with a stop in Ashford. Call 360-569-2331.

CAMPING AND LODGING

Five of the park's campgrounds charge a fee of $8 to $15 per night; there is no charge for use of the Mowich Lake Campground. The Cougar Rock and Ohanapecosh Campgrounds require a reservation from July 1 through Labor Day weekend. Call 1-800-365-CAMP, 301-722-1257, or 1-888-530-9796 TDD, or write to National Park Reservation Service, P.O. Box 1600, Cumberland, MD 21502. Other campgrounds are first-come, first-served. No campground has showers or RV hookups. There are public showers on the lower floor of the Henry M. Jackson Visitor Center at Paradise.

Sunshine Point Campground is half a mile inside the Nisqually entrance, at an elevation of 2,000 feet. It has eighteen individual sites; open year-round.

Cougar Rock Campground is 2.3 miles north of Longmire, at an elevation of 3,180 feet. It has 173 individual sites and five group sites; open late May to mid-October. Sites may be available upon arrival without reservations if the campground is not full (often the case Sunday through Wednesday nights).

Ohanapecosh Campground is 3 miles north of the southeast park boundary, at an elevation of 1,914 feet. It has 188 individual sites; open late May to mid-October. Sites may be available upon arrival without reservations if the campground is not full (often the case Sunday through Wednesday nights).

White River Campground is 5 miles west of the White River entrance off State Route 410, at an elevation of 4,400 feet. It has 112 individual sites; open mid-June to late September.

Ipsut Creek Campground is 6 miles east of the Carbon River entrance in the northwest corner of the park, at an elevation of 2,300 feet. It has twenty-eight individual campsites; open year-round, depending on snow conditions.

Mowich Lake Campground is in the northwest corner of the park at the end of State Route 165, at an elevation of 4,929 feet. It has thirty walk-in-only sites, about one-quarter of a mile from the parking lot; open mid-May to mid-October.

The two hotels in the park are managed by Mount Rainier Guest Services. The National Park Inn at Longmire is open year-round. The Paradise Inn at Paradise is open mid-May to early October. Both hotels have a full-service restaurant, lounge, and gift shop. For reservations, call 360-569-2275 or write to Mount Rainier Guest Services, P.O. Box 108, Ashford, WA 98304. Their Internet address is *www.guestservices.com/rainier.*

CLIMBING PERMITS

Climbing teams must register and get a backcountry permit from the National Park Service before leaving the trailhead. There is a special-use flat fee of $30 per calendar year collected from each climber. Fees finance the climbing ranger program and support projects that directly assist climbing on the mountain. These projects include: construction and maintenance of solar-assisted outhouses at Camp Schurman and Camp Muir, including helicopter flights to remove the waste, staffing of high camps and ranger stations, and other climbing specific information services. Up to date information can be found at: *www.nps.gov/mora/climb/climb.htm.*

Teams can register in person at any Wilderness information center. For an additional fee of $20 per party, high camp reservations can be made in advance of the climb by calling 360-569-4453 (or by e-mail at *mora_wilderness@nps.gov* or fax at 360-569-2255).

To register, a team fills out a card with information on the dates of the trip, intended route, desired high camp, emergency contacts, essential gear, team members, and climbing experience. If space is available at the intended high camp, the ranger will register the team and file the information card until the climbers return and check out. Data on the card is used if the team becomes seriously overdue or needs rescue.

If your team tries to register for a high camp that is already at permitted capacity, you'll be asked to choose another route or to come back later. You can avoid this problem by climbing during midweek or off-season or by selecting a lightly traveled route. If you must climb on a busy summer weekend or holiday, arrive early and have a backup plan. The Park Service requires solo climbers to obtain written permission from a permanent climbing ranger before ascending the peak. Additionally, climbers under the age of eighteen must provide written permission from a parent or guardian.

Parties may camp for a maximum of 14 days in the backcountry. Maximum

Camp Schurman and the Climbing Ranger hut in May

party size is twelve people, with any team larger than five considered a group party. There are limits on the number of people allowed in many of the high camps and alpine zones. Listed below are the limits for the most popular high camps:

Muir Snowfield	36 people
Camp Muir	110 people
Ingraham Flats	35 people
Camp Hazard	36 people
Kautz Alpine Zone	36 people
Inter Glacier (snow only)	2 parties
Glacier Basin	5 regular parties; 1 group party
Camp Schurman	48 people
Emmons Flats	24 people
Thumb Rock	12 people
Rainier Summit	36 people

Providing a guided climb or mountaineering instruction in exchange for money is illegal within the park, except by one of the following authorized concession services.

Alpine Ascents International: 206-378-1927
American Alpine Institute: 360-671-1505
Cascade Alpine Guides: 800-981-0381
Mount Rainier Alpine Guides: 360-569-2604
Rainier Mountaineering, Inc.: 360-569-2227

PROTECTING THE PARK

The National Park Service manages wilderness areas "in such manner as will leave them unimpaired for future use and enjoyment . . . " Some 97 percent of Mount Rainier National Park is designated by law as wilderness through the Washington Wilderness Act of 1988.

The park owes its existence in part to the efforts of early explorers and mountaineers. They viewed the mountain as a place worth preserving and lobbied to save it from unrestricted and abusive development. But as the park celebrated its centennial in 1999, the pressures of human activity were greater than ever.

Climbers have increasing reason to consider how their actions might affect the wilderness. Standard routes are clogged on summer weekends, and once-

Bivouac on Kautz Cleaver, 9,600 feet

pristine areas are starting to show the signs of climbing use and distress. Issues such as human waste management, overcrowding, and protection of the wilderness are paramount today.

Climbers should practice leave-no-trace principles. The leave-no-trace ethic means taking nothing away and leaving nothing behind: no gear, garbage, climbing wands, food, or anything else. It means the climber avoids creating new tent platforms or rock walls, builds no campfires, and keeps off the fragile alpine plants and meadows. The climber packs along a bag for garbage and carries "blue bags" for human waste disposal (see the later section on blue bags and sanitation). The goal is to leave no sign of your presence, no clue that you were ever there. Consider your actions, and ask yourself, "What impacts might be occurring."

Wilderness is a vital part of American culture and an essential component of our history and identity. Mount Rainier is a major climb that many mountaineers want to check off their list. It also stands as a vital part of America's priceless legacy of wilderness areas and the mountaineering tradition. Do your part to protect its future.

PLANNING A SUCCESSFUL CLIMB

Thoughtful planning and preparation greatly enhance the success and enjoyment of any Mount Rainier climb. Begin with an honest analysis of your mountaineering skills. Rainier is a technical climb requiring a high degree of self-reliance. If you're new to climbing, consider instruction through a mountaineering school or guide service. Or if you're fortunate, you may have friends with a lot of mountain climbing experience who can help you learn the fundamentals of crevasse rescue, routefinding, alpine campcraft, and other mountaineering skills.

Mountaineering is as much a mental exercise as it is a physical event. Sound judgment and mental stamina are important skills to possess. The ability to recognize and evaluate dangerous situations is a critical mountaineering skill. Climbers must constantly assess the abilities of each of their team members and the mountain conditions to ensure safety and success.

Know your strengths and weaknesses. Climbing with confidence (but not foolish pride) helps to avoid hardships and enables many experienced teams to succeed under adverse conditions. It's dangerous to pin your climbing hopes on fate or luck. Don't rely on other climbing teams or the Park Service; success is built on independence and realistic self-confidence.

Choosing the correct teammates is the most important preparatory step. You will be spending at least 2 days with them on the mountain, in the close confines of a tent or on the rope as you cross dangerous terrain. Be sure of your partners' skills and judgment; climb other peaks with them before attempting Rainier. Find out what they are about and how they perform in difficult situations. Other glaciated mountains such as Mount Hood, Mount Adams, and Mount Baker are excellent choices before attempting Rainier. Become familiar with your partners' habits, skills, strengths, and weaknesses. Remember that these people are your best resources if you need help in an emergency. They will share every step of the climb and greatly affect your success and enjoyment. Make sure your teammates' judgment and mountaineering skills are up to the demands of Rainier and your expectations.

PHYSICAL CONDITIONING

Do everything you can to be physically prepared for the immense challenge of Rainier. The climb is incredibly demanding, and lack of physical conditioning prevents many from reaching the summit. Don't let that happen to you.

Solid aerobic conditioning is vitally important. Hiking up hills with a 50-

Disappointment Cleaver, 12,300 feet. A climber pushes towards the summit on a beautiful day.

pound pack is good training. Intense bicycle riding is another great way to build leg and lung strength. Whatever your form of aerobic exercise, do it four times a week for at least an hour, preferably more. Your heart should be pumping hard. In addition, go on at least one extended climb every week during your training regimen. It should last upward of 6-10 hours, and you should be carrying a heavy backpack. Building stamina will pay large dividends on your summit attempt, as the slopes of the mountain are a bad place to discover that you're not in adequate physical condition.

MOUNTAINEERING

Whether climbing Rainier is a once-in-a-lifetime experience for you or just one more challenge in a lifelong passion for mountaineering, the demands are the same. The indifference of the mountain levels the playing field, and the same hazards confront inexperienced and veteran climbers alike. Climbing on Mount Rainier is a sport played always at full strength; there are no handicaps or special considerations for anyone, especially climbers with poor skills.

For dedicated climbers, mountaineering is a pursuit, a way of life, and a state

of being. It's more than ascending a peak. It's living, traveling, exploring, and coexisting within the mountains—off the trails and in the high places of the world. It's about goals, personal accomplishments, friendships, failures, and successes. Sometimes it's about survival. And when the climb is completed, summit or not, consider the next adventure and smile upon your time with friends in the mountains.

Public interest in mountain climbing has always been high. Adventure, successful ascents, and life-threatening danger help to create mountaineering's romantic image. Yet anyone who has climbed Rainier knows there is no glamour in wearing the same clothing for days, eating marginal food out of a pot, or sleeping next to a snoring, smelly partner. Mount Rainier is a place where climbers endure a rudimentary physical existence while pushing toward the extraordinary opportunity to stand on the summit.

In preparing for Rainier, some climbers set out to "conquer" the mountain. Rainier isn't an adversary and the mountain cannot be conquered. It can, however, test one's mettle and push personal limits. The true reward is just being there, ready to confidently proceed toward achieving the goal. Enjoy the experiences along the way. If you don't reach the summit, you'll still have the experience. And if the summit is an important goal, the mountain will always be there for future attempts.

Rainier is much more than physical hardship and climbing challenge. You can also expect your share of relaxation and mental recuperation amid the clean air, silence, and beautiful vistas. Even tent-bound days can be a welcome reprieve from traffic jams, appointments, and the stresses of school or job. Working with teammates toward a common goal forms strong bonds. Triumphs and losses, conversations and stories—all create the fabric of invaluable memories. Mountaineering is extremely demanding, but the joys and rewards outweigh the hardships.

EQUIPMENT AND CLOTHING

Mountaineers depend on specialized gear and clothing to survive extreme environmental conditions. The gear you bring will depend largely on the season, your experience, and on the route you intend to climb. You may be tempted to bring every piece of gear that might come in handy, but remember that weight is your enemy. A heavy pack can compromise both comfort and safety. On the other hand, be sure you have the proper gear to ascend the peak safely at your skill level. You don't want to be caught out at night with a dead headlamp battery, or on the glacier at noon without sunglasses. The Mountaineers recommend carrying the following ten essentials on every hike: extra clothing, extra food, a pair of sunglasses, a knife, fire starters, a first-aid

Climbers gearing up below Sunset Ridge, at the very top of the Colonnade

kit, matches in a waterproof container, a flashlight, a map, and a compass.

You can buy or rent many climbing related items for a Rainier climb at Summit Haus, a mountaineering store in Ashford (360-569-2142). It's best to buy all food for the climb before heading to the park, which offers only limited grocery items at the Longmire General Store.

The following lists give a rundown on gear and clothing you should consider for a Rainier climb. I have never carried everything on these lists at once, but I have carried each of these items at one time or another for a specific reason. Choose the items you will carry, based on the season, the route, and your style of climbing. Don't be overly concerned if you don't have the best pack, boots, Gore-Tex jacket, or ice tool. Just make sure that what you have works when you need it.

Personal Gear

Backpack (4,000 to 5,000 cubic-inch capacity)

Sleeping bag (for summer, a synthetic-filled bag rated between 20 and 40 degrees Fahrenheit; for winter, a synthetic or down bag rated between zero and 20 degrees Fahrenheit)

Insulating pad

Water bottles or water bladder bags (two-quart minimum)

Headlamp (with extra batteries and bulb)

Crampons (properly sized)

Helmet

Ice ax

Harness

Belay/rappel device

Rescue pulley

Snowshoes or skis

Trekking or adjustable ski poles

Runners (loops of webbing or cordage)

Rope-ascending system (mechanical ascenders work best for climbing out of a crevasse)

Carabiners

Knife

Compass, map, GPS receiver

Sunglasses or goggles

Sunscreen and lip protection

First-aid kit

Cup, bowl, spoon

Matches and fire starter

Plastic bags

Mountaineering boots (plastic or leather)

Socks (two pairs)

Long underwear, top and bottom (lightweight to midweight for summer, midweight to expedition-weight for winter)

Shorts

Insulating shirt

Synthetic pile jacket

Wind, snow, or rain jacket

Insulating pants

Wind, snow, or rain bibs or pants

Insulating hat

Sun-protection hat

Gloves or mittens (two pairs)

Gaiters

Specialized medication (prescription, allergy, etc.)

Toilet paper

Chemical heat packs for warming extremities

Book

Playing cards

Earplugs

Camera and film

Journal and pen

Group Gear

Tent or bivy sacks

Stove, cookset, and fuel (one pint per two people per day)

Ropes (60-meter rope for a team of four or five people; 50-meter rope for a team of two to four people)

Snow and ice protection (one snow picket per person, one to five ice screws per party, one or two snow flukes per party)

Climbing wands (25–75 for summer, 75–125 for late spring and early summer, 125–200 for winter)

First-aid kit

Avalanche transceivers and probes

Snow shovels

Snow saw

Repair kit (duct tape, two-part quick epoxy, needle and thread, utility knife with basic tools to adjust all hardware, tent-pole repair supplies, stove maintenance kit)

Altimeter

Cellular phone

Mountaineers Sunrise: Disappointment Cleaver Route, Emmons Variation

SANITATION AND BLUE BAGS

Since so many people visit the upper slopes of Rainier, the disposal of human waste requires special attention. Cold temperatures and lack of soil limit the number and activity of microorganisms that normally break down human waste, and the feces remains. Wind can also transport contaminated snow to clean areas. Not only is this aesthetically displeasing, but it also poses a serious health risk for climbers who gather snow from the area for water.

Outhouses are provided at Camp Schurman and Camp Muir. At other locations on Mount Rainier, use the blue-bag system for human waste disposal. The system utilizes a pair of plastic bags; sets of the bags are issued free when climbers register. During your climb, defecate on the snow away from camp or route. Use the inner blue bag as a glove to pick up the waste. Turn the bag inside out; secure it closed with one of the twist ties that are provided, and deposit it in the second, larger bag. Then twist-tie this bag shut also. Urine should not be collected.

Carry the bag in your pack until it can be properly disposed of. Along the principal Paradise and White River climbing routes, bags can be deposited in one of the black collection barrels placed at central locations. The barrels are flown off the mountain in the fall and the waste is incinerated. If there are no barrels on your route, ask a ranger if there is a drop location near the trailhead. All fecal waste should be blue-bagged and then carried until it can be deposited in a black barrel (not in an outhouse).

WHEN TO CLIMB

Choosing the date of the climb will depend partly upon your goals. If your overriding interest is in reaching the summit, you will probably climb in the summer months, which offer the highest likelihood of success. Those looking for solitude, independent challenges, or a more rigorous mountaineering experience often climb during the off-season.

Spring

Some of the best climbing conditions are found in April, May, and June. A great deal of winter snow remains on Mount Rainier's glaciers and rocky ridges, helping to minimize problems that intensify with the heat of summer: exposed icy sections, large crevasses, and loose, rotten rock. In the spring, the mountain has a pristine, fresh appearance, and you're more likely to have that classic wilderness mountaineering experience. Although you may see other climbers on popular routes, crowds and permit limits are less likely to be an issue.

The unpredictable factor during this time of year is weather. Spring storms are common, and unstable weather may persist for a week or more. If you're traveling from afar, allow 7 days to climb the mountain in case the weather turns sour.

Summer

July and August bring the highest summit success rates. Summer days are long and the weather is predictably better. And by that time, hundreds of preceding climbers have established the standard routes, kicking steps and placing route-marking wands. Summer storms may come, but they are generally short in duration and severity. Consider that summer climbing also means crowds on the popular routes and at high camps. Most teams need 2 to 4 days to reach the summit.

Autumn

September and October can offer excellent weather, but the days are shorter and the nights are colder. Winter snows, like the crowds of summer, have vanished by then, and the glaciers become hard and icy. Moderate ice climbing skills are needed due to the increased hazards of steep, icy terrain. You will also need good routefinding skills as the glaciers become broken, jumbled masses of crevasses and icefalls. The path to the summit will be circuitous. Sudden storms can arise, and your ascent may quickly turn into a winter climb. If you're intent on reaching the summit, give yourself 5 to 7 days for bad weather and difficult glacier navigation.

Winter

Climbing Rainier in winter is truly one of North America's great mountaineering experiences. The mountain is beautifully covered in snow, the routes are more direct, and the crowds of summer are five months away. But be forewarned, climbing Rainier may also be the most grueling and defeating trip imaginable. Short days, fierce winds, cold temperatures, and deep snow all contribute to make standard routes extremely difficult and successful winter ascents a rarity.

Much of your success will depend upon the weather, but there are some things you can do to lessen the chance of your climb turning into an epic. Give yourself a minimum of one week, preferably in late February or March. The days are longer than earlier in winter, and a week should be enough time to give you a chance at the summit.

Get in good physical and mental shape. Actually, get in excellent shape. Winter climbs are hard on the body and demand exceptional endurance. Take cold-weather gear that you've tested and know will keep you comfortable. Assume that you will be rained, blown, snowed, and sunned upon. Carry a spare pair of gloves. Have a full set of insulating synthetic garments—pants, shirt, jacket—topped by a rain jacket and rain pants. Your sleeping bag can have either synthetic or down fill. Down works great, but remember that moisture and down are a bad combination, and down won't dry out on the mountain.

If it's raining while you're still in the parking lot, wait. Staying dry in the rain on Rainier is nearly impossible, and the weather rarely gets better as you ascend. If you do insist on going, remember that constant exposure to the severe trio of rain, snow, and wind is demoralizing and hard on your constitution. Teams that sit out big storms on the mountain are usually eager to go home when the weather breaks, not head for summit. But if the weather is good at the parking lot, GO!

A winter gear list should include a good supply of bamboo wands (150 to 200) to mark your route to high camp and above. The wands are placed on the ascent, then picked up again on the descent. Each person should also carry a snow shovel and avalanche transceiver—along with the knowledge of how to use them and how to recognize avalanche hazards. Depending on conditions, you will probably want snowshoes or skis for a portion of the climb to keep you from postholing through the deep snow. Mount Rainier is noted for heavy snowfall. For many years it held the world record for snowfall within a single year at 1,122 inches (93 feet). A ski descent of at least part of your route can be an incredible experience. Crampons are required for areas where deep snow gives way to wind-scoured ice.

Think ahead about how you will establish your winter camp. Be prepared

Snow bridges and crevasse crossings become more hazardous and exciting late in the summer. The climber negotiates the upper Emmons Glacier in September.

to set up your tent in a storm while your hands are freezing and you're hungry and tired. Secure the tent with wide stakes that can hold in snow, not the thin aluminum stakes that came with it. In addition, you can secure the tent in the snow with extra ice tools, ski poles, or shovels.

In cold weather, check the elastic shock cords that hold the sections of tent poles together. The cords remain elongated when it's very cold, making it difficult to set up a tent because the elastic no longer pulls the poles together. You can retie the cords a few inches shorter or rewarm them in your jacket.

In selecting tent or bivy sites, figure out which way the wind has been blowing and build snow walls to protect your camp. Or build a snow cave, if you've learned how. A snow cave can be a lifesaving refuge during a storm and is much more comfortable than a tent if you're confined inside for any length of time.

How well does your stove work on snow? Does it need a stand to prevent it from melting into the snow? Comforts such as spare socks become invaluable after a few days. Think carefully about what is critical for your success. Always carry a backup or materials for repair for any item you cannot afford to lose. A storm can pin a team down for a week or more. What happens if your stove fails or the tent blows out?

Winter climbers who leave from Paradise must park their vehicles across from the Paradise Inn. This permits plows to remove any new snowfall in the upper parking lot for daily traffic. (Vehicles parked overnight in the wrong place can end up plowed in or buried with snow from the plows.)

During the late fall, winter, and spring, a gate at Longmire prevents uphill traffic toward Paradise at night and while snowplows are at work. It's not uncommon for the gate to remain closed till noon or later during large storms or when the avalanche danger is extreme. To avoid a long wait in Longmire, call ahead and ask when the road is scheduled to be open (360-569-2211, Ext. 2334). Have snow tires on your car and carry tire chains and a shovel. The Longmire Museum, the small building near the road gate, is the best place to get a climbing permit in fall, winter, and early spring.

DURATION OF THE CLIMB

If climbing Mount Rainier is a serious goal, don't limit your outing to 2 days, even in summer on a standard route. Be generous and allow extra days to make the most of the trip. The routine 2-day standard climb may seem attractive to people with limited time, but teams that spend several days on the mountain generally have the best experiences.

There are many advantages to a 3- or 4-day climb, the most obvious being versatility. Why limit the chance of success to 1 or 2 days after so much preparation? If something goes wrong, you'll have additional time to recuperate and try again. Foul weather frequently denies the summit even to strong, well-prepared teams. An extra day or two could allow a second attempt.

Teams can also use an extra day to rest and acclimatize before the summit push. Many climbers reach the top of Rainier at such great effort that they are unable to enjoy the success. That extra day of rest and acclimatization can help a climber stand strong and healthy on the summit, rather than feeling wasted and sick while worrying about the trip down.

Extra days also make trips safer. Teams that spend an extra day at high camp, or take a half day to climb to an advanced high camp, are better prepared for the demands of a long summit day. A well-positioned and rested team moves more efficiently. Being swift and strong enables rope teams to move through hazardous areas rapidly, spending less time exposed to uncontrollable mountain variables such as rockfall or avalanches.

For many people, climbing Mount Rainier is an adventure they have planned and dreamed about for months, if not years. Building in an extra day or two will give you a chance to enjoy all aspects of the climb. It's a margin for both safety and enjoyment—a simple way to acknowledge that there's no good reason to hurry through the climb only to rush back to the parking lot, the highway, and the daily routine.

SAFETY AND SURVIVAL

Climbing Mount Rainier can be deadly. This section of the book is dedicated to your safety and will address mountaineering hazards, how to avoid them, and what to do if you run into trouble. I've heard climbers dismiss warnings, claiming that their greatest danger lies in driving their car to the trailhead. Maybe, maybe not. Park Service statistics indicate that climbers are more likely than any other park visitors to be killed or seriously injured. The resources and technology exist to help make climbing safer, but the sport is inherently unsafe.

The objective dangers of mountaineering are evident. These are the hazards we have no control over: crevasses, avalanches, lightning, blizzards, high altitude, rockfall, and icefall. But you can learn to recognize these hazards and to reduce your exposure to them. (See the full discussion on avalanches in a later section of the text.)

Subjective hazards—the ones we have some control over—are equally threatening. They include such negative factors as improper training, inadequate equipment, or poor conditioning. Is your team physically and mentally ready for the rigors of mountain climbing? Can you rely upon your teammates if you are in trouble? Do you know how to perform a self-rescue? What happens if someone becomes sick from the altitude?

The most dangerous element on the mountain is the human one: the climbers themselves. Poor planning and bad decisions contribute to virtually every mountaineering accident. Humans cause most of the avalanches that kill. Many lost or distressed climbers ignore the obvious signs of deteriorating weather. Frostbite, hypothermia, dehydration, mountain sickness, and other medical problems all have precursors and are conditions that can be reversed in the field if identified early. (See the detailed section on medical problems in a later section of the text.) Climbers have the ability to control many of the dangers that can become life-threatening emergencies. The importance of being independent and prepared for any situation cannot be stressed enough. Self-reliance during an emergency is critical to your chances of survival and may prevent small incidents from turning into huge problems.

AS THE WEATHER TURNS

Inclement weather on Mount Rainier contributes to many mountaineering accidents, epics, and problems. Every year, climbers are rescued or bodies are recovered because bad weather forced them to make tough decisions. (See the

This National Park Service warning sign was destroyed by weather. The message, however, remains as true as ever. © Eric Simonson.

later section on weather for a full discussion of Mount Rainier's weather patterns, season by season.)

Climbing teams on the way to the summit from high camp should carry a map, compass, and GPS receiver, plus bivouac gear and a snow shovel. If the weather begins to deteriorate, reassess the situation. What will happen if conditions worsen? Are team members prepared to spend the night high on the mountain? What will happen if the storm persists for days? It's certainly OK to continue climbing in poor weather, but teams who do so need to possess the resources to help themselves. It's irresponsible to leave the proper gear back at high camp, expecting a rescue if an emergency arises.

Placing wands to mark the route, using a map, compass, and GPS receiver (I'm a fan of GPS), staying hydrated, and eating regularly may allow skilled and confident teams to reach the summit even under poor weather conditions. Teams that lack any of the essential equipment, water, or food should turn around in deteriorating weather—or expect the worst. Some practiced climbers choose to go extra light, leaving safety items behind in the interests of speed and reduced weight. This is an acceptable decision only for teams with a lot of experience in the mountains. Seasoned climbers understand the severity of poor weather and usually elect to turn back. A disregard for the weather can lead to deadly accidents. Open a mountaineering accident journal, and this scenario will be found occurring year after year, all over the world.

Whiteouts, blizzards, freezing rain, and high winds are the common weather conditions that frequently trouble climbers on Rainier. It's difficult to negotiate technical terrain in these circumstances. Climbers become disoriented and are unable to recognize other mountaineering hazards, such as crevasses, icefalls, or increased avalanche risk.

In a whiteout, as fog and clouds move in, the terrain and atmosphere merge into one. The light is flat and even, making it impossible to distinguish features and slopes. Objects appear to be in the distance but in reality are only one or two feet away. It even becomes difficult to tell up from down on the slope. When this happens, stop moving, dig in, and wait it out. Teams on a glacier should not attempt to navigate by map and compass, because these won't indicate crevasses.

Thunderstorms with lightning occur every year, particularly on the north and east sides of the mountain. The most common result of these storms is lower-elevation forest fires, but lightning is also a serious danger for climbers, who carry a plethora of metal objects—some quite long and thin that can act like lightning rods. The hut at Camp Schurman has been struck by lightning, and so have climbers on the Muir Snowfield. The best defense is to avoid buildings and high places. When large thunderheads begin to build or approach the mountain, descend immediately. Climbers on the north and northeast sides are at a disadvantage when storms rapidly circle the mountain from the south and catch them by surprise. If this happens, find cover, possibly in a crevasse that can be walked into. Stay low so you don't become a conductor.

AVOIDING ACCIDENTS

The best way to avoid climbing accidents or to stop them before they cause serious injury is to become familiar with basic climbing techniques such as roped glacier travel, ice ax arrest, team rescue and self-rescue from crevasses, and crampon techniques. You can test your skills on smaller glaciated peaks such as Mount Baker, Mount Hood, or Mount Adams before attempting Rainier.

Even after earnest training, the risk of having an accident remains. Climbing on Mount Rainier demands your complete attention. Accidents such as slips on steep snow or tripping on crampons are common. Be sure your crampon straps are tucked away and that your gaiters fit snugly. Keep crampons well-adjusted and tightly fitted to your boots. If they work loose, readjust them immediately in a safe location. Crampons ball up with snow during soft, wet conditions, so bang the snow out of the spikes with your ice ax. If conditions demand frequent banging, consider removing the crampons.

Most of the terrain on Mount Rainier is rated as moderate, but don't become complacent because the terrain lacks obvious technical difficulties or severe exposure. If a short slip isn't stopped immediately, the momentum quickly leads to a loss of control and a fast and dangerous slide down the slope. Practice self-arrest techniques individually and as a team, and make them second nature.

There will always be unavoidable hazards on Mount Rainier. Objective dangers such as rockfall, avalanches, crevasses, and icefalls can spell disaster for a team that is in the wrong place at the wrong time. (Avalanches are dealt with in detail in a later section.) Following are ways to limit your exposure to the dangers of rockfall, crevasses, and icefalls.

First of all, look with suspicion on any Rainier climbing route that involves exposure to rock. The rock on Rainier is volcanic—rotten and unstable. During cold periods, snow and ice help to hold the rock together. Warm weather and solar radiation melt the snow and ice, bringing a significant increase in rockfall hazard.

The best defense is to move quickly and to never take rest breaks in exposed

A climber with a broken ankle is lowered down the Inter Glacier.

locations. A helmet will afford protection from small falling rocks. In fact, a helmet is generally a good idea on Rainier, offering head protection during a crevasse fall and defense against any gear dropped by climbers above.

The glaciers on Mount Rainier are noted for large crevasses and for those especially steep, turbulent and chaotic sections known as icefalls. These areas change dramatically from season to season. Winter and spring snowfall blankets crevasses and fills in icefalls. Summer heat melts this snow, and the glaciers become broken and crevasses become more noticeable. As late summer and fall arrive, the glaciers become dry and icy, with a majority of crevasses exposed.

Crevasses and icefalls are dangerous any time of year, and it's strongly recommended that climbers rope up on any glaciated terrain. Extra care is needed in winter and spring, when crevasses are hidden under fresh snow and climbers are in danger of disappearing through hidden holes. Although crevasses become more apparent in the summer and thus are easier to avoid, there is still a danger of falling into them while crossing weakening snow bridges.

Icefalls melt throughout the spring and summer. As they do, large blocks of ice and snow tumble down the mountain, sometimes thousands of feet, destroying everything in their path. These large avalanches of ice seem to come at random, occurring both day and night, though activity is usually less during the colder periods. Later in the summer and early fall, glacier surfaces become hard and icy. Most of the snow bridges have melted out by then, and climbers must make an end run around crevasses. Icefalls are extremely broken, and climbing them would be time-consuming and dangerous.

Move quickly over snow bridges and under or through icefalls. As with rockfall hazard areas, don't stop for breaks; the less time in the danger zone, the better. Generally speaking, there is safety in a controlled speed. Climb when temperatures are below freezing, making the snow and ice more stable. In the summer, aim for an alpine start—getting under way well before dawn. On hard and icy terrain, move carefully and be aware that it's difficult to self-arrest on glacier ice.

Many climbers feel that seat glissading is an innocuous descent technique, but there are good reasons to avoid it. It can be difficult to get a good view of the terrain below while glissading, making it easy to slip into a crevasse. It's all too easy to catch a boot or crampon in the snow, then tumble, and lose equipment or sprain an ankle, dislocate a knee, or break a leg. Generally speaking, it's much safer to walk down.

TEAM DYNAMICS

Rainier guide Eric Simonson put it well: "Safety isn't just knowing how *you're* doing, it's knowing how *everyone* is doing." At the same time that you pay close attention to your own climbing, watch for signs of problems within the team.

If a member exhibits some continuing problem with the climb, stop to assess the situation and act to correct it.

Teams need to be able to recognize dangerous situations and take precautions to ensure the safety of all members. Belays and the placing of protection—such as ice screws or snow pickets—may be necessary to prevent crevasse falls or other slips that could result in catastrophe for the whole team. On the other hand, if the team decides to proceed without belays or protection, it may actually be safer not to rope up, so that the fall of one climber cannot result in the entire team careening down the mountain. This approach is usually taken on the Success Cleaver climb, for example.

Teams should stay together on the mountain, both on the ascent and descent. Some members of a party may be tempted to charge ahead of teammates who are not moving as rapidly. But leaving part of a team behind can lead to trouble, particularly when someone is having difficulties or during deteriorating weather. Teammates are responsible for each other until everyone is safely off the mountain and back at the car, and letting the selfish goals of a few supersede the needs of a team is dangerous. Teammates are the best resource for help during an emergency, but once a party splits up, that resource is seriously compromised. The mission of a true team is to stick together, work through tough situations, and support one another.

A CLOSE CALL

Michael Corroone, 51, and Dan Gallagher, 36, set out to climb Mount Rainier on April 11, 1999. Severe weather thwarted their summit attempt, and after a night at Camp Muir, they descended back to Paradise. High winds, low visibility, and whiteout conditions persisted through the descent, forcing the two to follow compass bearings down the Muir Snowfield. At around 8,800 feet, the un-roped pair simultaneously fell into a deceptively covered crevasse on the Paradise Glacier, at the eastern edge of the Muir Snowfield. Dan's backpack caught on the crevasse's slender entrance, and he was able to extricate himself. Michael, however, slipped through the crack and disappeared.

Dan set up a snow anchor and lowered a rope to to his partner, but Michael was wedged in such a way that he could do little to assist himself and could not tie off on the rope. After waiting for some time for cell service coverage, Dan used his cell phone and called 911, reaching an operator in Oregon. The call was transferred to the Mount Rainier communications center and Tom Mallard and I, were surveying winter damage to the Camp Schurman hut, were notified and asked to initiate a rescue. We reported that the weather was improving on the upper mountain, but below us the cloud deck was solid. A helicopter from Seattle managed to break through the ceiling and transported us from Camp Schurman to the 9,200-foot level on the Muir Snowfield above the accident site.

We descended to the crevasse where Dan reported that his partner had been trapped in the crevasse for over 2 hours and that there had been no communication between them for the last hour and a half. I quickly set new rescue anchors, fixed a rope, and hastily rappeled into the crevasse to assess the situation. I found Michael 80 feet below the surface. He was incredibly hypothermic and tightly wedged between the icy walls, suspended from his armpits by his backpack straps, like a parachutist trapped in a tree. By the time I arrived, he was unable to feel or use his arms and could do little more than press his legs against the crevasse walls to prevent slipping further.

Dangling from my rope, at times upside down, it took me an hour to cut off Michael's pack and snowshoes, free him from his precarious position, pull him onto a small ledge, and put him in a harness. Tom and Dan then hoisted him to the surface with a Z-pulley system, and I climbed out, helping along the way.

As the weather was improving, the helicopter returned to fly us all off the mountain. Shortly after it landed, a cloud enveloped the ship. Super-cooled rime ice quickly coated the rotors and turbine intakes. Pilot Doug Uttecht told us, "I don't want to, but I have to shut down."

With little daylight left and few bivouac resources the urgency of our situation was rapidly increasing. We scraped the ice from the rotors and turbine intakes of the helicopter with snow pickets. After 30 minutes of effort, the clouds again cleared, and Uttecht decided he'd try to lift off carrying only Michael. Fortunately, conditions rapidly improved, and he was able to return several times to retrieve Dan, Tom, and myself.

M.G.

RESCUES

No one plans to need rescue, but every year the Mount Rainier climbing rangers conduct numerous searches, rescues, or body recoveries. Rainier Mountaineering, Inc. and Mountain Rescue units from the region often assist by contributing strong field teams.

Self-reliance and team rescue is your best offense in the event of an emergency such as a crevasse fall, illness, or traumatic climbing injury. Do everything possible to handle the situation immediately. Specialized first aid and technical rope rescue training can prove invaluable in an emergency. The American Red Cross, climbing clubs, and community colleges are among the organizations that offer courses in cardiopulmonary resuscitation (CPR),

A Chinook helicopter lowers a climbing ranger via a hoist system. (12,200 feet, Kautz Cleaver)

mountaineering-oriented first aid (MOFA), standard and advanced first aid, emergency medical technician (EMT), and Wilderness First Responder (WFR) training. Team members with such training can contend with shock, serious bleeding, airway obstruction, broken bones, spinal injuries, and other medical emergencies.

There are also technical rope rescue schools. Many now specialize in wilderness and high angle rope rescue. These types of skills are of great value and provide confidence during intense rescue situations.

If the emergency becomes a crisis beyond the ability of your team, enlist the aid of other climbing parties. Generally accepted mountaineering etiquette asks that climbers assist each other during emergency situations. If the team remains in serious trouble after exhausting its own resources, one member should be sent to obtain help or another climbing party should be asked to pass the word. If a cellular phone is available, give it a try. Cell phones perform with mixed results on the upper mountain. Determine before the climb which emergency phone numbers would be helpful and bring them with you. During an emergency, call 911—but be aware that you may get a dispatcher in Yakima,

Seattle, Tacoma, Ellensburg, or in some cases Oregon, who will then have to transfer the call and information to the park. To reach the Park Service directly, call 360-569-2211, Ext. 2334. Save the phone's batteries for the emergency only. Don't call friends and relatives to inform them of the situation; reserve the phone for communicating with your rescuers and ask them to pass messages along for you.

Climbing rangers staff the high camps at Muir and Schurman during the summer. They have rescue gear, medical supplies, and Park Service radios. Climbers have access year-round to emergency radios inside the community hut at Muir and the hut at Schurman.

After the emergency is reported, a member of the team should keep a record of events. Record details such as how an illness or injury occurred, the patient's medical symptoms, duration of periods of unconsciousness, pulse and respiration rates, past medical history, medications used, and any other information that can assist diagnosis and care.

Continually reassess what can be done to facilitate the rescue. If a helicop-

Climbing rangers fix lines and lower off Liberty Cap. Climbers become injured or stranded on Liberty Ridge nearly every year.

ter is called, try to get the victim to a large, flat area for pickup. Many routes lack such locations, but they do exist here and there. If the rescue involves carryout on a litter, have patience while rescuers are on the way. Continue to eat, drink, and stay warm. Keep the patient comfortable, and treat the illness or injury as best you can.

Ground rescuers will be moving under heavy packs, carrying medical supplies, climbing and rescue gear, extra food, and other equipment to aid in the emergency. A team awaiting help can sometimes assist by descending part way down the mountain to meet rescuers. The lower on the mountain you can safely go, the quicker the rescue can proceed and the sooner the patient will be in the hands of a doctor.

A team in trouble cannot automatically expect helicopter rescue. The Park Service launches a helicopter only when there is a life-threatening or limb-threatening emergency and when weather and other conditions safely permit. Otherwise, ground rescuers will most likely respond to the emergency and may take a day or more to reach the team, especially in a remote location or during poor weather.

The taxpayer gets the bill for virtually every rescue, since climbing fees do not pay for such operations on Mount Rainier. If a climbing team is found to be grossly negligent, it can be billed for the cost of its rescue.

WEATHER

by Mark Moore and Mike Gauthier

The weather on Mount Rainier is as diverse and unforgiving as the terrain. Strong storms know no season; high winds, rain, snow, and subfreezing temperatures can occur any month of the year. Many mountaineering accidents are weather related, and climbers always need to factor the season and weather into their plans. Keeping track of mountain weather can be critical to a safe climb.

Mount Rainier generates its own weather. Because of local variations in wind flow, lifting air, sinking air, and Rainier's great height, amazing changes in weather are common from day to day, hour to hour, and elevation to elevation. Cool temperatures, light winds, and foggy skies near Paradise may give way to clear skies only an hour's hike above on a typical summer day. And Rainier's weather can be extreme. When it's wet, it's damp and penetrating; when it's windy, it's cutting and fierce; and when it's cold, it's brutally frigid.

Prepare for the weather by watching changes and trends. Use the radio, television, or Internet to get tuned into the weather situation before the climb. Up-to-the-hour weather observations for Paradise on Mount Rainier are available in late fall, winter, and early spring at the Northwest Weather and Avalanche Center's website: *www.nwac.noaa.gov*. The site includes other useful information such as daily mountain weather and avalanche forecasts. You can find out if the weather has been cold and wet or warm and dry; if it has been windy or calm. This knowledge will help in selecting the appropriate equipment and gaining a good idea of what's ahead: deep snow, ice, wind, sun, cold, or whatever. The phone number for the Northwest Weather and Avalanche Center is 206-526-6677. Begin with a solid forecast and then observe and mentally record meteorological events from the beginning of the climb. Maintain a mental picture of what is happening with the weather. The best way to learn weather is to keep your eyes open. Use telltale clues to continually update your weather information and your personal weather forecast. Then use this knowledge to modify routes, camp locations, and summit climb preparations.

When on the mountain, use the common clues that indicate deteriorating weather. Early storm signs include cloud caps (lenticular clouds); increasing cirrus clouds from the west or southwest; a lowering barometer (rising altimeter); and changing or backing winds. Increasing winds and precipitation are obvious signs of changing weather. Monitor these clues throughout the climb.

The weather on Mount Rainier can be dramatically different from what it is elsewhere in Washington. The mountain and its 12,000 feet of vertical relief

A team of climbers pushes through high winds, whiteouts and rime ice in August; Emmons Glacier.

directly influence what's happening on the peak. For example, moist air from the Pacific cools by approximately 3.5 degrees Fahrenheit (2 degrees Celsius) for every 1,000 feet (roughly 300 meters) that it rises. This cooling produces temperature differences of 30 degrees Fahrenheit or more between Paradise at 5,420 feet and the summit at 14,410 feet.

As the moist air rises and cools, it condenses, producing precipitation and whiteout conditions. A good example of this is a lenticular cloud sitting on the upper mountain. While this rising air can greatly increase precipitation on the windward side of the mountain, the sinking air common on the lee side may help to minimize precipitation as it warms and dries. Therefore it's not uncommon to find clearer weather on the Winthrop and Emmons Glaciers on the northeast side of Mount Rainier.

Other local weather effects induced by the mountain include small-scale wind eddies and turbulent swirls—formed as winds interact with ridges, ribs, valleys, gullies, and rock outcroppings. Also, solar heating and radiant cooling produce substantial daily cycles of rising and falling mountain winds. During the clear nights and early-morning hours of summer, heat loss off the snow, rock, and ice creates a river of cold, dense air that flows down the mountain.

Conversely, solar radiation warms air close to the surface during the day, producing an up-mountain wind during the late-morning and afternoon hours.

SPRING: APRIL TO EARLY JUNE

After months of harsh winter weather, storm cycles decrease their intensity as spring arrives. Storms are less frequent and less powerful in April and May. Breaks in the weather allow the sun to bring the year's first real warming to the mountain.

Spring storms are often followed by intense heating from the sun as days become longer. This causes a rapid warming and melting of snow as the air temperature at Paradise remains above freezing.

Spring days may seem like summer, but don't be deceived into thinking summer has arrived. During this transition in seasons, sudden and unexpected storms are still likely. April averages 10 inches of measurable precipitation and close to 70 inches of snowfall. Rain at Paradise means heavy snow on the mountain. Continue to watch for signs of approaching storms, and look for clues to a weakening snowpack and increased avalanche danger. Expect changing weather even during a pattern of apparent stability.

SUMMER: LATE JUNE TO EARLY SEPTEMBER

Summer weather provides the most stable opportunities for climbing. Good conditions make Rainier a popular summer climb.

Clear, warm weather is likely in late July, August, and early September. Even during the worst of years, Paradise has received only 6 inches of snowfall during August. Both July and September have recorded years of no measurable precipitation. A high-pressure ridge normally develops off Washington's coast during these months. It pushes storm energy to the north or splits and weakens its intensity while still offshore. It's not unusual for freezing levels to hover at 12,000 to 14,000 feet as precipitation dwindles significantly.

June and early July are a bit more temperamental than late summer. Springlike storms that deposit significant snow are common. The effects of solar radiation are the greatest during the long days of June and early July, particularly on clean, bright, reflective snow. Such reflection makes cirques and bowls seem like ovens, even above 10,000 feet. This can lead to significant surface snowmelt and the dangers to climbers of wet, loose avalanches, weakening snow bridges, rockfall and icefall, sunburn, snow-blindness, and dehydration.

Cold, clear nights result in radiant cooling of the snow. As the snow refreezes after the day's heat, a substantial crust is formed. This crust can make for good cramponing and climbing on crystal-clear days.

AUTUMN: MID-SEPTEMBER TO EARLY NOVEMBER

During late September and October, the jet stream begins to dip southward into the Pacific Northwest. The increased onshore flow associated with decreasing heat from the sun allows storms to bring a surge of prewinter conditions to the mountain. It's entirely possible to find a foot or two of snowfall at Paradise in September and October. But just as possible is the return of a summerlike high-pressure ridge, sometimes for a week or two. When this happens, expect brilliant clear days and cold nights, a so-called Indian summer.

With November and December approaching, the sun recedes lower on the horizon, producing a strong temperature contrast between the north and south poles. During this imbalance the onshore flow over the Pacific Northwest increases even more. Pacific-born storms now bring heavy rain, snow, ice, wind, and lowering freezing levels. Winter has started and climbers should be prepared for blizzard conditions.

WINTER: LATE NOVEMBER TO LATE MARCH

Winter on Mount Rainier generally means frequent clouds and heavy precipitation. Several major storms hit the mountain each winter. The storms produce heavy rain or substantial snowfall and high winds, particularly above tree line. Storms can last for a week or more and may deposit 80 to 100 inches of snow and bring temperatures below zero degrees Fahrenheit and winds in excess of 100 miles per hour. Anyone climbing in winter should be prepared for hostile conditions.

Due to Washington's temperate climate, it's not uncommon for the freezing level to rise above 9,000 feet in winter. During these periods, the avalanche hazard is greatly intensified and traveling on suspect slopes should be avoided.

Inevitably the freezing level will lower back to between 2,000 and 5,000 feet. Rain-soaked and windblown snow becomes stable, crusty, and icy, and pockets of wind-deposited snow fill the cracks of the glaciers, ridges, and rocks. The climbing can be very good at this time if significant snowfall doesn't follow immediately.

Climbers should be aware that storms change the appearance of the landscape. Whiteouts severely impair visibility, making navigation much more difficult. High winds can slowly blow climbers off track, even when using a compass. Rime ice attaches itself to any exposed object, cloaking the appearance of rocks. A few hours of heavy snowfall and high winds will quickly form new cornices, and rocks once visible may become buried. A boot track will vanish within 10 minutes. Recognize these added challenges of a winter storm.

Some winters experience a break in the westerly flow of storms. This happens when a large upper ridge of cold air flows over the Pacific Northwest, resulting in several days to a week or more of clear weather, especially at higher elevations. During this time, northeast and northwest winds commonly buffet the mountain.

As this high-pressure, cold-air ridge moves eastward over Washington, northerly winds yield to weak westerlies, increasing the high clouds in the sky and

the freezing levels on the mountain. The pressure gradient becomes great between the east and west side of the state, causing heavy cold air to sink under the warmer air aloft. Strong temperature inversions are likely between 4,000 and 6,000 feet, trapping low-level moisture as a blanket of low clouds or fog in the valleys.

As the pressure ridge continues east over the Cascades, south and southwest winds increase and return. This change breaks the inversion, mixing the moist surface air with drier air aloft. This turnover is often abrupt, resulting in dramatic changes in the weather and in the stability of the snowpack. The storm clock is ticking. During such air-mass transitions, extreme weather is likely and avalanches are certain. Winter weather returns as heavy precipitation and high winds again prevail.

Above Camp Muir, a climber ascends the Cowlitz Cleaver towards the Beehive on a windy, icy day.

AVALANCHES

by Mark Moore and Mike Gauthier

Mount Rainier is home to vast areas of classic avalanche terrain, with long, moderately steep slopes and massive annual accumulations of new snow. The mountain also sees thousands of enthusiastic climbers each year—many of them ignorant of the conditions that create and trigger the avalanches that could end their climb in tragedy.

Avalanche awareness is mandatory for safe travel on Mount Rainier. With such a wide variety of weather, terrain, and snowpack, avalanche hazard is likely somewhere on the mountain much of the year. Climbers should understand what causes avalanches, know how to assess conditions, and be prepared to rescue an avalanche victim.

The best approach is to learn to avoid being caught in an avalanche in the first place. But if you are swept away and buried, your best chance lies in a fast, efficient rescue from your teammates. In any venture onto potentially danger-ous avalanche terrain, every climber should carry an avalanche rescue beacon and know how to use it. Teams also need to carry strong snow shovels and ava-lanche probe poles.

TRAGEDY AT CADAVER GAP

Cadaver Gap, a rocky notch on the upper Cowlitz Glacier between Gibraltar Rock and Cathedral Rocks, earned its macabre name in 1929 when it be-came the recovery route for the bodies of two men who slid into a crevasse during a July blizzard. Today, Cadaver Gap is best known for a sudden ava-lanche on March 4, 1979, that claimed the life of one of the Northwest's most beloved climbers.

Willi Unsoeld was a Northwest climbing pioneer who promoted the credo that intense, firsthand experience of "the sacred in nature" resulted in per-sonal, life-affirming rewards. His willing embrace of risk pushed him to climb rugged mountains; he made more than two hundred successful ascents of Mount Rainier. In 1963, Unsoeld and partner Tom Hornbein completed the first ascent of Mount Everest's West Ridge, a harrowing climb that stranded the men below the summit in frigid darkness and left Unsoeld so stricken by frostbite that he lost nine toes. He later served with the Peace Corps in Nepal and helped develop and promote the Outward Bound program.

In 1979, when Unsoeld was a fifty-two-year-old professor at Evergreen State College, twenty-one of his students recruited him to lead a winter climb on Mount Rainier. Most of the party got as high as 13,000 feet on March 3 before wind and blowing snow forced them to abandon their attempt and return to their camp at 11,800 feet, next to Gibraltar Rock. That night, nearly 4 feet of fresh snow fell on Rainier's upper slopes.

En route to Camp Muir the next day, Unsoeld directed six rope teams of cold, slow-moving students down Cadaver Gap, figuring it was faster than winding through crevasses to the Ingraham Glacier. Unsoeld led the way down the steep slope, sharing a rope with students Peter Miller, Frank Kaplan, and twenty-one-year-old Janie Diepenbrock. Just after 1:00 P.M., a 3-foot slab beneath the climbers slid away. The avalanche pulled the roped-together party off their feet, sent them tumbling 500 feet down the mountain and buried them amid swirls of suffocating snow.

Kaplan quickly freed himself and located Miller. Others arrived, helped pull Miller from the debris and then traced the taut rope to Diepenbrock and Unsoeld. Both were found face down under several feet of snow. Attempts at resuscitation produced no signs of life. The surviving students stumbled exhausted down to Camp Muir and radioed news to the Park Service. Most of the students were led to safety March 6. Searchers recovered the bodies of Unsoeld and Diepenbrock on March 10.

S.C.

TYPES OF AVALANCHES

There are two distinct types of avalanches: loose and slab. Either type can be wet or dry, hard or soft.

Loose avalanches (loose slides; also sometimes called point-release avalanches) begin at a single point and gradually entrain more snow as they fan out, forming an inverted V-shape. Such slides are usually initiated by single snow grains that exceed their angle of repose, sliding downhill and bumping into neighboring snow grains as gravity takes over. Loose slides are frequent on steep, smooth slopes or cliff areas. Some loose slides are relatively small and harmless—simple sluffs. But others can grow large, even triggering dangerous slab slides as they descend. Even a moderate loose slide can be deadly if it carries an unwary climber into a terrain trap such as a crevasse, or over a cliff.

Slab avalanches occur when cohesion between snow grains allows entire layers of snow on a slope to give way at once. For a slab avalanche, all that is needed is the slab itself, a poor attachment of the slab to the layer below, and a sliding surface. A significant danger arises when buried weak layers of snow are unable to support the overlying snow as it constantly creeps downhill and adds

stress. The area of weakness may be small, or it may be widespread enough to cause an entire slope to fracture and release.

A variety of conditions can trigger slab avalanches. Changing weather may be the most common factor. This includes heavy snowfall or a rapid change (normally a rise) in air temperature. Rain can also be a prime instigator, adding weight without strength to the snowpack while weakening the surface snow and increasing its downslope motion. Other triggers include loose avalanches, rockfall and icefall, falling cornices and, most notably, climbers postholing through the snow. Regardless of the trigger, slab avalanches are deadly. It's not uncommon for them to become huge—sometimes incorporating several layers of snow from past storms, and in some cases the entire winter snowpack.

WEATHER, TERRAIN, AND THE SNOWPACK

Conditions for an avalanche are created by a combination of weather, terrain, and the snowpack. The weather interacts with the terrain to produce the snowpack. Then the weather and terrain continue to interact with the snowpack, constantly altering its characteristics and stability.

Snowpack and Weather

Constant variations in the weather can occur as snow falls. Changes in temperature, in wind speed and direction, and in precipitation type and rate cause snow to accumulate in a wide variety of layers—some weak, some strong; some thick, some thin. The bonds between these layers may range from rock solid to shaky. The vertical relationship of these layers largely determines the stability of the snow. Overall, the deposition of stronger layers (higher-density snow) over weaker layers (lower-density snow) produces less stability.

Increases in temperature, wind speed, or rate of precipitation often lead to an increasingly unstable snowpack. Rising temperatures with snowfall result in dense, heavy snow being deposited over weaker, lighter snow. Increasing winds produce higher-density, wind-slab snow over less cohesive and weaker snow. And high snowfall rates do not allow buried weak layers and newly deposited snow time to settle and stabilize. All of these scenarios can create an unstable snowpack that loads and stresses weak layers to the point of failure.

Snow-crystal shapes also affect the stability of the snow. Small, simple snow crystals generally produce more slab-like snow than larger more intricate snowflakes do. But high winds can break intricate crystals into smaller shapes, which makes for a more cohesive slab layer. Snow pellets (graupel) are an extreme example of crystals that contribute to instability; they often form a cohesionless

A small avalanche can quickly turn large and disastrous, as this one did in the upper Nisqually Basin, near Nisqually Cleaver. This slide released shortly after the morning sun hit the snow slope above.

layer in the snowpack. Hoar frost or surface hoar, the ice equivalent of dew, can also affect slope stability; if buried intact, this thin and notoriously weak crystal layer frequently produces avalanching.

Snowpack and Terrain

There is great variability in what can be considered avalanche terrain, from large, steep snow bowls to minor chutes and open faces. Most slides occur in well-defined paths with a starting zone, a running track, and a runout or deposition area. Avalanche terrain exists almost anywhere there is an unstable slab on a steep enough slope to slide. On Mount Rainier, this means much of the upper mountain.

Even during days of high avalanche hazard, however, careful routefinding can guide you to relatively safe avenues. Minimize your time in avalanche terrain by selecting a route subject to less hazard. Often the safest routes are along the crests of ribs or ridges, especially when they are windswept. Take into account, though, whether shifting winds could transport snow that loads both sides of the ridge, creating unstable cornices.

Cross any potential avalanche slope as high up as possible, one person at a time. Move quickly from anchor point to anchor point (exposed rocks and other safe areas), each person using the same track. In most cases, being caught near the top of a slide is better than being in the middle or bottom, where all the snow above can bury you.

Recognizing slope angles is a critical part of assessing avalanche danger. Slab avalanches are most common on slope angles between 30 and 45 degrees. Large slides from steeply angled slopes are less likely because frequent smaller slides reduce the stresses and the amount of snow. Slope angles below 30 degrees tend to compress and stabilize, though they too can slide if a particularly weak layer exists below. Be aware of even relatively minor changes in slope angle. The transition from 30 to 35 degrees may not seem like a big change to you, but to the snowpack it may mean the difference between stability and avalanche release.

RATING THE DANGERS

In analyzing avalanche danger, consider the three primary factors: weather, terrain, and snowpack. Rate the current conditions of each as a red (danger), yellow (caution), or green (safe). If any one of the three factors comes up as a red, stop and take a very close look at the other two.

If current snowpack conditions, for example, are clearly in the red—very unstable snow, with cracking or evidence of recent avalanches—make sure you've got a good, safe green for the terrain (you'll be traveling through flat areas or up on windswept ridges) and for the weather (temperatures are dropping and there's no wind). But if terrain or weather conditions are verging on yellow or red, change your route or come back another day.

Thinking about the three factors and their changing contributions to stability as red, yellow, or green lights is a very effective way to remain avalanche aware.

Learning avalanche awareness is as important as learning how to use an ice ax or crampons, especially on Rainier. The Northwest Avalanche Institute offers avalanche evaluation and forecasting courses that specialize in conditions in the Pacific Northwest and on Mount Rainier (39238 258th Avenue SE, Enumclaw, WA 98022; 360-825-9261; *www.avalanche.org/~nai*).

During late fall, winter, and early spring, mountain weather and avalanche forecast information is provided by the Northwest Weather and Avalanche Center. Information is available on the Internet at *www.nwac.noaa.gov* or by calling 206-526-6677.

GLACIERS
by Paul Kennard

Looming two miles above the surrounding mountains, and clad in over a cubic mile of ice, Mount Rainier sports more glacier ice than any other peak in the contiguous United States, more in fact, than all the other Cascade volcanoes combined. The vastness and beauty of its 34 square miles of perennial ice is impossible to comprehend from afar, and climbers from around the world flock to the mountain, in large part to experience the magnificent glaciers firsthand.

These flowing glaciers are not a passive backdrop to the mountain but active agents of change. Shiva-like, the massive glaciers helped shape the mountain when it formed and now are working relentlessly to destroy it. These ice rivers are also "living" systems, exquisitely in tune with their environment—expanding and contracting in size in response to subtle changes in climate. But the impassive beauty of the flowing ice belies the danger and occasional terror wrought by the ice fields to climbers and other park visitors.

THE BASICS

A glacier is a body of perennial ice that is of sufficient size to flow like a very thick liquid. Glaciers form in areas where more snow accumulates than melts. As new snow falls, it buries and compresses the underlying snow and, through a variety of processes, light, fluffy snowflakes are transformed into ice crystals. While in Antarctica, for example, it can take centuries for snow to become glacier ice, at Mount Rainier ice forms in just a few seasons, the metamorphosis being hastened by rain and snowmelt percolating through much of the snowpack.

Ice formation occurs in the upper portions of the glaciers of Mount Rainier, in areas called accumulation zones; the ice then flows downhill, replenishing areas where there is much more melt than snow accumulation. Glaciers advance when a surplus of ice flows to the lower glacier and retreat when the advancing ice melts faster than it flows.

In addition to moving by deformation, ice also slides along its base at the ice-rock interface, lubricated by meltwater. The speed of glacier movement has been measured on the Nisqually Glacier by the USGS. Near the glacier's equilibrium line (which separates the accumulation zone from the depletion area below) the Nisqually moves only about 8 inches a day in November. In late May and early June, when meltwater is available to promote glacier sliding, the glacier has been measured as moving almost 29 inches a day.

Mount Rainier has more glacial ice than any other mountain in the contiguous U.S.
For years, it held the world record for snowfall (over 93 feet) in a single twelve month
period, July–June.

Crevasses

While glaciers flow like a fluid, they also act like a solid, developing cracks (or
crevasses) near the surface. Ice's behavior can be likened to that of Silly Putty.
When a ball of Silly Putty is left out overnight, it flattens under its own weight,
but if it is quickly jerked apart, it snaps.

A crevasse may appear bottomless when you peer over its edge. However,
because ice flows at a different rate at various depths, most crevasses are actually
80 to 100 feet deep, and very seldom are they more than 150 to 200 feet deep.

Ice tends to move more quickly (and be thinner) in steep areas and move
more slowly (and be thicker) in flatter areas. As ice moves down the mountain
it moves faster as it approaches an icefall or other steep area, and the tendency
for crevasses to form intensifies (for example, Ingraham Icefall). At the bottom
of an icefall, or other area where the steepness moderates, the ice is slowing
down and compressing, and there are fewer crevasses (Ingraham Flats).

Marginal crevasses form on the edges of glaciers, where the friction exerted by the valley walls slows the flow. Crevasses also form where ice is being stretched, such as in accumulation areas or where ice flows over bulges. Splaying crevasses are often found near the terminus of the glacier. Since these types of crevasses are controlled by the underlying topography, the crevasse patterns are stable in location and form, even though ice is continually moving through the areas.

Other crevasses are affected by glacier-ice dynamics and can vary widely from season to season. This is the case on the Nisqually Glacier where ice bulges formed in response to years with much more snow than melt can cause accelerated movement (kinematic waves). In another example of seasonal effects, widespread breakup on the upper Emmons Glacier in the 1960s was attributed to increased volcanic heating.

Since the accumulation areas tend to be snow-covered throughout the year, many crevasses are hidden. Lower elevations on the glacier that experience less snowfall can be exposed in the summer and fall, leaving all the crevasses visible. In some years when there has been exceptional snow and ice melt, crevasses can be revealed in unlikely places. In the past few years, crevasses have been forming on the Muir Snowfield.

The uppermost crevasse on a glacier, known as a bergschrund, separates thin, stagnant ice from the thicker, moving ice below. On several of Rainier's climbing routes, such as the Emmons/Winthrop Glaciers, bergschrunds can be a formidable climbing obstacle.

Moats are fissures that form next to the valley wall and are caused by ice melt, rather than ice movement. The darker rock absorbs more sunlight than the ice, warms up, and melts the ice. Like crevasses, moats can be hidden by snow and can present quite a challenge when you are entering or leaving the glacier.

The Mighty Wind

Another glacier phenomenon that bedevils glacier visitors occurs during fair, calm weather when glacier ice cools the air above it, making it heavier. This air drains down valley as a glacier (katabatic) wind. A strong katabatic flow can transform a glacier campsite that seemed ideal in the morning, into a cold wind tunnel later in the day.

THE GLACIERS OF MOUNT RAINIER

Mount Rainier shoulders vast amounts of perennial ice, 156 billion cubic feet of it. That's enough ice to fill a line of dump trucks, placed bumper-to-bumper, that would span the distance from the mountain to the moon over eighteen times!

The glaciers of Mount Rainier are among the most accessible in the United

States. Road access is maintained year-round to within less than a mile of the lower Nisqually Glacier. The spectacular terminus of the Carbon Glacier is also an easy 4-mile hike from the end of the Carbon River road, which is typically passable all year.

The largest glacier by area is the Emmons (4.3 square miles), but the Carbon Glacier wins the medal for most impressive, having the most volume (25.1 billion cubic feet of ice), the lowest terminus in the contiguous United States (3,600 feet), and the deepest ice, with a measured ice thickness of 705 feet.

Most of Rainier's ice is distributed in twenty-five major glaciers, and many of the glaciers well-known to climbers, such as the Carbon, Emmons, Winthrop, Tahoma, Ingraham, and South Tahoma, are among the ten largest on the mountain. The Kautz Glacier, surprisingly, barely cracks the top twenty.

Many of the classic types of alpine glaciers are well represented at Mount Rainier. Cirque glaciers, located near ridges in amphitheaters (often of their own carving) are abundant. These glaciers include the Inter Glacier, and the less well-known Flett, Sarvent, and Williwakas Glaciers.

Valley glaciers, the true rivers of ice that flow over cliffs, around corners,

Glaciers are rivers of ice; here, the torrent creates beautiful crevasse patterns.

and into the valleys include the Nisqually, Tahoma, Emmons, and Carbon.

Hanging glaciers terminate abruptly at the edge of cliffs and, while beautiful, can pose considerable hazard to those climbing below. Notable hanging glaciers at Rainier include the Kautz, the Nisqually, and the Liberty Cap Glacier above the Willis Wall. In all the above instances, the tumbled ice reorganizes itself back into a glacier called a *remainé* below the ice cliff. The Liberty Cap is particularly successful in this regard, with the deepest ice on the mountain being found below the Willis Wall.

BEAUTY AND TERROR

When climbing or visiting the glaciers of Mount Rainier, be sure to keep an eye out for unusual glacier phenomena that abound. Wildlife is rare but not entirely absent, from Rainier's upper slopes. Mountain goats and marmots are frequent visitors, and other animals occasionally traverse glaciers. Elk tracks have been observed at 10,000 feet on the Emmons Glacier at least once. Ravens rule the sky above the mountain, and it is not unusual to be buzzed by a humming bird, temporarily mistaking you for a large flower.

Besides snow fleas, the ice worm is the only animal known to actually live on glaciers. For many glaciologists, the presence of ice worms is what proves an ice mass is a real glacier. Related to the common earthworm, but only about one-tenth of an inch long, ice worms can often be found on perennial snow overlying ice, out of the direct sunshine, and near patches of red algae (which is known as watermelon snow, but don't eat it), thought to be a food source for the worms.

Interesting glacier features come in a variety of dimensions and sizes. The alternating light and dark wavelike bands of ice on the surface of a glacier are called ogives. The lighter wave crests rise up to 30 feet higher than the darker troughs. Taken together the width of a light and dark band represents how far ice moves in one year. Ogives are thought to form when dirt concentrates in crevasses from snowmelt in the summer (resulting in the darker bands below the icefall), followed by clean snow filling the crevasses in the winter.

One of the easiest places to see ogives at Mount Rainier is on the lower Cowlitz Glacier, which is visible from Cowlitz Rocks, an area easily reached from Paradise Visitor Center.

On a smaller scale, glacier tables are curious ice pedestals capped by a large rock. The rock insulates the underlying ice and the reduced melt eventually results in a glacier table. Deposits of human waste can cause mini-tables, so always follow the park's recommended sanitation practices.

Smaller still, and dauntingly ephemeral, are Thompson flowers, which are actually large ice crystals that form in stagnant pools of water on glacier ice. To see one, find a water-filled crevasse on relatively inactive ice, and drop a rock down the edge of the pool to dislodge the crystals. If you are lucky, you will be rewarded with a series of Thompson flowers floating to the top of the pond.

Cathedral Rocks is one of several striking polychromatic ridges that provide a spectacular early morning backdrop for climbers. Radiating out from the mountain, these ridges, including Paradise Ridge, Rampart Ridge, and Emerald Ridge, have intrigued and deceived scientists for decades. For years, conventional wisdom held that the ridges were formed by massive lava flows, and that what we see today is the reverse topography of a past landscape. That is, the lava flowed down valleys, filling them, and glaciers later eroded the older and weaker rock next to these flows, "flipping" the landscape and creating ridges where there were once valleys. Scientist have recently dated the lava flows and found some are only 40,000 years old, too short a time to erode valleys into ridges.

What more likely happened is that during prehistoric eruptions of Mount Rainier, torrents of lava streamed over the glacier-mantled volcano, resulting in an epic combat of fire and ice. In most cases the ice won. The glaciers were formidable thermal and physical barriers, forcing most of the lava flow to the margins of the ice, where it formed ridges, where it is visible today. When climbing or hiking the mountain, keep an eye out for hexagonal columns in the rock or a glassy texture, telltale signs of rapidly cooled lava.

Mount Rainier's valleys are not only glacially molded but glacially eroded as well. Some weary climbers may take solace in the fact that the flowing glaciers have reduced the height of the mountain by 1,000 feet in the last six thousand years. Other climbers may be delighted to find out that the most sculpted and challenging climbing areas higher on the mountain will only become more challenging as the glacier ice movement continues to relentlessly tear away and steepen Rainier's crests, cirques, and ridges.

In addition to being one of the most sublimely beautiful mountains, Mount Rainier is considered the most dangerous mountain in the United States because of its volcanic and geologic hazards, and the resultant risks to the surrounding population. The mountain is capable of large, destructive volcanic eruptions, as well as massive mudflows (lahars) that can affect large areas outside the park and which sometimes occur without warning.

Glaciers can contribute to these hazards. During the catastrophic eruption of nearby Mount St. Helens in 1980, 70 percent of its glacier ice was blown off the mountain, contributing to the devastating downstream flooding. It is also known that much of the groundwater that has contributed to massive lahars on Rainier in the past came from glacial meltwater.

Increased volcanic heat can affect ice dynamics, sometimes with surprising results. Increased geothermal activity was the culprit in the abnormal breakup of the upper Emmons Glacier in the 1960s. In August 1967, in response to an increase of geothermal heat, there was a spectacular glacier outburst flood *(jökulhaup)* on the South Tahoma Glacier. Water stored inside the glacier catastrophically broke out of the glacier surface at an elevation of 7,000 feet, severing the lower glacier in two. The flood developed into a debris flow, a destructive slurry of mud, old-growth trees, and boulders, with the consistency of concrete. The flow obliterated the former Tahoma Creek campground, which fortunately had just been evacuated because of fire danger.

Since 1984 there have been at least thirty-five debris flows, many of which started as glacier outburst floods. Unlike the Tahoma event in 1967, which was likely related to volcanic heating, these other glacier outburst floods are weather driven and commonly occur during prolonged spells of unseasonably warm weather. Historically, the Kautz and Tahoma Creeks, the Nisqually River and West Fork of the White River, have experienced *jökulhaups*. Climbers and hikers should exercise due caution when hiking in valleys downstream of glaciers and immediately get at least 50 feet above the valley floor if they hear a noise similar to that of a train.

Debris flows driven by glacier floods can be expected to increase as Rainier's glaciers recede, exposing large piles of loose unstable rock that was formerly buttressed by glacier ice.

Climbers should keep in mind that in addition to normal glacier hazards, such as crevasses and routine icefall, collapse of ice in ice caves has injured, and running water in ice caves has drowned, people on Mount Rainier in the past.

GLACIER RESEARCH

The glaciers of Mount Rainier are not relics from an earlier ice age—rather they are finely attuned to the present conditions and react by shrinking and expanding in response to subtle climate shifts. Glaciers on the south side of the mountain, such as the Nisqually, respond most quickly to both changes in snow accumulation and summer melt.

This is because the southwest side of the mountain bears the major brunt of winter storms and receives the most snow. Measured snowfall near the Nisqually, at the Paradise Ranger station at 5,400 feet in elevation, is world class. Snowfall has been recorded in every month of the year, and one year over 90 feet of snow fell (the average is over 56 feet). In the summer, the south side of the mountain receives the most sunshine and experiences the most glacier melt. Summer ice melt of over 30 feet has been measured on the lower Nisqually Glacier.

Scientists estimate that if it ever stopped snowing completely on the Nisqually (a very unlikely event), the glacier would effectively disappear in about thirty years. Starting in 1931, surveys of the lower Nisqually Glacier have been regularly made to determine changes in the elevation of the ice surface. These surveys, one of the longest running glacier monitoring programs in the United States, show how the Nisqually quickly responds to changes in snow accumu-

Glacier scientists for the NPS place probes in the snow and ice to measure the snow accumulation and rate of decline on the glaciers.

lation. When higher than normal snowfall builds up in the accumulation area of the glacier, a "bulge" forms and can be tracked as it moves down the glacier, like a consumed mouse moving though a snake.

These bulges, called kinematic waves, can exceed 80 feet in height and can move down the glacier at speeds up to six times faster than the ice itself. When the wave reaches the bottom of the glacier, the terminus usually advances dramatically. In the case of the Nisqually, the time delay between changes in snowfall, and the glacier advance is about fifteen years. Without the wave, the delay would be much longer.

During the time that Nisqually Glacier surveys have been taken, three kinematic waves have been detected. The first two resulted in healthy glacier advances. The third wave was predicted to reach the glacier snout in 2003. Due to an exceptionally dry and sunny summer and fall that year, however, glacier melt overwhelmed the advancing wave. The glacier retreated and is fast approaching its historic minimum.

The terminus positions of six of Rainier's large glaciers were last mapped in 2002 using satellite imagery. In addition to the Nisqually, the Winthrop, Tahoma, South Tahoma, and Carbon Glaciers are at or near their smallest historic size. Anomalously, the Tahoma made a small advance between 1994 (its historic minimum) and 2002. The Emmons Glacier has remained relatively stable, most likely because the lower glacier is covered with a thick insulating blanket of rocks, from a massive rockfall in 1963.

Despite a series of relatively recent advances and retreats, the overall trend for hundreds of years has been a retreat of the glaciers at Mount Rainier. Until 1936, the Nisqually Glacier reached to within a half mile of the Nisqually Bridge (now over a mile away). In the 1840s (during the little Ice Age), the glacier was hundreds of feet below the present road. Even the more sedate glaciers on the other side of the mountain are not immune. The Emmons has retreated over a mile since the mid-1700s.

Between 1913 and 1994, according to the most recent detailed measurements available, the combined area of Mount Rainier's glaciers has been reduced by a fifth and total glacier volume by a quarter. While these changes may seem excessive, they are within the range of normal glacier behavior, in response to climatic changes.

GLACIERS AND RADAR

After Mount St. Helens erupted in 1980 and there was great interest in estimating the volcanic and mudflow risks to surrounding communities, I was involved in a team using a backpack ice radar unit to measure the level of ice on the mountain. The equipment we employed was made possible by a tragic discovery during World War II.

During the war there was a spate of airplane crashes into the Antarctic ice sheet. It turned out that the radar used to detect the plane's altitude was not reflecting off the ice surface. Rather it penetrated the ice, with terrible consequences. This ability of radar to penetrate ice was exploited in the development of instruments used for modern ice radar measurements.

There is a long and illustrious history of glacier research at Mount Rainier. While the amount of research has been greatly scaled back from historic levels, core programs continue, largely in response to concern among the public and the scientific community about climate change, both natural and human-induced. The sensitive and dynamic response of glaciers to variations in both temperature and precipitation makes them excellent indicators of regional and global climate change.

P.K.

HEALTH
by Jim Litch, M.D.

This was the first of our eighteen summit climbs that season as climbing rangers for Mount Rainier. We had pulled over the top of the Kautz Headwall and were suddenly struggling against an invisible force. Our pace slacked off as we hauled ourselves up the last 300 feet to the summit. As I congratulated my partner, he suddenly bent over and vomited. This veteran of twenty-four Rainier summits looked up with a smile and said, "Every year on the first summit of the season I lose my stomach and get wasted, but I recover quickly while descending. After a few weeks acclimatization, it'll be a different world up here."

The climb of Mount Rainier is unusual for North American mountains in that nonacclimatized climbers routinely travel from their home at sea level to a trailhead at 5,000 feet and on to the summit at 14,410 feet in less than 48 hours. This is a greater altitude gain than the trip from base camp to the summit of Denali (Mount McKinley), which takes most climbers 10 to 14 days. This rapid gain in altitude—the invisible force that hit me and my partner on our way up Rainier—requires special attention because it significantly endangers performance and safety.

HIGH-ALTITUDE ILLNESSES

Above 8,000 feet, any further gain in altitude forces our bodies to contend with a significantly lower level of oxygen in our bloodstream. The summit of Rainier has a third less oxygen than sea level as a result of the lower atmospheric pressure. If climbers were willing to be patient enough to achieve the same gain in altitude by gradual ascent over a week or more, their bodies would have time to adjust, and they would perform much better. Ultimately a climber's only protection from the effects of a rapid ascent of Rainier is to descend before these effects of altitude progress to life-threatening illness. On a typical ascent of Mount Rainier without prior acclimatization, climbers are racing the clock.

The most common form of altitude illness is known as acute mountain sickness (AMS), and its relatively mild symptoms include headache, malaise, lassitude, poor appetite, nausea, vomiting, dizziness, and irritability. Nearly 70 percent of climbers on Rainier suffer from acute mountain sickness during their summit climb.

AMS is not life threatening, but ignoring it is. The illness may worsen, over hours or days, as dangerous collections of fluid develop in the lungs and/or the brain. Significant fluid in the lungs (high-altitude pulmonary edema, or HAPE) results in shortness of breath while at rest and a further reduction of oxygen transfer to the body. Increasing fluid in the brain (high-altitude cerebral edema, or HACE) causes loss of balance, confusion, and hallucination. If descent or oxygen supplementation is not accomplished within hours, coma and death may ensue.

How to Avoid Altitude Illness

Gradual ascent of Mount Rainier over several days reduces the likelihood of acute mountain sickness because your body has time to adapt. Only rarely do climbers have this luxury of time, however. Most climbers simply accept the symptoms of AMS during a summit climb as part of the overall experience.

It's possible to help prevent the symptoms of AMS with the use of simple drugs like acetazolamide (250 milligrams twice a day or 500 milligrams slow-release once a day), acetaminophen (325 milligrams up to four times a day), or aspirin (325 milligrams three times a day) at the start of the climb. Acetazolamide is particularly useful in improving poor sleep at high altitude and is very effective for preventing the periodic breathing that occurs during sleep. However, these medicines do not protect against the development of the more serious forms of altitude illness HAPE and HACE.

Gingko biloba and garlic were both recently studied for use in the prevention of AMS and results have not been impressive (no or limited benefit beyond that of the placebo).

Some nondrug measures can decrease the symptoms of high-altitude illness and help performance. They include the following:

- Begin a high-carbohydrate diet 1 or 2 days before the climb and maintain this diet through the climb.
- Make climbing plans that take into account your decreased work capacity at high altitude.
- Reschedule the climb if you come down with an upper respiratory or other active infection.
- Avoid overexertion on the climb by maintaining a reasonable pace and not overloading yourself with nonessential gear.
- Drink enough fluids on the climb to offset increased fluid loss. Passing urine that is clear is a good sign that you're drinking enough fluids.
- Avoid nonessential medications and remedies. There are no shortcuts or quick fixes; they only make issues more complicated.
- Provide good ventilation for camp stoves used in confined places.

Symptoms and Treatment

The critical point about altitude illness is to not let acute mountain sickness progress to life-threatening HAPE or HACE. It's not uncommon for climbers to dismiss their symptoms as other maladies and push on. If anyone in your party is experiencing even mild symptoms, do not ascend farther to sleep at a higher camp. If the symptoms are worsening, the person should descend. Do not let your team member descend alone. The decision to descend must be made well before the patient loses the ability to walk down. In HAPE, the climber should sit upright, and be prevented from physical exertion, while the descent is conducted by the group.

An actual incident illustrates how early symptoms of altitude illness can proceed to something far worse. A small research team ascended over 3 days to camp in Rainier's summit crater. One member of the group had developed AMS at a previous camp but attributed his malady to overexertion. The climber's condition worsened that evening, and he could not help in establishing camp on the summit due to the illness, which now included shortness of breath while at rest and poor balance.

At sunset, the team leader alerted climbing rangers, who were also on the summit. They found the patient in his tent, disoriented and unable to support himself. Attempting a descent at night with a physically impaired climber would have been too dangerous. Shortly thereafter, the patient became unconscious and intermittently required assisted breathing. Climbing rangers from Camp Muir attempted to carry up oxygen but were unsuccessful due to poor weather. Fortunately, the patient was still alive at dawn, when the weather improved enough to permit a helicopter evacuation from the summit. The climber, suffering from HACE, had a blood oxygen saturation of 38 (95 to 100 is normal) but later recovered fully in a hospital.

The red-flag symptoms that indicate the need for **immediate descent** include shortness of breath while at rest; the coughing up of pink, frothy sputum; poor balance; confusion; a decreased level of consciousness. Descent must not be delayed if any one of these signs is present. The seriousness of these signs cannot be overstated. Without descent or supplemental oxygen, death may occur within hours. Waiting for a rescue, without some form of supplemental oxygen, is a desperate option.

Medications may help with severe altitude illness, but only rarely do they make a critical difference and thus they cannot be relied on. Each has benefits, but they can also cause harm if not used correctly. They include the following:

Acetazolamide is very safe, and is used to treat AMS and HACE. Take 250 milligrams twice a day or 500 milligrams slow-release once a day. It should not be taken by people with a known intolerance to sulfa drugs. Side effects commonly include increased urine output and tingling of hands, feet, and lips.

Dexamethasone is safe when used for treatment of HACE while descending. It may also be used to treat patients with HAPE if you suspect HACE may also be present. The dosage is 4 milligrams every 6 hours. The drug is dangerous if given as an aid to ascent.

Nifedipine is a potentially dangerous medication in a mountaineering environment. Although it is used by health professionals for treatment of HAPE, nifedipine has severe side effects that bottom out blood pressure and thus make it unsuitable for use by climbers who lack specialized training and supplies.

PREEXISTING MEDICAL CONDITIONS
In addition to high-altitude illnesses, any number of other medical emergencies can occur during a Rainier climb. The sustained strenuous climbing can precipitate a variety of medical problems. The related dehydration can seriously impact the blood levels of individuals taking certain medications. If you have a condition that limits your activity at home or that is managed with medications, check with your doctor before venturing high on Rainier. During a climb, descent can only help not hurt any medical condition that develops at high altitude. When in doubt, descend.

COLD-WEATHER HAZARDS
The cold temperatures encountered during a Mount Rainier climb can have serious health consequences. Climbers can learn to effectively guard against hypothermia and frostbite and to treat the conditions if they occur. Like altitude illness, prevention of hypothermia and frostbite is key.

Hypothermia
Hypothermia is a drop in the core body temperature to below 95 degrees Fahrenheit (35 degrees Celsius). Hypothermia can occur rapidly after a sudden event like immersion in cold water or a radical change in weather. It can also develop slowly if the body's metabolism isn't adequate to meet ongoing environmental exposure.

Hypothermia occurs both ways on Mount Rainier. A person who falls into a crevasse while lightly dressed for a sunny mid-afternoon glacier crossing will be at risk if not extricated quickly. More slowly but just as surely, hypothermia can affect a climber who has eaten little food while climbing through the day with a heavy pack, leaving the body with lessened ability to produce heat as the sun drops and the wind kicks up. Most deaths from this slow form of hypothermia occur at relatively mild temperatures, between 30 degrees and 50 degrees Fahrenheit (-1 degree to 10 degrees Celsius). You can die of hypothermia in the summer.

Prevention is a matter of minimizing excessive heat loss and ensuring adequate heat production. This is achieved through:
- proper choice and use of clothing and shelter
- staying dry
- adequate nutrition and hydration
- avoidance of overexertion
- preparation for sudden changes in the conditions of the climb.

Hypothermia is progressive. Symptoms of mild hypothermia include a loss of judgment and of fine-motor coordination. The patient shivers to keep warm. This is readily reversible in the field. Patients can warm themselves once they are protected from further heat loss and are given rapidly absorbed high-energy food. A reasonable initial maneuver is for the patient to huddle with other members of the party behind some form of wind barrier, gaining warmth from the teammates. Early recognition and treatment of mild hypothermia may avoid the progression to profound hypothermia.

As profound hypothermia sets in, shivering ceases and the patient becomes confused, with loss of coordination progressing to apathy, stupor, and coma. People with profound hypothermia cannot warm themselves. Provide the patient with wind protection, remove wet clothing, and apply prewarmed insulation (including a ground layer) to prevent additional heat loss. It's essential to provide warming by applying heat packs or hot water bottles next to the patient's body; cuddling with the patient inside a sleeping bag or bivy sack also is effective. Begin these procedures as soon as possible. If the patient is in a stupor or unconscious, use gentle handling to avoid triggering an irregular heart beat. Never assume that the patient has died; continue the rewarming process.

Frostbite

Frostbite is a localized area of frozen tissue. It occurs most commonly at the end of extremities and uncovered areas during exposure to subfreezing temperatures. The risk of frostbite increases with extreme cold, high winds, high altitude, dehydration, and overexertion. Wearing tight clothing or footwear or using alcohol, tobacco, or other drugs also increases the risk. Especially vulnerable are parts of the body that are in contact with metals or liquids or that have been frostbitten in the past.

Superficial frostbite results in pale, cold skin with underlying tissue that is pliable and soft. Treat with skin-to-skin contact or by immersion in water that is just warm to the touch of the caregiver's elbow (104 to 108 degrees Fahrenheit). If the frostbite produces blisters, the patient should be evacuated to receive further treatment. If the frostbite is on the foot, the patient shouldn't try to walk.

Deep frostbite involves the skin and deep structures that become hard and nonpliable. The decision to thaw deep frostbite depends on the situation. Rewarming requires both proper technique to minimize tissue damage and the use of a strong painkiller or narcotic. To prevent further damage, don't use the affected part after thawing. Thawing in the field usually isn't called for on Mount Rainier, however, because rapid evacuation can often be organized.

Corneal frostbite is rare but can occur in extreme cold and high winds. Irreversible damage may occur, requiring a corneal transplant. If you travel in such harsh conditions, wear goggles and cover exposed skin.

OTHER MEDICAL CONCERNS

Mount Rainier can confront climbers with a number of other medical problems. Here are several notable issues relevant to Mount Rainier.

Heat Sickness, Exhaustion, and Dehydration

These conditions can disable even a strong, fit climber. They are common on Mount Rainier, where climbers face frequent and rapid extreme changes in weather conditions during a sustained period of physical activity. The conditions result from a lack of attention to basic nutrition, hydration, and regulation of body heat by adjusting clothing layers. Each of these ailments points to its own cure. Heat sickness (dangerous overheating) requires urgent rapid cooling. Heat exhaustion warrants rest and high-energy food. Dehydration, and the resulting electrolyte imbalance, requires the drinking of water containing reasonable concentrations of salts (sodium and potassium) and sugar.

The symptoms of these conditions overlap with those of altitude illness. Sorting out these potentially dangerous conditions can be difficult. Carefully evaluate a patient's symptoms and closely follow the responses to initial therapy, while maintaining a suspicion that altitude sickness is involved. More than one illness may be occurring at the same time.

Snow-Blindness and Sunburn

These conditions are surprisingly common on Mount Rainier despite well-known preventive measures. Both snow-blindness and sunburn result from direct tissue irritation by the ultraviolet (UV) rays of sunlight. The UV dose is dependent on the intensity and duration of exposure to sunlight, which increases with altitude. Although both ailments may occur throughout the year, they are more common in the sun-intense spring and summer, especially on snow-covered slopes.

For sunburn, barrier methods are very effective, such as light clothing to cover extremities. Apply sunscreen (SPF 15 or higher) or zinc oxide paste frequently to sun-exposed areas when you are perspiring.

High-quality sunglasses filter out most UV light, and when combined with side shields they offer extremely effective eye protection. Cheap sunglasses can actually increase the risk of snow-blindness because they do not filter out a significant proportion of the UV rays but still permit pupils to dilate.

Preexisting Visual Problems

At the altitudes found on Mount Rainier, contact lenses are tolerated without the difficulties that are common with their use at extreme altitude. Corrective lenses (eye glasses) can be bothersome in poor weather conditions and may lead to serious problems if required for adequate vision. Prescription goggles are available.

Surgical corrections of nearsighted refractive errors, such as radical kera-totomy (RK) and laser keratectomy (LASIK and PRK), have recently become popular. Although RK can lead to visual changes at altitudes above 9,000 feet, typically approximately 24 hours of altitude exposure at 14,000 feet are neces-sary for significant visual problems (fully reversible at sea level) to arise. LASIK and PRK are more stable procedures and do not result in visual changes at altitudes below approximately 17,000 feet; typically visual problems don't occur until approximately 27,000 feet.

High-Altitude Cough Syndrome

This is a persistent debilitating cough that develops following exposure to very high altitude, usually above 14,000 feet. It is not so much a problem on Mount Rainier as it is in higher ranges.

Accidents/Trauma

The great majority of serious accidents on Mount Rainier are related to poor conditions on the route. Be informed before setting out and apply your own critical analysis of conditions as you climb. To climb using your brain, not your legs, is arguably the most challenging aspect of climbing. Use your head, be-fore you get in over it.

COMMERCIAL GUIDING
by Eric Simonson

The story of the early years of Rainier guiding is well told in Dee Molenaar's *The Challenge of Rainier*, a book I read countless times as a boy growing up in Tacoma. That book inspired me to learn the history of Mount Rainier, and to make my own mark. I made my first ascent of Rainier in 1970 as a fifteen-year-old and began my guiding career in 1973 as an apprentice with Rainier Mountaineering, Inc. (RMI). Over the years I have taken literally thousands of people up Rainier, most of them novice climbers. I've learned firsthand the joy of success, the frustration of failure, and the sorrow of tragedy. Perhaps most satisfying is that I've been able to share with so many people my knowledge of this incredible place.

In any profession, no one reaches his or her fullest skills in a vacuum. For me, learning to be a good Rainier guide has meant observing other climbers carefully for over thirty years. My friends Phil Ershler and George Dunn, both lifelong guides at Rainier with over 400 ascents each, have taught me a lot. Their commitment has inspired a whole generation of guides. I've learned that the success of a climbing team is often as much about people skills and preparation as it is about brute strength and technical climbing prowess.

WHY HIRE A GUIDE
Many people who climb Rainier with friends who have more experience than they do are essentially entering into a guiding relationship. Over the years my colleagues and I have seen many versions of guiding—ranging from well-led independent teams to a group outfitted with garden hoes, another with their harnesses on backwards, and another team tied into the rope with wrist loops. Phil Ershler once encountered a team high on the mountain with no ice axes at all. Asked where their tools were, they replied that they didn't need any because their guide was God and he was taking care of them. Phil's comeback line was a classic: "Up here, even God uses an ice ax!" For the purpose of what follows, guiding is defined as a contractual relationship in which money is paid by a customer to a guide, or guide service, who is legally permitted to conduct business in the National Park.

While climbing techniques and equipment have changed remarkably in the past century, the reasons to go with a guide have remained essentially the same. Often the prospective climber just wants to get to the summit but lacks the mountain craft to keep out of trouble. In this case, the guide's job often starts with instruction. More experienced climbers may choose to climb with guides when they are ready to try something more challenging, like a different route or a winter climb. Many climbers who travel to Rainier from out-of-state don't know enough potential partners to create a self-sufficient rope team. Some climbers choose to go guided because they feel safer, while others consider the statistically higher success rate of guided versus nonguided climbs in reaching the summit to be worth paying for. Finally, many climbers have developed close relationships with certain guides and simply want to climb with someone they know and trust.

For individuals captivated by mountaineering who want to learn the skills they need for future climbs and expeditions, Rainier is truly the most accessible alpine training ground in the country. It is a natural starting point for many climbers and often their first chance to climb with a professional guide.

To avoid disappointment, it always helps when both guides and clients can clearly communicate their respective motivations and expectations. When considering hiring a Rainier guide, prospective climbers need to consider some important variables: route difficulty, number of days required, fitness level, guide ratio, and the weight of the packs to be carried. For example, if you are in excellent physical condition and just want to take a quick trip to the summit, then a 2-day climb might be perfectly suitable for you. However, if your physical fitness is insufficient for such a strenuous climb, you will have a tough time. Do you have snow camping skills and the ability to carry a decent-sized backpack? Do you enjoy being with a group of people? In this case you would do fine on a longer program with a larger group. Alternatively, if you have done little camping and climbing or feel you need detailed instruction, both you and your guide would be happier if you were on a program with a lower client/guide ratio, enabling the guide to work with you on a personal basis. If you are in good physical shape, not cost-sensitive, and ready to try a different route, then a custom, privately guided climb would be a blast.

WHAT TO CONSIDER ONCE YOU HAVE DECIDED TO HIRE A GUIDE

It has probably been a while since you were a student, perhaps even longer since you put your faith in another person, let alone one that you hardly knew. It is tough sometimes, especially for people who are used to being in control, to cede to someone else decisions that affect their security and safety. From the standpoint of the guide, the most desirable clients are those who are fully engaged in the climb, who are cognizant of the hazards, and who can work with us to mitigate them. Both you and your guide will be evaluating each other from the moment you first meet. For both the guides and the customers, the old adage "you only have one chance to make a good first impression" holds true. To get things off on a good start, it is important to gain mutual trust by being on time, appropriately equipped, mutually respectful, and willing and able to communicate clearly.

Many people consider a paid guided climb to be a simple commodity. It is not. When you hire a guide you are really renting their "bandwidth," i.e., their experience, knowledge, and skill. The more experienced the guides, the more bandwidth is available for their clients. Similarly, a lower client/guide ratio will allow the guide to give the customers more individual attention. A guide has only a finite amount of bandwidth. This becomes stretched in bad weather, difficult conditions, with multiple clients, or when a "high maintenance" client demands most of the guide's attention. Experienced guides know that focusing too much on one individual's issues detracts from seeing big-picture problems, and that this is a situation to be avoided.

I once turned a whole group around halfway up Disappointment Cleaver on a perfect sunshiny, blue-sky day. Because it had rained the night before, the route was slick and frozen, and I knew the clients I had with me didn't possess the cramponing technique that the Cleaver demanded that day. Predictably, several people complained later about not getting their money's worth. One climber in the group, however, was so impressed that he came back to climb Rainier with me on another trip, and from there we went to climb McKinley, Vinson, and Everest. In short, even an "unsuccessful" climb often provides an unexpected upside. I've never had a trip up Rainier that didn't teach me something, and the unsuccessful trips often are the most generous in this regard.

Making the summit is one way to measure success on a mountain, and a guide can help a customer achieve this goal. For the client interested in learning more about the mountain and about climbing in general, the guide can be a great resource; I really appreciate the person who asks questions rather than following blindly everything I say. It forces me to articulate what I am thinking and keeps me in touch with the old guide's adage "have a reason for what you do." It is not uncommon among guides to have different ideas about the best way to handle a situation. What is important is that the guide can identify clearly the issues involved in his or her decision. It all comes down to seeing the big picture, and understanding what it really means to be successful. For a beginning climber, struggling with all kinds of problems, just getting to the top of Disappointment Cleaver might be a huge success. Alternatively, a climber who takes unnecessary risks to reach the summit or puts others at risk by his or her behavior is arguably not much of a success at all. A guide who can help his clients understand the bigger issues involved in safety is providing a real service. It is not always easy.

When I rope up to a group I hardly know, it is not without some trepidation, because I realize we are depending on each other and worry whether we are all up to the task, myself included. While I have many times spotted falling

Surveying the route, climbers eyeball the Tahoma Sickle from the 11,300 foot camp near upper St. Andrews Rock.

rocks, arrested falls by my clients, or prevented some mistake from becoming a disaster, I've also been at the receiving end of assistance. Once I was smashed by a falling rock in the dark at about 2:00 A.M. on the traverse across the nose of Disappointment Cleaver and sent tumbling over the edge, only to have my clients put the brakes on me and keep me from going all the way to the glacier below. Another time on a winter climb, I was dragged down by a slab avalanche that I had triggered on the upper Cowlitz Glacier and was stopped from a very long ride because my rope team executed perfectly the team arrest we had practiced only a few hours before. I've had numerous crevasse falls, both on Rainier and McKinley, including a spectacular plunge on the upper Ingraham Glacier when a 30-foot-wide snow bridge crumbled below me, sending me down with tons of ice blocks into a blue hole and certain death. But my rope team stopped me. It makes one appreciate one's team!

SOME TIPS TO HELP YOU MAXIMIZE YOUR CHANCES OF SUCCESS

Many things you have little control over on a climb: your partners' fitness, the weather, the route conditions, or other parties on the mountain. To be successful, you need to focus as much as possible on the things over which you do have control, including your own fitness, efficiency, food, gear, and attitude. The Planning a Successful Climb and On the Mountain sections of this book contain a wealth of valuable information on physical conditioning, equipment, and supplies, and, of course, you should pay close attention to any guidelines your guide provides in advance. Outlined below are a few specifics you may find useful.

As for physical conditioning, there are certainly times on a Rainier climb where you need to be able to put the "pedal to the metal," but the majority of the climb will actually be done on "cruise control." Knowing how your body runs, and how to make very subtle adjustments to your "throttle" is crucial. During your training hikes, pay attention to how small adjustments to your pace, step length, and breathing rate translate into big improvements in the "mileage" you are getting.

Rest breaks on climbs are misnamed—there is rarely time for much rest. It is a time for making adjustments. You'll want to be familiar with your equipment and how the clothing layers work in conjunction with each other, so you can make fast and accurate changes that are appropriate to the temperatures you encounter.

Lou Whittaker used to say "You can't run a bulldozer on a pint of diesel," which loosely translates to "You can't expect to climb all day without eating." Bring plenty of lunch! Many people just don't bring enough calories for a long, hard day. That means that for a typical 2-day climb you'll need at least a dozen candy/energy bars or the equivalent in terms of calories.

At rest breaks, climbers should eat and drink even when they may have zero appetite. Knowing where clients are on their "gas gauge" is one of the most important skills a guide can develop. Many times I have had customers who became tired or disheartened and convinced that they can't make the top. By encouraging them to eat and drink, and helping to sort out some of their problems, I have been able to help them summit. On the other hand, I can remember getting fooled a few times by people who seemed strong going up, but who made it to the summit only on fumes and then were totally out of gas for the trip down. This can be a guide's real nightmare, especially in bad conditions when fatigue makes slips and errors more likely.

I am always amazed by customers who invest a lot of money to do a trip, and then choose to disregard the recommended equipment list. In particular, many people bring insufficient warm clothes. One of the things a client buys is the guide's familiarity with the route, which means the guide can often push on to reach the summit in marginal conditions that would turn back less experienced climbers. This is only possible, however, if everyone is prepared.

A list of common equipment problems starts with carrying too much and may include boots that are too stiff (which causes blisters), problems with headlamps (bring extra bulbs and batteries), the inability to keep sleeping bags and extra clothes dry in case of driving rain on the way to high camp (bring plastic bags), and poorly fitted crampons (avoid those shaped liked "cookie cutters" with vertical side rails). Make sure your pants have side zips for better ventilation and for ease in getting them on and off over boots and crampons.

Renting gear is recommended for beginners. Better to spend some money to try out some different options and see what works for you than to commit a lot of treasure to expensive stuff that might be wrong. When fitting boots my suggestion is "when in doubt, go big" and bring extra socks. Get an ice ax that is long enough (at least 70 cm), not a short technical tool. You'll be wearing a helmet, so bring a bandana or ball cap to go underneath. On a hot day going up a glacier to your high camp with a big pack, you'll appreciate light gloves and a loose fitting long-sleeved shirt that vents well. Make sure you have a down parka that is big enough to go on over the top of your other layers.

I want my clients to be a little bit selfish and let me worry about the other people in the party. When each person on the team can efficiently manage his or her own eating, drinking, and clothing adjustments, it is a guide's dream. While still stressing details, I like to try to get my team to consider the bigger picture, starting with something as simple as looking uphill. It is no exaggeration to say that most of what is bad on Rainier comes from above. A climber needs to be habitual about frequently looking up. Remember to situate yourself at rest breaks where you can keep an eye uphill in case something cuts loose.

Get used to the feeling that you are being watched! Most guides will initially take a pretty conservative approach with their clients in order to appraise their capabilities and limitations. The goal is to take that appraisal, combine it with the guide's experience, anticipate where problems are likely to arise, and then make proactive decisions. In any climbing situation, the more you know, the better you can anticipate on behalf of yourself and your team members, and the better you will be at dealing with problems while you still have options. This is an important element of maintaining a margin of safety.

A MEMORABLE CLIMB

My 250th ascent of Mount Rainier was special for a number of reasons besides the fact that it was a numerical milestone. It was a February ascent, one of about twenty times I've been to the top during the winter, and I was climbing with a great group of guides and clients. The weather was good, so we left early, ascended the Gibraltar Route to the summit and were able to go across to Columbia Crest. The trip back down to Camp Comfort at the top of Gib was uneventful, and our plan was to continue down the ascent route. At this point, I realized I was really getting warm, and experience told me that the well-frozen conditions on the Gib Ledges we had seen in the morning would now be replaced by lots of falling ice and rocks. Our beautiful day had become a trap. After weighing the alternatives, I decided to attempt a descent of the Ingraham Glacier Direct instead, despite crevasses and routefinding challenges. We started off by setting an anchor and lowering everyone one-at-a-time down a rope length from the top of Gibraltar, over the bergschrund, and down to a stable slope. I left a snow picket when I rappelled down as the last person. Then, we re-roped for serious glacier travel, picking our way down the Ingraham Glacier. By taking our time, we put the puzzle together perfectly and soon we were down on the Flats. A quick trip to Cathedral Gap, then down and back across the Cowlitz Glacier, and we were at Muir again. What a great day, a great climb, made all the better by having to go digging into the bag of tricks. That is what mountaineering is all about.

E.S.

ON THE MOUNTAIN

The first part of a Rainier climb is the journey from trailhead to high camp, a trek that can take anywhere from 3 hours to 2 days depending on the climbing route you've chosen. In some cases, the trip to high camp can be longer and more arduous than the summit climb itself. Leave early to maximize the use of daylight hours. Problems such as blisters, equipment troubles, or struggling teammates may arise on the way. Arriving at base camp early allows extra time to set up, prepare, and rest. Drink and eat at regular intervals on the hike to camp and after you get there. Keeping fluid and energy levels high will help you acclimatize and perform better.

On the way to high camp, you'll pass through different ecological zones, the most fragile of which are the subalpine and alpine zones between 5,000 and 11,000 feet in elevation. What may appear to be bare ground can actually be home to small plant colonies thousands of years old. Stay on the trails; if there are none, simply watch your footing and try not to crush these alpine plants, which rely on the short summer season for growth and reproduction. Unfortunately the meadows and fields above Paradise show signs of distress, with random trails and shortcuts causing erosion and plant damage.

HIGH CAMPS AND BIVOUACS

High camps vary greatly on Mount Rainier. You may find yourself in the crowded community shelter at Camp Muir or alone on the Tahoma Glacier, at popular Camp Schurman or at a bivy site on the Kautz Glacier route. In choosing a tent location, look for an area that offers protection from the weather and from objective hazards. Avoid sites that expose you to high winds, lightning, rockfall, or avalanche terrain. On a glacier, probe the site to ensure you haven't pitched your tent above a crevasse. Camp on snow whenever possible to avoid damage to vegetation; snow walls can be built to help protect camp and offer privacy. Never build new rock walls, windbreaks, or tent platforms on bare ground because they kill vegetation, cause erosion, and leave scars that last for decades.

Camp Muir, at an elevation of 10,080 feet, qualifies as a small community with A–frame ranger hut, guide/cook shack, client hut, three outhouses, and a 75-year-old public shelter that was remodeled in 2004 with new skylights and additional cooking and storage space. Use of the stone shelter, which can sleep up to twenty people on two long bunk platforms, is on a first-come, first-served basis. Climbers who can't find room in the shelter or who prefer not to stay there set up camp on the snow outside.

The Muir shelter is spartan, but it provides great protection during stormy weather. Be forewarned: the shelter is not for light sleepers. It is every bit a climbers' shack, with more snoring, smelly, restless climbers than you ever thought you'd spend a night with at 10,000 feet. Naturally it's important that every climber who stays here cleans up his or her own mess and never leaves a thing. Leftover food only attracts mice, and any other abandoned items simply add to the clutter. The restroom just outside the shelter is equipped with a park-frequency radio for emergency use.

The only structures at Camp Schurman are the ranger hut and an outhouse. Climbing rangers staff the hut in summer. During an emergency when no rangers are there, climbers can use the two-way radio on the outside of the hut next to the door to contact the National Park Service.

At most high camps, you'll have to melt snow for drinking water. Get rid of contamination by using water filters or iodine tablets, or by boiling the water for 1 minute.

EVENING ON THE MOUNTAIN

Climbing camps are generally social places, and it's common to find other teams with similar summit plans or climbing experiences. Here you may find future climbing partners, advice both good and bad, or a piece to that broken stove. Returning teams may have recent route information or stories to share. Don't be afraid to ask around if you have questions or need help.

At the same time, privacy and solitude are pleasures that some climbers seek. Climbers can respect each other's space and the wilderness experience by not camping too close together and by keeping noise and voice levels low. Sound carries extremely well on those quiet mountain evenings, and few people enjoy a neighbor's music, singing, yodeling, or conversation while looking for peace and quiet. I've heard all sorts of musical instruments on the mountain, and most climbers agree that the sound of a harmonica is no more appealing at 10,000 feet than at sea level if you're trying to get some sleep. Early risers can also help by keeping noise levels down for the benefit of parties opting for a later start.

At best, however, it may be difficult to get a good night's sleep before summit day. Hit the sack early to maximize rest; a few hours of sleep before the climb will help immensely. Climbers who think it's easier to skip sleep and head toward the summit after sunset often hit a wall after a few thousand feet.

Most people have no problem sleeping after the hard climb to high camp, but others may find that excitement and anxiety keep them awake. Avoid

A climber fords Tahoma Creek on the approach to Tahoma Cleaver. Fording creeks and crossing glacial moraines are some of the challenges that face climbers on the way to high camp.

napping before bedtime. When it's time to get into your sleeping bag, make yourself as comfortable as possible, and remember that lying horizontal is restful to the body even if you're unable to sleep. Try earplugs to help block noise from wind, other climbers, or your snoring tent partner. Doctors who specialize in high-altitude medicine recommend against use of sleeping pills, which reduce the breathing rate and may contribute to acute mountain sickness.

Before going to bed, complete all the final preparations for summit day. Get ropes and climbing gear ready, and double-check essential gear such as crampons, headlamps, and backpacks. Make the final decisions about your rope teams. Most rope teams put the leader in front, the second-most experienced climber in the back, and the least-experienced climber or climbers in the middle. Other teams choose rope order depending on fitness level, with the best pacesetter in front and the rope leader in the back. Consider the best scenario for your team and stick to it.

SUMMIT DAY

The planning and preparation all come down to this day. This is when you may discover that all your careful work does not necessarily guarantee success. You may go to bed on a star-filled night, feeling good, and waken to a headache and a stormy day. Or you could go to sleep during a storm, only to find excellent climbing conditions when you arise. If your body and the mountain both cooperate, you'll soon be heading toward the summit, which I often recommend teams at least try. Many find it much more satisfying to turn around on the mountain while headed to the summit, than to bag the trip from high camp because things appear dubious higher up.

Prepare for a long day. Most teams need between 6 to 10 hours to reach the summit from high camp and another 3 to 5 hours for the return trip to high camp. A predawn departure—an alpine start—is the norm in order to make the most of the day and to ascend and descend in the cooler hours when snow and ice are more stable.

What to Bring

Mountaineers differ on what should be carried in a summit pack. The most conservative plan is to carry all your gear from high camp so you'll have everything you need in case you get stuck for an extended period on the mountain. Every year, climbers get pinned down high on the mountain by storms, injury, or illness. On the other hand, a lighter pack feels better and allows you to move more quickly. If you go light, consider the consequences of stormy weather or an accident. Will you be able to help yourself and your teammates, regardless of the proximity of other parties or of rescue rangers? Carry the items you feel will be necessary in an emergency. Weigh the virtues of a heavier pack versus a light

Climbers enjoy the sunset and view of the Puget Sound from Columbia Crest.

rucksack. Both have their advantages, and on any given day one may be preferable to the other. The decision is yours.

Recommended team gear during a summit climb includes a snow shovel, stove with pot and fuel, insulating pad, bivy sack, first-aid kit, wands, repair kit for crampons and other essential items, and gear for belays and crevasse rescue. Personal essentials on a summit climb include a headlamp with extra batteries and bulb, food, two quarts of water, warm jacket, sunglasses, sunscreen, map and compass, matches, knife, and personal medication. Think about your summit climb and ask, "What will I need to safely continue climbing if conditions degenerate?"

When and What to Eat

Your body will perform better if it's adequately hydrated and fueled from the start, so give yourself the advantage of drinking and eating before leaving on the climb. A food rich in carbohydrates, along with a quart of water, makes for a good pre-climb breakfast.

Excitement, anxiety, high altitude, and other factors can commonly make the prospect of food unappealing. If this is the case for you, after you arise on summit day, at least try snacking on a candy bar or energy bar and having some-thing to drink. But don't make yourself sick by forcing something down. If you feel OK, start the climb anyway and try eating during the breaks. Hopefully you'll regain your appetite as you move up the mountain.

Continue to eat and drink every hour or two during the climb. Bring food you enjoy, but don't indulge in a lot of sugary snacks that may leave you feeling empty later. I often enjoy precooked red potatoes, yams, and sweet potatoes on summit day; hard candies and gum quench my thirst while moving. Keep some food easily accessible for short rest breaks.

Pace and Breaks

Set a good pace from the start. There's a fine line between too slow and too fast. A good pace allows climbers to breathe rhythmically, think clearly, and get up the mountain in a timely fashion. If you're struggling to maintain your footing, to keep your crampons off the rope, and to stay up with your teammates, you probably won't be able to continue for long. If you trained properly, a steady pace with breathing at every step will take you to the summit. Communicate with

Climbers ascending the Sunset Amphitheater, Headwall Couloir, also know as "Backstage Pass."

your rope leader about the pace. Try for a rhythm that team members can maintain for an elevation gain of 1,000 to 1,500 feet before requiring a break. Climb steadily. It's not a race; steady upward movement is what counts.

Most people feel good for the first 1,000 to 2,000 feet of elevation gain above high camp. A few will quickly realize they're in over their head and opt to stop or turn back, while some others will make it even higher and then call it quits. The breaking point for most teams is around 12,500 to 13,500 feet—after 5 to 6 hours on the standard routes. The effects of altitude and physical exhaustion really kick in. That great pace you set may pull you through, but be prepared for the psychological battles as you try to continue when your body is screaming to stop. Even the best athletes slow near the summit. Don't be discouraged. Fortitude has pulled many people up the last thousand feet.

There is no doctrine on when or how long you should rest during the ascent. Breaking more than once an hour, however, will significantly slow the team down. Stop only in safe locations, avoiding areas of crevasse, rockfall, or icefall hazard. If your team must stop in an exposed location, anchor the climbing rope and secure your pack and any other loose items that may blow away or slide down the mountain. Use breaks to eat, drink, check your gear, take pictures, and discuss plans. If you need to defecate, step off the climbing route and make use of a blue bag, but stay tied in to a rope. Pack the blue bag with you, and deposit it later in one of the barrels at the popular high camps or in a trailhead collection barrel.

Passing

On a busy route, don't be surprised to find yourself passing other parties or having other parties pass you. Rope teams passing each other as they climb can be a hazardous and stressful operation. If possible, pass while the other party is taking a break. As in backpacking, it's considered polite to allow faster teams to pass. Stepping off route for a minute or two will allow a faster party to pass safely without cutting you off.

Fast or impatient teams may try to pass if they're stuck behind a slower party. I've witnessed many arguments over who should go first and who is faster—confrontations and "horse races" that tire team members. Let impatient parties pass. And if your group would like to pass another rope team, talk with the last person on the rope ahead and ask if you can get by. This usually works. If you still can't get around the slower team, it's time to try a little patience: Focus on your surroundings and take in the view. Soon enough, you'll find a safe way to move ahead.

The Summit and Crater

You may believe you're home free once you see the rocks along the summit crater rim, but many climbers feel that this only marks the hardest part of the climb. Keep your head down and stay with your pace. Soon you'll reach the rim and enter the crater.

Most parties reach the crater rim at a point where they can seek protection from the elements. Parties generally unrope and take a break here. You're now at the summit—almost. You'll still need to walk a quarter-mile across the flat floor of the small crater if you want to stand on Columbia Crest. This highest point, at 14,410 feet, is a small snowy knoll on the west rim of the crater. With the air considerably thinner than at sea level, tired climbers often find this walk through the crater a lot more difficult than it appears.

From Columbia Crest on a clear day, you can see for a hundred miles in any direction. The summit plateau is so broad, however—more than a mile across— that Rainier's shoulders obscure lower parts of the mountain and other peaks within the park.

If the weather is particularly nice and you're feeling well, there are many things to explore while on the summit. The summit plateau has two other notable high points: Liberty Cap, at 14,112 feet, to the northwest, and Point Success, at 14,158 feet, to the southwest. Both can be a pleasant stroll for climb-

Caves and tunnels lace much of the crater's rim. Here, a scientist collects high-altitude water samples from the grotto lake 150 feet below the summit crater ice cap.

ers who are still in good shape. The two points appear to be close by, but don't be deceived. It usually takes 1½ to 2 hours for the round trip from Columbia Crest to Liberty Cap and about an hour for a similar round-trip hike to Point Success. Point Success is on a narrow ridge that offers a unique view of Rainier's south side, including the Tahoma Glacier and Paradise. Liberty Cap is a snowy point that quickly rolls away to the precipitous north and west flanks of Rainier.

You can also explore the steam caves created in the summit crater by hot volcanic gases within the mountain. Numerous fumaroles (vents) let gases escape through the soft mud and rock under the snowcap. From inside the crater, you can sometimes see steam venting in small clouds. The crater entrances to the caves change throughout the year depending on snowfall, but the passages themselves remain more or less the same. The network of tunnels is extensive, and scientists have mapped them over the years.

Some of the tunnels are small and require visitors to crawl. Others are large and cavernous. One tunnel houses the remains of a small airplane that crashed on the summit in 1990 and melted through the ice; it now resides in a mangled heap on the cavern floor. It's even possible for knowledgeable explorers to enter the caves at one point, cross beneath the crater snowcap, and exit a quarter-mile away on the opposite side by linking the correct tunnels. Visitors to the caves can expect to get wet from the steam and muddy from the volcanic clay. The caves are a unique feature that have provided shelter for many climbers caught on the summit, including Hazard Stevens and Philemon Beecher Van Trump during the mountain's first documented ascent in 1870.

Sleeping is another popular pastime in the crater. But keep an eye on the time. Those rare days when skies are clear and winds are calm can quickly change, and I've found the summit to be most typically a place where you prepare for your descent.

Descending

Going down the mountain can be as physically demanding and dangerous as going up. Acute mountain sickness, fatigue, hunger, and other problems can make it difficult to stay focused for a safe descent. A majority of mountaineering accidents occur during the descent, and parties need to take extra care to avoid mistakes that can lead to accidents.

On the standard routes, most teams need 3 to 5 hours for a safe descent to high camp. Before leaving the summit, check critical equipment such as crampons, ropes, and harnesses. Knots or crampon straps may have loosened during the climb. Tie back in to the climbing rope and check with your teammates to ensure everyone is ready and nothing is left behind. Most teams put the most experienced or strongest climber last on the rope for the descent. If anyone falls, this person can respond quickly both as an anchor and leader.

Going downhill is aerobically easier than climbing up—you don't have to breathe as hard—but it's tougher on the body. Again, pace is important. The leader should set a pace that everyone can follow without tripping or without stepping on the rope. Continue periodic eating and drinking to stave off dehydration in the sun and to keep your body well fueled.

Try to get back to high camp before the afternoon heat weakens snow bridges and increases rockfall and icefall. The snow often becomes sticky and soft in the sun. Crampons collect soft snow between the spikes, making it difficult to gain traction. Banging them with your ice ax will remove the snow temporarily; some climbers remove their crampons if the snow is particularly stubborn. Generally it's safer to leave them on, however, in case you run into icy sections. Avoid the temptation to glissade on the upper mountain, which can lead to uncontrolled slides, injuries, or falls into crevasses.

Back at high camp, relax and refuel before heading down to the trailhead. If you're at one of the popular high camps, deposit any blue bags you have into the collection barrels; otherwise pack it out to the trailhead. Again inspect your gear and clothing for damage. Go through camp and check that your team left no trace of its presence, picking up all trash, gear, and leftover food. Then it's a trek back to the trailhead. Check out at the ranger station, and your summit climb of Mount Rainier is history.

HOW TO USE THIS GUIDEBOOK

The forty principal climbing routes described in this guidebook are organized into four main sections, based on the area where climbers will leave the trailhead. These main sections are Paradise; Longmire and the Westside Road; Mowich Lake and Carbon River; and the White River area. An additional route on Little Tahoma, Washington State's third-highest peak and another significant mountaineering destination within the National Park, is also included.

From each of these general starting areas, the routes are categorized by nearby prominent features and place names on the mountain. For instance, the Longmire/Westside approaches allow access to three prominent mountain features—Success Cleaver, Tahoma Cleaver, and Puyallup Cleaver—which encompass eight distinct summit routes. (Cleavers are the prominent ridges that separate adjoining glaciers.)

Distances are given in miles, and elevations are listed in feet. To easily convert miles to kilometers, multiply by 1.6. To convert feet to meters, divide by 3.3.

THE ROUTE DESCRIPTIONS

Every route description begins with a short discussion of the route's particular qualities and features. This includes aesthetic value, views, points of interest, and other bits of information that help create a mental picture of what the route is like. Each description then provides entries with the following information.

Elevation gain: From the trailhead to the principal high point at the top of the route: Columbia Crest (elevation 14,410 feet), Point Success (elevation 14,158 feet), or Liberty Cap (elevation 14,112 feet). For the walk from Point Success to Columbia Crest, allow about half an hour. For the walk from Liberty Cap to Columbia Crest, allow about 45 minutes to 1½ hours. The listed elevation gain does not include the ups and downs in elevation that may be part of the overall ascent.

What to expect: Information on rockfall and other hazards, slope steepness, additional climbing factors, and the route's grade rating.

Time: Estimated number of days for a successful ascent and descent during favorable weather and climbing conditions. Also included are hour estimates for teams to ascend or descend the route between high camp and the summit. These estimates are generous and are based on consistent observations of independent climbers. Consider that larger teams move more slowly at high altitude, especially when they are roped together or include inexperienced climbers. Teams that have previously climbed together and are comfortable with the terrain and altitude can subtract a few hours here and there.

Season: The usual best months to climb that particular route. These recommendations consider the seasons, snow cover, access, and generally recognized optimum time and conditions to climb. The actual climatic conditions at the time of the climb will determine much of a route's difficulty.

First ascent: The climbers and the year of the original ascent and major variations.

High camp: Suggested camp for each route. Although bivouac options exist, the camps listed are generally the best and most direct for that particular climb. Exceptional bivy sites also are noted.

The full climbing descriptions are supported by detailed photos and written information about approaches, high camps, ascents, and descents. Many routes require glacier navigation. Glaciers change constantly and so do the routes. In these situations, the most common route is described. However, any glacier navigation may require extra routefinding skills as conditions change.

HOW THESE ROUTES WERE SELECTED

The routes for this guidebook were chosen based on popularity, usage trends, name recognition, and realistic climbing value. Some climbers contend Mount Rainier may have as many as eighty routes. While this is arguable, in reality only about seventeen routes are regularly attempted from year to year. This guide includes forty-one routes and numerous variations, though some are rarely climbed anymore. These include the logical lines mountaineers take as they ascend the peak and are based on prominent geological features.

If the routes on Mount Rainier were categorized by chute, approach, couloir, ice runnel, rock band, face, or other features and variations, you might come up with a thousand routes. If you consider that only a few feet may separate distinct routes at major sport-climbing venues like Smith Rock in Oregon, imagine the number of potential routes Rainier would provide.

CHOOSING YOUR ROUTE

Many climbers have heard of a few well-known routes on Mount Rainier and will choose to climb one of them based on name recognition. A great way to discover a route is through firsthand information and recommendations from reliable climbers and friends. If none of the routes are known to you, consider the mountain as a place to explore. Read about the routes here and then choose one that suits your goals, skills, and resources.

New climbers should consider one of the popular standard routes and allow a few extra days to give plenty of time for the approach to high camp, mountaineering practice, and becoming accustomed to mountain life. The

Climbers making their approach to high camp over rocky alpine slopes

Ingraham Direct/Disappointment Cleaver route and the Emmons Glacier route are the most climbed on the mountain. They offer relatively good access to high camps and glaciers where teams can practice climbing skills. Professional guide services also use these routes. However, don't become lulled into a false sense of security by the presence of so many other climbers.

If solitude, independence, and getting off the beaten track are among your goals, look to routes on the west side of the mountain or climb in the fall, winter, or early spring. Teams that are ready to hike through forest, scramble up and down moraines, break trail, negotiate glaciers, and find their own way will enjoy routes that depart from Longmire, the Westside Road, or Mowich Lake. Many of these routes go without ascents year after year. And if teams are looking for something daring, seasoned mountaineers can test their skills on the challenging Grade IV and V routes. These routes are rarely climbed.

Training Possibilities

Mount Rainier is not just a summit destination, it is also a training destination. Quick access to glaciers and alpine snowfields provide mountaineers with wonderful opportunities to practice glacier, snow travel, ice climbing, and other mountaineering-related skills. In fact, Rainier makes a realistic and appropriate training ground for expeditions to Denali and the Himalaya precisely because of its altitude, glaciation, and potential for bad weather.

At 1½ hours from Paradise, it's hard to beat the Nisqually Glacier for crevasse rescue practice or for honing glacier-climbing techniques. In May and June, crevasses begin to really open up and accessing them is rather straightforward (see the approach section to the Kautz Glacier Route).

The Nisqually Glacier is also an ice-climbing destination. This is particularly the case in the fall before the winter snows arrive and waterfall ice forms around the region. In September and October, most of the previous winter's snowpack has melted, leaving steep crevasse walls and seracs that make for dramatic ice tooling. Few of the glacier ice walls are very large (most are under 70 feet) so climbs can be top roped. It's a great place to practice; however, keep in mind that it's glacier ice and not water ice. Access the Nisqually Glacier below Glacier Vista above Paradise; the crevasses and ice should be visible from the moraine.

In the winter and spring, climbers and mountain rescue teams often practice rope ascending and crevasse rescue techniques on the steep/vertical snow walls around the Paradise parking lot. Though not as aesthetically pleasing as the glaciers in the wilderness area, the access can't be beat and the simulation of the crevasse "edge" is generally excellent. If you only have a short day, this is a good place to go.

Another great glacier training area is the Paradise Glacier, east of the Muir Snowfield between 8,000 and 8,800 feet. It's close to Paradise and Camp Muir but off the beaten path, and is great for a loose group of climbers with experience who might better come together as a team if they practice together. The Inter Glacier offers similar experiences on the Emmons Glacier approach. Breaking up the climb for training purposes is a popular option for loose-knit teams and first-time climbers on Mount Rainier.

Alternate Plans

If you're serious about having a good time during your trip to Rainier, make sure you have alternative plans. Don't base a trip on one particular route or a 2-day weather window. Always choose an alternative route or two. All the permits may be taken, or the route conditions may be unfavorable forcing you to look elsewhere on the mountain.

There are many days when the summit is inaccessible, but climbing and adventuring on other peaks and areas in the park is still possible. Research peaks like Little Tahoma or other backcountry destinations. Little Tahoma, or a cross-country jaunt in the park, may satisfy some of those alpine desires.

If worse comes to worst and the weather is just downright nasty, there are always the adjacent ski areas, Crystal Mountain and White Pass. If it's summer, check out the movie theaters in Enumclaw and Eatonville.

THE GRADING SYSTEM

The difficulty of mountaineering routes is measured in Roman numeral grades from I to VI, with I the easiest and VI the most difficult. Most climbers are familiar with the class ratings of rock climbing, such as a 5.10 rock climb or a Class 3 scramble. These ratings measure the difficulty of the hardest move. Mountaineering grades are determined by the overall difficulty of the entire climb. Factors that contribute to the grade selection include elevation gain, duration of the climb, altitude, number of pitches, objective hazards, weather, level of commitment, and physical difficulty.

Snow, ice, and glacier climbs are challenging to grade. The technical difficulties of this type of climbing change with the weather, season, and year, making it difficult to give a climb a specific rating. The changeable current conditions are as critical as the more permanent known hazards of the route. Liberty Ridge, for example, typically has a steep, exposed, icy pitch near 12,500 feet; however, late-season climbers claim the hardest part of the route is crossing the Carbon Glacier to approach the ridge.

Grade I climbs may have any number of challenges, but the route can usually be completed in half a day or less, providing a quick escape and low commitment level. Rainier does not have any summit routes rated Grade I.

Grades II and **III** involve more time on the route, perhaps a full day for the summit portion, plus some technical climbing. Many routes on Mount Rainier are Grade II or III because of their strenuous nature, altitude gain, steep terrain, glaciers, and level of commitment.

Grade IV ascents include a full day of technical climbing, with pitches that require belays and with routefinding difficulties.

Grade V routes demand 1 to 2 days of hard climbing involving difficult rock- and ice-climbing moves.

Grade VI routes call for difficult free-climbing on rock (5.10 and above), aid climbing, and ice climbing over 2 days; no routes on Rainier are rated Grade VI.

Grade II climbs may include the Emmons Glacier, Disappointment Cleaver, Gibraltar Ledges, Success Cleaver, and Kautz Cleaver routes. Grade III climbs include Liberty Ridge, Sunset Ridge, Nisqually Ice Cliff, and Nisqually Cleaver. Grade IV climbs include Ptarmigan Ridge, Curtis Ridge, Willis Wall, and Tahoma Cleaver. Routes that can be Grade V include the North Mowich Headwall and the Central Rib of Willis Wall. These climbs change with conditions. There may be a steep, icy section that becomes rock or mud as the season progresses. A straightforward climb in May could become very difficult by late August. Expect some surprises.

A NOTE ABOUT SAFETY

Safety is an important concern in all outdoor activities. No guidebook can alert you to every hazard or anticipate the limitations of every reader. Therefore, the descriptions of roads, trails, routes, and natural features in this book are not representations that a particular place or excursion will be safe for your party. When you follow any of the routes described in this book, you assume responsibility for your own safety. Under normal conditions, such excursions require the usual attention to traffic, road and trail conditions, weather, terrain, the capabilities of your party, and other factors. Keeping informed on current conditions and exercising common sense are the keys to a safe, enjoyable outing.

The Mountaineers

ROUTE OVERLAY LEGEND

 Climbing route

······ Major variation

▲ Camp or bivy (permanent or temporary)

● Landmark

① Route number referred to in list

Part II

THE ROUTES

THE ROUTES	GRADE	ELEV. GAIN	DAYS
PARADISE APPROACHES			
Camp Muir Routes			
Ingraham Glacier Direct	II	9,000	2–3
Disappointment Cleaver	II	9,000	2–3
Gibraltar Ledges (Gib Ledges)	II	9,000	2–3
Gibraltar Chute (Gib Chute)	II	9,000	2–3
Nisqually Ice Cliff	III	9,000	2–3
Nisqually Cleaver	III	9,000	2–3
Nisqually Icefall	II–III	9,000	2–3
Wapowety Cleaver and Kautz Routes			
Fuhrer Finger	II	9,000	2–4
Fuhrer Thumb	II	9,000	2–4
Wilson Glacier Headwall	II–III	9,000	2–4
Kautz Glacier	II–III	9,000	2–4
Kautz Headwall	III	9,000	2–4
Kautz Cleaver	II	9,000	2–4

Crevasses and climbers, Emmons Glacier

LONGMIRE AND WESTSIDE ROAD APPROACHES

Success Cleaver Routes

Success Couloirs	II	11,400	2–4
Success Cleaver	II	11,400	2–4
South Tahoma Headwall	III	11,400	2–4

Tahoma Cleaver Route

Tahoma Cleaver	III–IV	11,400	2–3

Puyallup Cleaver Routes

Tahoma Glacier	II	11,500	2–4
Tahoma Sickle	II	11,500	2–4
Sunset Amphitheater Ice Cap	III	11,400	2–4
Sunset Amphitheater Headwall Couloir	III	11,400	2–4
Sunset Ridge	III	11,400	2–4

MOWICH LAKE AND CARBON RIVER APPROACHES

Mowich Face Routes

Edmunds Headwall	III	9,200	2–3
Central Mowich Face	III–IV	9,200	2–4
North Mowich Headwall	IV	9,200	2–4
North Mowich Icefall	IV	9,200	2–4

Ptarmigan Ridge Routes

Ptarmigan Ridge	IV	9,200	2–4
Ptarmigan Ice Cliff	IV	9,200	2–4

WHITE RIVER APPROACHES

Lower Curtis Ridge Routes

Liberty Wall Ice Cap	IV–V	9,700/11,800	2–5
Liberty Wall Direct	IV–V	9,700/11,800	2–5
Liberty Ridge	III–IV	9,700/11,800	2–4
Willis Wall: Thermogenesis	III–IV	9,700/11,800	3–5
Willis Wall: West Rib	IV–V	9,700/11,800	3–5
Willis Wall: Central Rib	IV–V	9,700/11,800	3–5
Willis Wall: East Rib	IV–V	9,700/11,800	3–5
Willis Wall: East Willis Wall	IV	9,700/11,800	3–5
Curtis Ridge	IV	9,700/11,800	3–5

Camp Schurman Routes

Winthrop Glacier/Russell Cliffs	II–III	10,000	2–3
Emmons/Winthrop Glaciers	II	10,000	2–3

Little Tahoma

Standard Route	II	6,000/7,400	2–3

PARADISE APPROACHES

Thirteen climbing routes encompass most of Mount Rainier's south side and can all be accessed from the Paradise area.

These climbs are categorized by proximity to Camp Muir, Wapowety Cleaver, or the Kautz Glacier area.

Camp Muir routes
Ingraham Glacier Direct
Disappointment Cleaver
Gibraltar Ledges (Gib Ledges)
Gibraltar Chute (Gib Chute)
Nisqually Ice Cliff
Nisqually Cleaver
Nisqually Icefall

Wapowety Cleaver routes
Fuhrer Finger
Fuhrer Thumb
Wilson Glacier Headwall

Kautz routes
Kautz Glacier
Kautz Headwall
Kautz Cleaver

Paradise is the major destination for most visitors coming to Mount Rainier National Park. There you'll find the Henry M. Jackson Visitor Center (the large, distinctive round building), the Paradise Ranger Station, the Climbing Information Center, and Paradise Inn. Register and secure your climbing permit at the Climbing Information Center, located in the historic Guide House across from the inn at the upper end of the parking lot. If the center is closed and the Jackson Visitor Center is open, get your permit there; it's .25 mile back down the road.

JOHN MUIR ON MOUNT RAINIER

Naturalist and author John Muir climbed Mount Rainier only once. But like the colonial-era inns visited by George Washington, Muir's backcountry bedrooms have developed special significance. Rainier's most popular climbing camp bears Muir's name because of a single sleepover in August 1888.

As he recounted in his story "An Ascent of Mount Rainier," Muir climbed the peak with Philemon Beecher Van Trump, who with Hazard Stevens had made the first recorded ascent in 1870. Among those accompanying Muir and Van Trump were Edward S. Ingraham, for whom the Ingraham Glacier is named, and photographer Arthur Warner, who hauled more than 50 pounds of primitive camera equipment to the summit. Their path took them past the wildflowers of present day Paradise, a spot the fifty-year-old Muir called "the most luxuriant and the most extravagantly beautiful of all the Alpine gardens I ever beheld in all my mountain top wanderings."

Setting off the next day at noon, the men trudged easily up to what Muir described as "a narrow ledge, at an elevation of about ten thousand feet above the sea, on the divide between the glacier of the Nisqually and Cowlitz." Some historical accounts suggest Muir chose the campsite after seeing pumice that he thought indicated the ledge was protected from wind. Ingraham soon after named the site Camp Muir. The well-traveled snowfield below the camp took Muir's name years later.

The men endured a cold, windy night before setting off for the summit at 4:00 a.m. The party climbed briskly up the narrow shelf of the Gibraltar Ledge, past a field of ice pillars above Gibraltar Rock, then through a tangled maze of crevasses. Most reached the summit by noon.

After two hours atop Rainier, the group headed down. The descent was marked by several close calls. Volleys of rock fell nearby. One climber lost his footing on an icy slope and went shooting past the others so fast that Muir thought he "seemed to be going to certain death." Instead, the man dug in his alpenstock and stopped his slide. Another broke through a slim bridge spanning a crevasse; his momentum carried him to the far side, but he lost his alpenstock and had to be lowered much of way down by rope. Finally, the men reached the tree line—tired, hungry, sunburned, but otherwise in good shape.

Muir and Van Trump maintained a friendship for years after the 1888 climb. In 1893, Van Trump became one of the first people from outside California to join the Sierra Club, and he served with Muir on a club committee that pushed to make Mount Rainier a national park. Both men lived to see the dream realized: Muir died in 1914, Van Trump followed in 1916.

S.C.

Paradise Approaches

1. Ingraham Glacier/
   Disappointment Cleaver
2. Gibraltar Ledges
3. Gibraltar Chute
4. Nisqually Ice Cliff
5. Nisqually Cleaver
6. Nisqually Icefall
7. Fuhrer Finger
8. Fuhrer Thumb
9. Wilson Headwall
10. Kautz Glacier
11. Kautz Headwall
12. Kautz Cleaver

CAMP MUIR ROUTES

Seven climbing routes are best accessed from Camp Muir and the upper Muir Snowfield. Camp Muir has Rainier's shortest high-camp approach, and the climb from Paradise to Muir is one of the most popular in the park. Most parties take 4 to 8 hours to climb the 4,500 feet of elevation gain to Muir. Even the lower part of the route is often covered in snow till mid-June, but the trail to Pebble Creek at 7,200 feet melts out by midsummer. Near the start of the trail, climbers pass through Paradise Meadows, one of the park's most popular visitor attractions. Expect hundreds of day hikers and sightseers in summer.

Getting to Camp Muir: From the Paradise upper parking lot (5,420 feet), take the Skyline Trail 1.5 miles to Panorama Point (6,900 feet). In summer, follow the trail to Pebble Creek (7,200 feet), where Muir Snowfield begins. When this section is heavily snow-covered, continue along the broad ridge above Panorama Point, staying west of McClure Rock (7,385 feet) to Muir Snowfield.

Once on Muir Snowfield, ascend north-northwest to Camp Muir at 10,080 feet. Along the way, climbers get dramatic views of Mount Adams, Mount St. Helens, Mount Hood, and sometimes even Mount Jefferson in central Oregon. The snowfield occasionally gets small crevasses in late summer, and the terrain is deceiving and difficult to navigate without the aid of a compass during storms and whiteouts. A map that includes compass bearings between Paradise and Camp Muir is available from the Park Service; you can ask for one when you get your permit.

Camp Muir has a ranger hut, guide/cook shack, client hut, outhouses, a public shelter, and tent camping areas near the shelter. The shelter building can accommodate thirty climbers overnight. An emergency radio is kept inside. The shelter is open year-round, but during the winter and spring the door is frequently blocked with spindrift snow that accumulates after storms, and climbers should then expect to dig for an hour to get in.

Ingraham Glacier Direct
and Disappointment Cleaver

These routes, the most popular on Mount Rainier, see more than six thousand climbers attempting the summit every year. These mountaineering classics begin where teams leave Camp Muir and cross the Cowlitz Glacier to Cathedral Rocks, a volcanic rock ridge, and then move onto the Ingraham Glacier. The route offers great views of Little Tahoma and Gibraltar Rock as teams ascend the steeper sections of the Ingraham Glacier or Disappointment Cleaver to access the upper mountain. The final push onto the upper Ingraham and Emmons Glaciers leaves the smaller peaks of the Cascade Mountains behind as Glacier Peak and Mount Stuart in the north come into view and the crater rim and summit are reached.

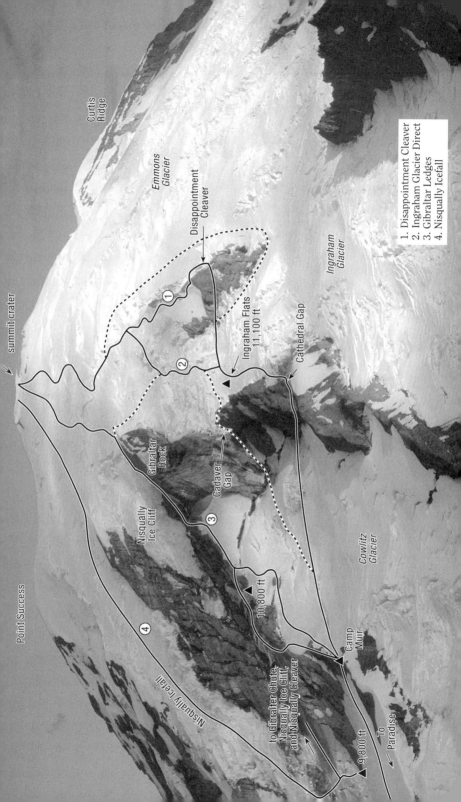

summit crater

Point Success

Curtis Ridge

Emmons Glacier

Disappointment Cleaver

① Disappointment Cleaver

② Ingraham Glacier

Ingraham Flats
11,100 ft

Cathedral Gap

Gibraltar Rock

Cadaver Gap

Nisqually Ice Cliff

③

10,800 ft

Cowlitz Glacier

Camp Muir

Nisqually Icefall

④

to Gibraltar Chute,
Nisqually Ice Cliff,
and Nisqually Cleaver

9,800 ft

To Paradise

1. Disappointment Cleaver
2. Ingraham Glacier Direct
3. Gibraltar Ledges
4. Nisqually Icefall

Although these routes are rewarding to climb, their popularity leads to heavy use and crowds. Do not expect a wilderness experience. There will be other climbers, and possibly even lines, at tight locations along the route. Rainier Mountaineering, Inc. leads more than three thousand climbers up the DC—Disappointment Cleaver—every year. The guides do an excellent job ensuring that the route remains climbable throughout the summer—digging out the route, fixing hundreds of feet of rope, and sometimes even carrying ladders high onto the mountain to bridge small crevasses. Teams that leave Camp Muir late and fall behind a guided team should not become frustrated. Consider the route and its popularity, and enjoy the view.

ELEVATION GAIN • 9,000 feet from Paradise to Columbia Crest.

WHAT TO EXPECT • Rockfall and icefall hazards; 35- to 45-degree snow and ice slopes. Grade II.

TIME • 2 to 3 days; 6 to 8 hours from high camp to summit, 3 to 4 hours for descent to high camp.

SEASON • May through September.

FIRST ASCENT • Uncertain; possibly Allison L. Brown and six or seven Yakama Indians in 1885 or 1886.

HIGH CAMP • Camp Muir (10,080 feet) or Ingraham Flats (11,100 feet).

From Camp Muir, traverse the Cowlitz Glacier to Cathedral Gap (10,640 feet) and continue left along scree, frozen rock, and ice (snow-covered in early season) to Ingraham Glacier and to Ingraham Flats at 11,100 feet. The Ingraham Flats glacier camp enjoys dramatic summer sunrises and is a great high camp for teams wanting a shorter summit day. Climbers must use the blue bag disposal system at Ingraham Flats.

An option for the route from Camp Muir to Ingraham Flats is to climb through the higher pass in Cathedral Rocks called Cadaver Gap. From Camp Muir, ascend north-northwest up the Cowlitz Glacier, skirting the bergschrund to the 11,250 foot gap, arriving just above Ingraham Flats. This variation has a reputation for avalanche and is a bit steeper than going over Cathedral Gap, but some climbers prefer it for its directness.

From Ingraham Flats, there are two principal routes: the Ingraham Glacier Direct and Disappointment Cleaver.

In the early season, most climbers prefer the **Ingraham Direct route** because it is shorter and is less exposed to avalanches than the entrance and nose of Disappointment Cleaver. From Ingraham Flats, ascend westerly to the Ingraham Icefall. Move rapidly in the lower section of the icefall to avoid falling blocks, which occasionally cut loose and sweep parts of the route. Once in the icefall, continue up 25- to 30-degree slopes as you weave around crevasses and seracs to connect with the top of Disappointment Cleaver (12,250 feet). Occasionally, parties will

2. Ingraham Direct
3. Cadaver Gap
4. Gibralter Ledges
5. Gibralter Chute
6. Nisqually Ice Cliff
7. Nisqually Cleaver
8. Nisqually Icefall

Cowlitz Glacier

▲ Ingraham Flats

Camp Muir ◄

To Paradise

Nisqually Glacier

Photo taken from Camp Muir

1. Ingraham Glacier Direct/Disappointment Cleaver
2. Cadaver Gap variation
3. Gibraltar Ledges

climb to the left, or southerly, side of the glacier and connect with the top of Gibraltar Rock (12,600 feet), ascending slopes as steep as 50 degrees.

The **Disappointment Cleaver route** becomes more popular in June and July as the Ingraham Direct melts out and crevasse navigation becomes problematic. From Ingraham Flats, head westerly to gain the cleaver on a ledge system of crumbling rock 300 feet above the Flats. Move quickly and watch for icefall from seracs on the Ingraham Glacier while accessing the lower cleaver. Once on the cleaver, be extra conscious of other parties. This is a bad area for passing other rope teams, and it is noted for its high rockfall potential. The boots and ropes of other climbers loosen rocks, as do the warmer temperatures later in the day. The lower section of the cleaver is steep—30 to 45 degrees—and switchbacks up rock or southerly exposed snow slopes as it climbs to gentler terrain. Eventually the route reaches the top of the cleaver at 12,250 feet, a good rest spot. Another summit variation passes below the Disappointment Cleaver, and climbers ascend the Emmons Glacier instead. It is a bit longer; some teams prefer this variation over Disappointment Cleaver or Ingraham Glacier Direct because they wish to navigate their own glacier route to the summit.

The Ingraham Direct and Disappointment Cleaver routes join here at the top of the cleaver. Ascend the Ingraham and Emmons Glaciers to the summit on 25- to 30-degree slopes, negotiating crevasses and unstable snow bridges along the way. Climbers who choose to ascend from Ingraham Flats to the top of Gibraltar Rock will find similar conditions on the way to the summit. The routes reach the crater rim at 14,150 feet. From there it's about a 20-minute walk to Columbia Crest, the true summit, at 14,410 feet.

Descent: Descend the route you climbed. Move quickly in dangerous areas, and plan rest breaks for safe locations. The late-morning and afternoon heat weakens snow bridges and greatly intensifies rockfall hazard.

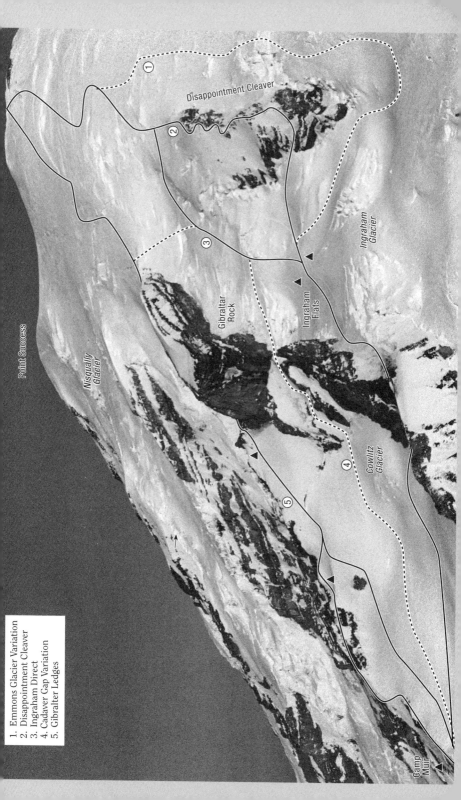

Point Success

Disappointment Cleaver

①

②

③

Ingraham Glacier

Gibraltar Rock

Ingraham Flats

Nisqually Glacier

④

Cowlitz Glacier

⑤

Camp Muir

1. Emmons Glacier Variation
2. Disappointment Cleaver
3. Ingraham Direct
4. Cadaver Gap Variation
5. Gibralter Ledges

FIRST WOMAN TO CLIMB RAINIER

She wore a skirt, boy's shoes, a straw hat, and bloomers. She traveled to Paradise for a summer outing, talked her way onto a party heading for the summit and vowed "to climb until exhausted." And on August 10, 1890, Fay Fuller, a twenty-year-old schoolteacher from Yelm, scrambled up Gibraltar Ledge and became the first woman to climb Mount Rainier.

Fuller was born October 10, 1869, in New Jersey and moved west at age twelve with her father, Edward Fuller, the owner of several small newspapers. In August 1890, she accompanied Philemon Beecher Van Trump, his wife, and ten-year-old daughter on an outing to Paradise. En route they met a group of Seattle climbers led by the Reverend Ernest C. Smith, and the enthusiastic Fuller later won permission to join their the summit attempt.

The group set off from Paradise on Saturday, August 9, at 11:00 A.M., reached Camp Muir by 5:00 P.M., awoke the next day at 4:30 A.M., and quickly started for the summit.

Fuller's climbing outfit consisted of thick, blue flannel bloomers (a garment "considered quite immodest," she later recalled), wool hose, a loose blouse, mittens, goggles, a heavy flannel coat and skirt, and a small straw hat. Rugged boots were unavailable for women, so Fuller wore calfskin boy's shoes and drove long caulks and brads into the soles. She carried a U.S. government canteen, an alpenstock fashioned from a shovel handle and three days' provisions wrapped inside two blankets looped over her shoulder.

Fuller and four male companions climbed to the base of Gibraltar Rock, picked their way along the sloping ledge's loose scree, then chopped steps to scramble up steep ice to the top of Gibraltar Cliff—with Fuller reportedly refusing offers of assistance. Beyond, they negotiated crevasses, crossed snow bridges, and fought fierce winds but finally reached the summit's highest point at 4:30 P.M. Low clouds obscured Puget Sound, but the party could see other Cascade peaks and numerous valleys, rivers, and prairies.

Too tired to descend at that late hour, the party entered an ice cave on the east rim of the summit crater and made camp amid vents of stinky, sulfurous steam. The five climbers spread out blankets, took off their shoes, and bathed their feet in whiskey. Cold and nauseated, Fuller vomited but soon "felt all right and ready to enjoy the night." Warmed by two blankets apiece, the small party spent the cold night peering at stars and listening to the rumble of avalanches. Fuller was the only member of the group to claim a few hours sleep.

They awoke to find their shoes frozen and ice coating the men's moustaches. Snow had fallen, and the windstorm was now a gale. At 6:30 A.M., they emerged into the inhospitable conditions and began their tricky descent. By the time they reached Paradise that afternoon, Fuller's lips, face, and wrists were so sunburned and swollen that she could do little for the next few days besides rest and let the pain subside.

Her account of her climb was published in her father's newspaper on August 23, 1890. She wrote that she hoped to return someday to the summit, "but now I am satisfied. . . . I have accomplished what I have always dreamed of and feared impossible."

Fuller reached the summit again in 1897, as one of fifty-eight members of the Portland-based Mazamas. Her journalism career later took her to Chicago, Washington, D.C., and New York, where she met and married attorney Fritz von Brieson. Fay von Brieson died May 27, 1958, in California.

S.C.

Gibraltar Ledges
(Gib Ledges)

The Gibraltar Ledges provided the original summit route, first climbed by Hazard Stevens and Philemon Beecher Van Trump in 1870. Now regarded as the standard winter route, it is also one of my personal favorites on Rainier. The climb ascends from Camp Muir up the Cowlitz Cleaver, a rocky ridge dividing the Cowlitz and Nisqually Glaciers. This ridge affords great views of the Nisqually Glacier, Ice Cliff, and Icefall, which provide a showcase of avalanches and icefalls that can be safely observed from the route. Once at Gibraltar Rock, one of the most visible mountain features from Paradise, this classic mountaineering route follows a narrow and exposed ledge system of challenging and steep climbing to the high glaciers and upper mountain. The route should be traveled in colder conditions and preferably before the sun hits the south face and loosens rocks above the ledge.

ELEVATION GAIN • 9,000 feet from Paradise to Columbia Crest.
WHAT TO EXPECT • Serious rockfall hazard; 35- to 50-degree snow and ice slopes. Grade II.
TIME • 2 to 3 days; 6 to 8 hours from high camp to summit, 3 to 4 hours for descent to high camp.
SEASON • December through June.
FIRST ASCENT • First recorded ascent was by Hazard Stevens and Philemon Beecher Van Trump; August 17, 1870.
HIGH CAMP • Camp Muir (10,080 feet) or the Beehive (10,800 feet).

From Camp Muir, ascend the Cowlitz Cleaver or the left side of the Cowlitz Glacier to the base of Gibraltar Rock at 11,600 feet. You will pass the well-protected

1. Disappointment Cleaver
2. Ingraham Direct
3. Cadaver Gap Variation
4. Gibraltar Ledges
5. Gibraltar Chute

Cadaver Gap

Cowlitz Cleaver

Beehive

Cowlitz Cleaver

Camp Muir

Muir Snowfield

9,800 ft

and excellent bivy sites at the Beehive (10,800 feet) and an unnamed camp at 11,400 feet, while ascending the 25- to 45-degree slopes. If you climb the glacier, be aware of possible crevasses and bergschrunds.

Once you reach the base of Gibraltar Rock—at a spot sometimes called Camp Misery, not a recommended bivy site—find the obvious ledge that leads out to the left side (west side) of Gibraltar. This ledge system is usually covered with snow or ice, but may become rocky and melted out in June and July. It is strongly recommended that climbers wear helmets and move quickly while ascending the ledges. Gibraltar is notorious for rockfall, particularly on warm days.

Traverse and ascend the ledges (do not rappel or downclimb!) to Gib Chute, a 40- to 50-degree frozen snow or ice slope that leads to the top of Gibraltar Rock, 12,600 feet. This location is also known as Camp Comfort. However, climbers should avoid camping here as the site is exposed and thus offers little protection. Ascend the upper Nisqually and Ingraham Glaciers from Camp Comfort to the crater rim (14,150 feet), negotiating crevasses and unstable snow bridges along the way. From the rim, it's about a 20-minute walk to Columbia Crest, the true summit, at 14,410 feet.

Descent: Descend this route or the Ingraham Direct or Disappointment Cleaver routes.

Gibraltar Chute
(Gib Chute)

To ascend Gibraltar Chute and three neighboring routes—Nisqually Ice Cliff, Nisqually Cleaver, and Nisqually Icefall—climbers enter the upper Nisqually Basin, a fabulously wild cirque that is noted for frequent avalanches and ice-falls from the upper glacier and ice cliff. The car-size blocks of rock and ice that litter the glacier attest to this activity.

For these climbs, teams often camp at the base of the Cowlitz Cleaver (9,800 feet) on the edge of the Nisqually Glacier, a 5-minute walk from Camp Muir. The camp at the base of the cleaver offers excellent views of the routes, including any avalanche activity. Staying overnight here can be a humbling experience as avalanches roar off the upper Nisqually and send clouds of light snow through the camp.

Since Gib Chute and the three neighboring routes have substantial objective hazards, it is strongly recommended that climbers have high-level skills and the ability to move fast on steep technical terrain. Try to use a safer route for the descent; good choices include the Ingraham Direct, Disappointment Cleaver, and Gibraltar Ledges.

Gib Chute is arguably the most direct route to the summit. This prominent

Previous page: A climber ascends Gibraltar Ledges before it connects with the upper Gibraltar Chute. Mount St. Helens is in the background.

Gibraltar Rock

①

②

1. Gibraltar Ledges
2. Gibraltar Chute

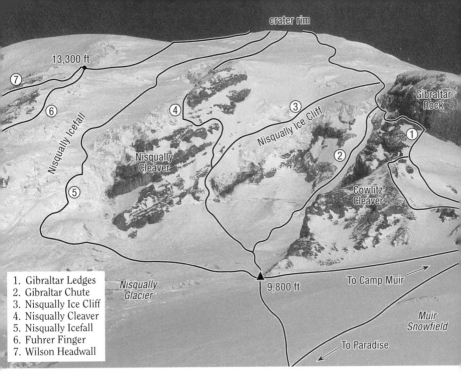

crater rim

13,300 ft

⑦

⑥

Nisqually Icefall

④

③ Nisqually Ice Cliff

Nisqually Ice Cliff

Gibraltar Rock

①

②

Nisqually Cleaver

⑤

Cowlitz Cleaver

1. Gibraltar Ledges
2. Gibraltar Chute
3. Nisqually Ice Cliff
4. Nisqually Cleaver
5. Nisqually Icefall
6. Fuhrer Finger
7. Wilson Headwall

Nisqually Glacier

9,800 ft

To Camp Muir

Muir Snowfield

To Paradise

snow chute (or rock chute, in late season) lies between and below the Nisqually Ice Cliff and Gibraltar Rock. Although perfect for rapid ascents due to its directness, the route also exposes climbers to substantial rockfall and icefall from the Ice Cliff and Gibraltar Rock. Climbers must be prepared to accept a certain amount of risk.

ELEVATION GAIN • 9,000 feet from Paradise to Columbia Crest.

WHAT TO EXPECT • Substantial exposure to rockfall and icefall; 35- to 50-degree snow and ice slopes. Grade II.

TIME • 2 to 3 days; 6 to 8 hours from high camp to summit, 3 to 4 hours for descent to high camp.

SEASON • December through June.

FIRST ASCENT • Paul Gilbreath, Stan de Bruler, and a climber named Hewitt; July 1946.

HIGH CAMP • At the base of the Cowlitz Cleaver, just below Camp Muir, on the edge of the Nisqually Glacier (9,800 feet); or at Camp Muir (10,080 feet).

From the base of Cowlitz Cleaver (9,800 feet), head northwest out onto the Nisqually Glacier, climbing the right-hand side toward the chute, which is below the Nisqually Ice Cliff. Continue up the glacier toward the base of the chute; beware of rockfall from Gibraltar Ledges above. There may be a bergschrund to cross as you leave the glacier and head up the chute.

The route becomes gradually steeper as you ascend 1,200 feet to the narrowest point, or hourglass, below the Ice Cliff, where the angle reaches 45 degrees. Move quickly through this section, which particularly exposes climbers to rockfall and icefall. The slope angle increases to 50 degrees after the chute, but ascends under less stressful and hazardous conditions to the top of Gibraltar Rock (Camp Comfort). The chute may have sections of hard ice if icefall activity has recently scoured the route.

From Camp Comfort, ascend the upper Nisqually and Ingraham Glaciers to the crater rim (14,150 feet), negotiating crevasses and unstable snow bridges along the way. From the rim, it's about a 20-minute walk to Columbia Crest, the true summit, at 14,410 feet.

Descent: Descend the Ingraham Direct, Disappointment Cleaver, or Gibraltar Ledges back to high camp.

Nisqually Ice Cliff
and Nisqually Cleaver

Deep winter snowpack and quick access from Paradise make these routes excellent winter and spring climbs. The upper Nisqually Basin, a glacier war zone of avalanches and icefalls, is crossed to access the steep ice slopes that ascend the Ice Cliff and the Cleaver. On the routes, climbers must negotiate crevasses, seracs, ice cliffs, and rock bands amidst uniquely beautiful glacier chaos. A speedy ascent is demanded for safety. Once the technical pitches are completed, the slope decreases and the routes move on to gentle glacier terrain. Late-season climbs are discouraged as these routes become too crevassed and the ice cliffs above avalanche frequently.

For additional general information related to these routes, see the introduction to the Gibraltar Chute route.

ELEVATION GAIN • 9,000 feet from Paradise to Columbia Crest.

WHAT TO EXPECT • Substantial exposure to rockfall and icefall; 35- to 60-degree snow and ice slopes. Grade III.

TIME • 2 to 3 days; 6 to 9 hours from high camp to summit, 3 to 4 hours for descent to high camp.

SEASON • December through June.

FIRST ASCENT • Nisqually Ice Cliff—Barry Bishop and Luther Jerstad; August 13, 1962. Nisqually Cleaver—Fred Dunham and James Wickwire; June 19, 1967. Nisqually Cleaver Variation, Right—Jason Edwards and Todd Kelsey; May 22, 1999.

HIGH CAMP • At the base of the Cowlitz Cleaver, just below Camp Muir, on the edge of the Nisqually Glacier (9,800 feet); or at Camp Muir (10,080 feet).

Leaving camp at 9,800 feet (base of Cowlitz Cleaver) heading on to the Nisqually Glacier

From the base of Cowlitz Cleaver (9,800 feet), head northwest onto the Nisqually Glacier, climbing to a large snow ramp that provides access to the lower left-hand side of the Nisqually Ice Cliff. There is a high objective hazard as you traverse and climb the Nisqually. Move quickly to avoid avalanches and ice blocks that liberate themselves from above and litter the glacier. Access the ramp by crossing the bergschrund, which is typically filled with debris from snowslides above. Climb the 55-degree ramp to a rock band directly overhead and a little to the right. This gains access to the shelf that forms the ice cliff itself. The ramp is at its steepest just below the rock band. Traverse and climb right, along the ice shelf. The ice cliff and cleaver routes separate at about 11,400 feet, shortly after the rock band.

To ascend the **Nisqually Ice Cliff route,** ascend right (east) along the top of the ice shelf. The route becomes less steep, but crevasses and short sections of icefall must be crossed. There is still substantial exposure to objective hazards as the route continues along this slanting shelf to the top of Gibraltar Rock (Camp Comfort) or the upper Nisqually Glacier. This section of the route changes from year to year. Glacier movement pushes the old shelf onto the Nisqually Glacier and usually creates another shelf behind it.

To ascend the **Nisqually Cleaver route,** climb the steep face and snow chutes, keeping the rock bands on the left and the Nisqually Ice Cliff and shelf to the right. Variations exist that may include short water-ice steps to 80 degrees. The rock bands at 12,500 feet can either be climbed (moves are easy but exposure is great) or circumnavigated as seasonal conditions dictate. The route is quite airy

Climbers above 12,000 feet on Nisqually Cleaver, with the Nisqually Glacier Falls below © George Beilstein.

through this section. After the rock bands, traverse and climb left around the nose or crest of the upper cleaver to the upper Nisqually Icefall. Stay close to the cleaver and climb another chute, angled at 40 degrees, to the termination of the cleaver.

After this climb of either the Nisqually Ice Cliff or Cleaver, ascend glacier slopes to the summit crater rim. It's a 20-minute walk to Columbia Crest from the crater rim.

Descent: Descend the Ingraham Direct, Disappointment Cleaver, or Gibraltar Ledges back to high camp.

Nisqually
Icefall

The Nisqually Icefall, like the Nisqually Ice Cliff and Cleaver, is a great winter and spring climb. Ascending the largest glacier on the south side of the mountain, this route avoids many of the hazards that make Gibraltar Chute, Nisqually Ice Cliff, and Nisqually Cleaver so dangerous. However, there still are objective hazards and they can be substantial depending on the year. The icefall's charms include excellent views of the Nisqually Basin and river drainage and the Paradise area and a close-up look at such glacier features as seracs, jumbled ice blocks, and crevasses. Climbers need good routefinding and glacier navigation skills; a speedy ascent is strongly recommended. Avoid the icefall late in the summer, when the glacier becomes extremely broken and navigation too circuitous.

For additional general information related to this route, see the introduction to the Gibraltar Chute route.

1. Gibraltar Chute
2. Nisqually Ice Cliff
3. Nisqually Cleaver

Nisqually Glacier

Nisqually Glacier

Nisqually Cleaver

Nisqually Cleaver

Nisqually Glacier

Nisqually

To

1. Gibraltar Ledges
2. Nisqually Icefall

Camp Muir

To Paradise

Muir Snowfield

Cowlitz Cleaver

① Cowlitz Cleaver

9,800 ft

② Nisqually Glacier

Nisqually Glacier

ELEVATION GAIN • 9,000 feet from Paradise to Columbia Crest.
WHAT TO EXPECT • Substantial exposure to icefall; 35- to 60-degree snow and ice slopes. Grade II or III.
TIME • 2 to 3 days; 7 to 10 hours from high camp to summit, 3 to 5 hours for descent to high camp.
SEASON • Winter through June.
FIRST ASCENT • Dee Molenaar and Robert Craig; July 15, 1948.
HIGH CAMP • At the base of the Cowlitz Cleaver, just below Camp Muir, on the edge of the Nisqually Glacier (9,800 feet); or at Camp Muir (10,080 feet).

From the base of Cowlitz Cleaver (9,800 feet), climb and traverse west onto the Nisqually toward the lower and western lobe of the glacier. There is some danger of rockfall and icefall from the upper Nisqually, so move quickly. Begin climbing the icefall at 10,800 feet, negotiating crevasses, seracs, and other features.

The glacier is not very steep, but there may be short sections of vertical ice where belays and protection are needed to navigate around obstructions. Beware of hidden crevasses; winter snowfall deceptively hides a very active and broken icefall.

Ascend to 12,500 feet, where the steepness of the icefall decreases. The Nisqually Cleaver is on your right, and the top of upper Wapowety Cleaver will be on your left; ascend gentle glacier slopes to the crater rim. It's a 20-minute walk to Columbia Crest from the crater rim.

Descent: Descend the Ingraham Direct, Disappointment Cleaver, or Gibraltar Ledges back to high camp.

▼▼▼

WAPOWETY CLEAVER AND KAUTZ ROUTES

The Wapowety Cleaver and Kautz routes on the south side encompass some of Mount Rainier's most noted climbs. These are moderately popular climbs for mountaineers seeking ascents on nonstandard routes. The high camps are primitive. The routes see little guided activity and are considered good alternatives to the most crowded tracks: the Ingraham Direct, Disappointment Cleaver, and Emmons Glacier. They are all Grade II or III, yet each has its own unique character.

The upper Wapowety Cleaver is a large triangular rock formation with steep snowfields and numerous snow chutes that melt out late in the summer. It separates the upper Kautz Glacier on its left (west) and the Nisqually Glacier on its right, and the bottom perimeter marks the beginning of the Wilson Glacier. From the Wilson Glacier, climbers have access to three climbing routes: the **Fuhrer Finger,** the **Fuhrer Thumb,** and the **Wilson Headwall.**

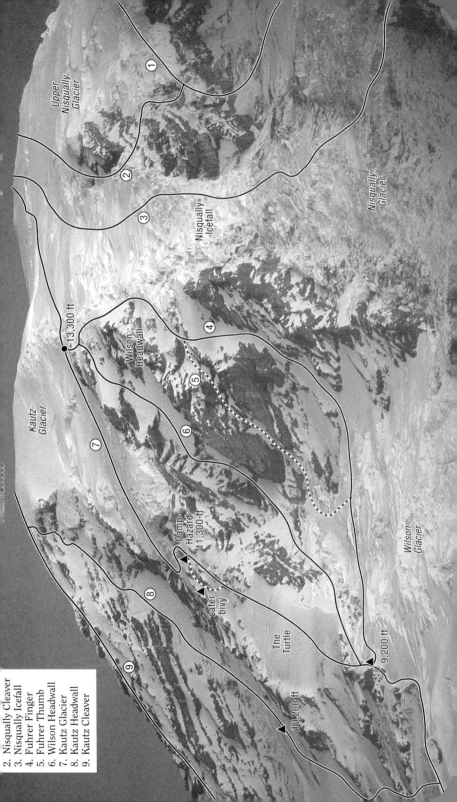

2. Nisqually Cleaver
3. Nisqually Icefall
4. Fuhrer Finger
5. Fuhrer Thumb
6. Wilson Headwall
7. Kautz Glacier
8. Kautz Headwall
9. Kautz Cleaver

① ② ③ ④ ⑤ ⑥ ⑦ ⑧ ⑨

Upper Nisqually Glacier

Nisqually Glacier

Nisqually Icefall

13,300 ft

Wilson Headwall

Kautz Glacier

Camp Hazard 11,300 ft

safer bivy

The Turtle

Wilson Glacier

9,200 ft

10,200 ft

1. Fuhrer Finger
2. Wilson Glacier Headwall
3. Kautz Glacier
4. Kautz Headwall
5. Kautz Cleaver

Columbia Crest

Nisqually Glacier

Wilson Glacier

Kautz Glacier

Camp Hazard

Kautz Glacier

Wapowety Cleaver

Success Glacier

The **Kautz Glacier** flows from the summit along the western edge of the Wilson Headwall. The glacier has a prominent lobe and ice cliff that can be seen from Paradise. The **Kautz Headwall** and **Kautz Cleaver** routes ascend the volcanic rocky spur that originates at Point Success. The Kautz Cleaver is a ridge that divides the Success Glacier and its headwall from the lower Kautz Glacier. The cleaver also forms the headwall for Kautz Basin, where the upper Kautz Glacier empties from a massive ice cliff.

Getting to the high camps: Of the two principal approaches to these routes, most climbers prefer the one that begins at Paradise. The alternative approach begins much lower—at the Comet Falls trailhead (3,600 feet), 4 miles above Longmire. Starting in the forest, this approach follows the trail along Van Trump Creek, passing Comet Falls and continuing up to Van Trump Park (5,600 feet). It ascends subalpine and alpine meadows north-northeast along the lower Wapowety Cleaver, which separates the lower Kautz and Wilson Glaciers. A very beautiful hike, this approach requires substantially more elevation gain, and many climbers prefer not to walk the extra distance.

The usual approach begins at the Paradise upper parking lot (5,420 feet) and follows the Skyline Trail for 1 mile to Glacier Vista (6,336 feet), a popular day-hike destination with excellent views of Mount Rainier, Mount Adams, Mount St. Helens, and Mount Hood. The vista overlooks the Nisqually Glacier, where climbers descend 400 feet to cross the lateral moraine and get onto the glacier.

Rope up—the Nisqually has numerous hidden holes—and continue northwest across the glacier. Look for a prominent snow chute on the other side of the glacier that provides access to the west side (left side) of the Wilson Glacier and to the upper Wapowety Cleaver. A large rock buttress marks the right side of this chute, known as the Fan. There may be a bergschrund at the entrance to the chute and a creek is usually flowing from the buttress. During the early season, it is possible to ascend the Nisqually Glacier directly to the Wilson Glacier. On some occasions, this can provide a more direct approach. The way melts out early, so be prepared to climb the Fan.

Put your helmet on; the chute is notorious for rockfall and avalanches, and usually has a large cornice directly above. Ascend the 25- to 35-degree slope for an elevation gain of 800 feet, to where the grade relaxes and provides a good rest area with views of the Nisqually Glacier, Paradise, and Muir Snowfield.

Continue north and uphill; the grade increases to 40 degrees as it climbs around another rock buttress, this one on your left, to reach the crest of Wapowety Cleaver. Travel along the broad, snowy crest of the cleaver, heading north toward the mountain. The Wilson Headwall and Kautz Glacier are straight ahead, and the route you intend to climb will determine where you make high camp.

To reach high camps for the Fuhrer Finger, Fuhrer Thumb, Wilson Headwall, and Kautz Glacier routes, continue up the mountain, selecting a site within the

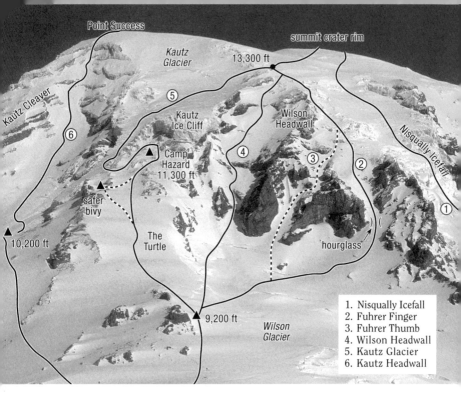

Point Success
Kautz Glacier
13,300 ft
summit crater rim
Kautz Cleaver
5
Kautz Ice Cliff
Wilson Headwall
Nisqually Icefall
6
Camp Hazard 11,300 ft
4
3
2
safer bivy
1
10,200 ft
The Turtle
hourglass
9,200 ft
Wilson Glacier

1. Nisqually Icefall
2. Fuhrer Finger
3. Fuhrer Thumb
4. Wilson Headwall
5. Kautz Glacier
6. Kautz Headwall

permitted zone that best suits the needs of your climb. Excellent bivies exist along the cleaver, where occasional rock outcroppings provide great weather protection. Camp Hazard (11,300 feet) is the highest camp along the cleaver. The camp has established rock walls and collection barrels for blue bags, and the unique location provides great views of the southern Cascades and the Kautz Ice Cliff. Unfortunately the camp is exposed to significant rockfall and icefall from that same ice cliff. Consider a safer camp at a lower elevation, where you won't have to carry your high-camp gear so far.

To reach high camps for the Kautz Headwall and Kautz Cleaver routes, traverse westerly across the broad Wapowety Cleaver to the edge of the lower Kautz Glacier.

Fuhrer Finger
and Fuhrer Thumb

The Fuhrer Finger is a wide, steep couloir up the eastern face of the Wilson Headwall. The vastness of the headwall dwarfs climbers, with large volcanic spires standing out sharply as teams cross the upper Wilson Glacier to access the Finger. The Fuhrer Finger route is recessed into the headwall, providing nonglaciated access up the wall and onto the upper western edge of the Nisqually Glacier. The route is often said to be the fastest way up the mountain, but it's not, because you spend too much time dropping down to the Nisqually Glacier and crossing it. The Gibraltar Chute offers faster access from parking lot to summit. The Fuhrer Thumb is a narrow couloir immediately west of the Finger.

This flank of Rainier receives a lot of sun. The snow may be firm early in the morning, but the routes can be an oven on clear, sunny days when the snow becomes deep and sloppy. Warmth also means rockfall; the routes demand helmets and call for a true alpine start. The routes eventually lead to the top of the Wilson Headwall (13,300 feet), where gentler glacier slopes then take climbers to the summit crater rim and Columbia Crest.

ELEVATION GAIN • 9,000 feet from Paradise to Columbia Crest.
WHAT TO EXPECT • Rockfall hazard; avalanche danger; glacier travel; 30- to 45-degree snow and ice slopes. Grade II.
TIME • 2 to 4 days; 5 to 7 hours from high camp to summit, 3 to 5 hours for descent to high camp.
SEASON • December through early August.
FIRST ASCENT • Fuhrer Finger—Hans Fuhrer, Heinie Fuhrer, Joseph Hazard, Peyton Farrer, and Thomas Hermans; July 2, 1920. Fuhrer Thumb—Jim Wickwire, Charlie Raymond, and Tom Stewart; May 27, 1972.
HIGH CAMP • On the west edge of Wilson Glacier, at 9,200 feet, next to a large rock buttress that provides excellent weather protection.

From the 9,200-foot high camp, traverse north-northeast across Wilson Glacier toward the eastern flank of the Wilson Headwall. Take care along the Wilson Glacier because many crevasses run parallel to the route, and arresting a crevasse fall is problematic.

The **Fuhrer Finger route** is a prominent snow couloir with an hourglass funnel. Ascend the glacier to the base of the Finger at 10,000 feet, where there may be a bergschrund late in the season. Begin the 2,000-foot climb up the couloir. The route looks steep from a distance; however, the slope angle is between 30 and 45 degrees. Move quickly, as rockfall is prevalent in the hourglass, a feature more prominent in the summer. The Finger broadens above 11,300 feet.

The **Fuhrer Thumb route** ascends one of the snow couloirs immediately west of the Fuhrer Finger. From the 9,200-foot high camp, approach the Fuhrer Finger, but head west and instead climb the prominent narrow couloir between the Wilson Headwall and the Finger. The Thumb has similar slope angles and hazards as the Finger, but it is considerably narrower. This couloir reconnects with Fuhrer Finger around 11,500 feet. (Avoid the temptation to continue up snow couloirs that ascend the headwall more directly; they end in cliffs.)

From 11,500 feet, Fuhrer Finger continues until it tops out onto the eastern edge of the Wilson Headwall, next to the Nisqually Glacier, at about 12,000

1. Fuhrer Finger
2. Fuhrer Thumb
3. Wilson Headwall

Note Icefall through Camp Hazard

Nisqually
Glacier

Kautz
Glacier

Camp
Hazard
11,300

The
Turtle

feet. Climb along the edge of the glacier to the crest of the headwall at 13,300 feet. From here, it's a short climb to the summit crater rim and Columbia Crest.

Descent: There are several choices. Teams can descend the Fuhrer Finger, the Kautz Glacier route, or a standard route back to Camp Muir.

Teams that descend the Finger are often tempted to glissade, but don't. This route has slid on many parties, and is the perfect angle for such an incident. Move quickly, and beware of avalanches in spring and early summer.

The recommended descent is via the Kautz Glacier. This descent provides a loop trip back to high camp on the west edge of Wilson Glacier, and doesn't require climbers to traverse back across the upper Wilson Glacier.

A descent via the Ingraham Glacier Direct, Disappointment Cleaver, or Gibraltar Ledges to Camp Muir and down to Paradise is popular with teams that want to sleep on the summit, carry over, or avoid the climb back out of the lower Nisqually Glacier up to Glacier Vista.

Wilson Glacier Headwall

The Wilson Glacier Headwall is a steep cirque of snowfields and rock bands accessed through narrow couloirs off the northwest head of the Wilson Glacier. The headwall comprises the central and western side of Wapowety Cleaver and tops out at 13,300 feet, the cleaver's apex. The climb is best attempted when snow covers most of the face. There is substantial exposure to icefall from the Kautz Ice Cliff when accessing the headwall. Climbers should use helmets and get an alpine start, especially in summer, when the headwall gets a lot of sun. Once on the route, the climb is moderately steep with great exposure as the lower headwall and Wilson Glacier fall away below.

ELEVATION GAIN • 9,000 feet from Paradise to Columbia Crest.
WHAT TO EXPECT • Rockfall and icefall hazards; glacier travel; 30- to 50-degree snow and ice slopes. Grade II or III.
TIME • 2 to 4 days; 6 to 9 hours from high camp to summit, 3 to 5 hours for descent to high camp.
SEASON • Winter through July.
FIRST ASCENT • Dee Molenaar and Pete Schoening; July 21, 1957.
HIGH CAMP • On the west edge of Wilson Glacier, at 9,200 feet, next to a large rock buttress that provides excellent weather protection.

From the 9,200-foot high camp, climb directly to the headwall and across the top of the Wilson Glacier. There may be a bergschrund in late season. The headwall is accessed through 30-degree snow chutes (at 10,000 feet) that expose climbers to icefall from the Kautz Ice Cliff. Move quickly.

Stay left of the prominent rock buttress in the center of the headwall and ascend 30- to 45-degree slopes for 3,000 feet. The steepest sections are lower on the face, increasing the feeling of exposure higher on the route. Small rock bands at 11,300 feet and 12,200 feet can be climbed or bypassed on the sides.

Slope angle decreases higher on the snowfield, but larger bands of rock near the top of the upper Wapowety Cleaver may require fifth-class moves and protection. These can be avoided by exiting on the eastern snow chute toward the upper Nisqually Glacier. Either way, continue to 13,300 feet—the top of the headwall and of Wapowety Cleaver. From here, it's a short climb to the summit crater rim and Columbia Crest.

Descent: Teams usually descend the Kautz Glacier route, which provides a loop trip back to the high camp, or carry over the summit and take a standard route back to Camp Muir. It's best to avoid descending the headwall because the hazards loom larger later in the day, and the steepness of the route makes descent difficult.

A descent via the Ingraham Glacier Direct, Disappointment Cleaver, or Gibraltar Ledges to Camp Muir and down to Paradise is popular with teams wishing to camp on the summit, carry over, or avoid the climb back out of the lower Nisqually Glacier up to Glacier Vista.

THE INDOMITABLE PETE RIEKE

Scientist Pete Rieke was an avid climber until a 1994 rock-climbing accident cracked his spine and left him paralyzed from the waist down. But the handicap didn't prevent him from becoming the first paralyzed climber to reach the summit of Mount Rainier.

Unable to walk to the mountaintop, Rieke designed and built a mechanical "snow pod" from bicycle gears, inline skate wheels, and studded snowmobile treads. Seated atop the 56-pound contraption, Rieke could hand-crank his way inch by inch up mountains, using the pod's forty-nine speeds to surmount snow, ice, and rock. In typical conditions, Rieke's snow pod could cover about 100 horizontal feet per minute and climb 1,000 to 2,000 vertical feet a day.

In 1998, Rieke and a support team cranked their way to 12,600 feet, near the base of Mount Rainier's Disappointment Cleaver, before conditions halted the climb. The next year, Rieke chose the steeper but more direct Kautz Glacier. He turned around at 11,600 feet amid a flurry of avalanches, but the experience taught him the Kautz route was a better fit for the pod's machinery.

Climbers made the first winter ascent of the Wilson Headwall in 1975–76. The Kautz Ice Cliff looms in the background. © Eric Simonson.

In 2000, at age forty-five, Rieke tried a third time to crank his way up Mount Rainier. After receiving the necessary permission to ride a mechanical vehicle in a National Park Wilderness, Rieke and his team left Paradise on June 8 and started inching up the peak.

Conditions were far from ideal, and Rieke's team spent many days bogged down by heavy snow, high winds, and the threat of avalanche. Most travel took place at night so the pod's treads could more effectively grip the cold, firm snow. By June 17, after the storm abated, Rieke had passed Camp Hazard and established high camp at 12,600 feet.

He and six other climbers set off the next day shortly after midnight, cranking steadily uphill amid 60 mph winds. By sunrise, the team had reached 14,153-foot Point Success. But between Rieke and the true summit lay a field of ice pillars, some 2 feet tall. His team chopped a path through the pillars with ice axes to allow Rieke to crank to the crater rim.

Rieke crossed the crater and rolled up the final rise to 14,410-foot Columbia Crest. "Base camp, base camp. This is the summit," he breathlessly radioed at 12:23 P.M. "We have done it." Rieke spent just 15 minutes atop the windswept summit before beginning his descent. He reached Paradise June 21 after spending 13 days on Rainier.

S.C.

Kautz
Glacier

The Kautz Glacier was the original line taken by Lieutenant August Valentine Kautz and his party when they nearly reached the summit in July 1857. A long approach combined with glacier travel and steep pitches of frozen snow or ice make this route an attractive choice for mountaineers desiring a challenging intermediate climb of Mount Rainier.

The Kautz Ice Cliff looms above climbers as they approach the route. Camp Hazard (11,300 feet) has the distinction of being the highest established camp on the mountain. The camp has protective rock walls piled up by climbers long ago, and collection barrels for blue bags. Despite the amenities, climbers should avoid staying here. The camp lies directly below the massive Kautz Ice Cliff, which occasionally dumps truck-size blocks of ice and debris into the camp, and sometimes even down onto the Turtle, the snowfield below. There are good protected bivy sites on the western edge of the Turtle and lower, near 9,200 feet.

Above Camp Hazard, climbers on the Kautz Glacier route get up-close and personal with the ice cliff, its seracs, and blue ice pinnacles. From 1939 to 1950, the Kautz Glacier was the standard route for guided parties.

ELEVATION GAIN • 9,000 feet from Paradise to Columbia Crest.

WHAT TO EXPECT • Rockfall and icefall hazards; glacier travel; 50- to 60-degree snow and ice slopes. Grade II or III.

TIME • 2 to 4 days; 5 to 10 hours from high camp to summit (depending on the high camp), 3 to 5 hours for descent to high camp.

SEASON • A great climb year-round; late-season ascents demand good technical ice skills to move through dangerous areas quickly.

FIRST ASCENT • Three women and seven men were reported to have climbed the route in 1913. The first recorded ascent was by Hans Fuhrer, Heinie Fuhrer, Roger Toll, and Harry Myers; July 28, 1920.

HIGH CAMP • Bivouac platforms can be dug in the snow along the western edge of the Turtle, a broad, rolling snow slope below Camp Hazard, between 9,800 and 11,000 feet.

From high camp, climb to the base of the Kautz Ice Cliff (11,300 feet). Head left (west) and descend 200 feet down an ice gully walled off on the right by the ice cliff and on the left by steep, rocky cliffs. Move quickly and wear a helmet; this is a run out for ice-cliff debris. Some years, usually early season, it is possible to ascend vertical steps and steep snow and ice chutes through the ice cliff itself. This variation avoids the descent down the chute.

Columbia Crest

Kautz Glacier

Camp Hazard

The Turtle

Wilson Glacier

The Fan

Nisqually Glacier

Glacier Vista

Paradise

1. Early Season Variation
2. Fuhrer Finger
3. Kautz Glacier

Only teams with strong ice climbing skills should elect to do this.

Continue along the base of the ice cliff and skirt its bottom. Then ascend steep snow and ice slopes that provide access to the glacier above the ice cliff. There are two pitches of 50- to 60-degree frozen snow or hard glacial ice, separated by about 100 yards of gentler glacier. The second pitch is a bit longer and steeper than the first; ice screws or pickets are recommended for protection.

The angle relaxes at the top of the second steep pitch, and glacier travel resumes to the apex of Wapowety Cleaver (13,300 feet). Continue along the upper Kautz and Nisqually Glaciers to the south side of the summit crater rim. From there, the true summit at Columbia Crest is a 15-minute walk away.

Descent: Climbers usually descend the Kautz Glacier, though some choose a summit carry-over and a standard route back to Camp Muir. When descending the Kautz Glacier, use extra caution on the steep icy pitches. Climbers with limited experience should descend on belay or consider rappelling. Ice pinnacles or constructed bollards make possible rappel anchors.

Descending the Ingraham Glacier Direct, Disappointment Cleaver, or Gibraltar

Ledges to Camp Muir is popular with teams wishing to camp on the summit, carry over, or avoid the climb back out of the lower Nisqually Glacier up to Glacier Vista.

Kautz
Headwall

The Kautz Headwall, which is rarely climbed, is one of the longest headwalls on Mount Rainier. A lengthy approach and ominous appearance discourage many climbers from attempting the route. High camp on Wapowety Cleaver sits above the lower Kautz Glacier. From there, climbers have an excellent view of the route, which crosses under the lower lobe of the Kautz Ice Cliff and ascends the right side of Kautz Cleaver to Point Success.

The headwall has moderately steep snowfields, rock bands, and occasional short sections of water ice in June and July. The route ascends technical climbing terrain for over 3,500 feet, making for some exciting climbing with great exposure. As with other headwalls, the climb has late-season rockfall problems.

ELEVATION GAIN • 9,000 feet from Paradise to Columbia Crest.
WHAT TO EXPECT • Rockfall and icefall hazards; glacier travel; 50-degree snow and ice slopes with rock bands. Grade III.
TIME • 2 to 4 days; 6 to 9 hours from high camp to summit, 3 to 6 hours for descent to high camp.
SEASON • December through July.
FIRST ASCENT • Pat Callis, Dan Davis, and Don Gordon; July 8, 1963.
HIGH CAMP • Bivouac platforms can be dug in the snow between 9,500 and 10,200 feet on the edge of Wapowety Cleaver.

Access the lower Kautz Glacier by dropping off Wapowety Cleaver and descending scree and snow slopes. The Kautz Headwall lies directly north; however, climbers must first cross under the lower lobe of the Kautz Ice Cliff. Debris on the glacier will indicate recent activity. Move quickly through this area of high objective hazard. Continue climbing toward the headwall, looking for a good location to cross the bergschrund and access the face.

The grade starts at 30 degrees, but sections of the climb may reach 50 or 60 degrees, depending on the season. Summer ascent teams may even find short sections (10 to 20 feet) of water ice over some of the rock bands. Continue to ascend chutes and snowfields left toward the crest of Kautz Cleaver. The final rock bands can either be climbed directly or skirted to the left, where a short terraced ledge leads to Point Success. Bring pickets for protection. From Point Success, cross the narrow col and ascend gentle slopes for the half-hour walk to Columbia Crest.

Descent: Descend the Kautz Glacier route. Take caution on the steep icy pitches, where climbers may elect to downclimb on belay or possibly rappel.

1. Kautz Headwall
2. Kautz Cleaver

Point Success

Columbia Crest

Kautz
Glacier

Kautz Cleaver

①

②

Wapowety Cleaver

To
The Fan

To
Van Trump
Park

Kautz
Cleaver

The Kautz Cleaver is a long rocky ridge that separates the Success and Kautz Glaciers. Beginning at 8,800 feet, the cleaver rises over 5,000 feet through snow ramps, rock bands, and scree slopes to Point Success. This route is best climbed when there is plenty of snow covering the loose rock and pumice that makes up most of this ridge. Although the route is technically easy, it sees little climbing activity due to its long approach.

The quickest approach may be via the Comet Falls trailhead, 4 miles up the road from Longmire, instead of from Paradise; it's a toss up. The Comet Falls approach begins much lower—at 3,600 feet, instead of the Paradise elevation of 5,420—but it's more direct, sending climbers straight up Wapowety Cleaver. The Kautz Cleaver is a great moderate climb for teams looking to get off the beaten track, away from crowded high camps and routes.

ELEVATION GAIN • 9,000 feet from Paradise to Columbia Crest (or 11,200 feet from the Comet Falls trailhead to Columbia Crest).

WHAT TO EXPECT • Rockfall hazard; glacier travel; 30-degree snow slopes with rock bands. Grade II.

TIME • 2 to 4 days; 7 to 10 hours to high camp, 7 to 10 hours from high camp to summit, 3 to 6 hours for descent to high camp.

SEASON • Winter through July.

FIRST ASCENT • George Senner and Charles Robinson; September 1, 1957.

HIGH CAMP • On the Kautz Cleaver (at 10,200 feet) or on Wapowety Cleaver (at 9,000 feet).

From 8,000 feet on Wapowety Cleaver, descend to the lower Kautz Glacier and navigate through crevasse fields to the toe of Kautz Cleaver at 8,800 feet. Gain the west side of the cleaver at 9,000 feet and ascend 20- to 35-degree slopes on the left (west) of the crest to the good bivy site on the cleaver at 10,200 feet.

An alternative is to make high camp at 9,000 feet on Wapowety Cleaver. From camp, descend onto the lower Kautz Glacier and traverse across crevasse fields to Kautz Cleaver. Gain the eastern side of the cleaver on 30-degree snow slopes at about 9,500 feet. Ascend directly to the ridge crest and saddle at 10,200 feet.

From 10,200 feet, the climb offers a variety of options. Ascend the ridge via any number of chutes and gullies, generally staying on the western flank. At 12,000 feet, the cleaver broadens and the Success Cleaver route joins in. From

Close Up of Upper Kautz Cleaver and Kautz Glacier
1. Kautz Glacier
2. Kautz Cleaver

Columbia Crest

Point Success

A climber descends Kautz Cleaver in July; note severe sun cupping.

here, stay east of the cleaver's crest, climbing high above the Kautz Headwall. The slope angle increases to 40 degrees for a short pitch before topping out at Point Success. From Point Success, cross the narrow col and ascend gentle slopes for the half-hour walk to Columbia Crest.

Descent: Descend the climbing route.

LONGMIRE AND
WESTSIDE ROAD APPROACHES

There are nine major climbing routes and several variations on Mount Rainier's southwest aspect. All can be accessed from the Westside Road and Longmire area.

These climbs are categorized by proximity to prominent mountain features: Success Cleaver, Tahoma Cleaver, or Puyallup Cleaver.

Success Cleaver routes
Success Couloirs
Success Cleaver
South Tahoma Headwall

Tahoma Cleaver route
Tahoma Cleaver

Puyallup Cleaver routes
Tahoma Glacier
Tahoma Sickle
Sunset Amphitheater Ice Cap
Sunset Amphitheater Headwall Couloir
Sunset Ridge

The routes in this section represent some of the longest and most challenging on Mount Rainier. They see limited use, though most are climbed annually and are popular with climbers familiar with Cascades volcano mountaineering. The long approaches, technical difficulties, and sporadic climbing activity make these routes committing. Climbing them requires self-reliance, as rangers and other mountaineers are few and far between. These cautions only serve to enhance the solitude that is so much a part of the wilderness experience. To preserve the integrity of the area the Park Service has instituted tighter backcountry camping limitations.

Many of these routes top out on either Point Success (14,158 feet) or Liberty Cap (14,112 feet). Both destinations require an additional hike to the true 14,410-foot summit at Columbia Crest. From Point Success, it's a half-hour walk to Columbia Crest. From Liberty Cap, it's a walk of nearly a mile to Columbia Crest, and climbers must descend to the col at 13,600 feet before regaining the gentle slopes to 14,410 feet.

Longmire is a popular stopping point for visitors on the way to Paradise.

Longmire and Westside Road Approaches

1. Success Couloirs
2. Success Cleaver
3. South Tahoma Headwall
4. Tahoma Cleaver
5. Tahoma Glacier
6. Tahoma Sickle
7. Sunset Amphitheater Icecap Glacier
8. Sunset Amphitheater Headwall Couloir

Longmire has a Park Service museum, Wilderness information center, and hotel with restaurant and gift shop. Obtain climbing and backcountry permits for these routes at the Wilderness information center during the summer and at the museum in the fall, winter, and spring. There are no services along the Westside Road, from which many of these routes are best approached.

The unpaved Westside Road leaves the main park road at a point 1 mile east of the Nisqually Entrance (and 5 miles west of Longmire). The Westside Road is closed at Fish Creek, 3 miles from the turnoff, at a small parking lot. The Westside Road previously gave vehicle access to the interior of the park's west side and the Wonderland Trail until severe flooding from Tahoma Creek in 1986 washed out the road. Attempts to repair it have met with opposition from the creek. The Park Service has been considering a van shuttle service to carry visitors up the road beyond the washout, unless an affordable way can be found to permanently repair the road.

SUCCESS CLEAVER ROUTES

The Success Cleaver routes—**Success Couloirs, Success Cleaver,** and **South Tahoma Headwall**—have the distinction of being some of the longest on Mount Rainier, starting at 2,880 feet on the Westside Road or at 2,760 feet at Longmire.

Some teams elect to spend 2 days approaching these climbs. This eases the work of ascending more than 11,000 feet to the summit. These routes see little activity; expect postholing through soft snow that impedes even the strongest teams. All three of these routes should be climbed when there is plenty of snow covering the rotten rock and pumice that make up the terrain.

Getting to the high camps: These routes have different high camps and three possible approaches. All approaches share an incredible hike through old-growth forest to the subalpine meadows of Indian Henrys Hunting Ground. There, they join together at the Mirror Lake Trail and continue towards the mountain.

For the **approach from Longmire** (2,760 feet), take the Rampart Ridge Trail for 1.4 miles to the Wonderland Trail. Take the Wonderland Trail north to Indian Henrys Hunting Ground, passing Devil's Dream Camp (5 miles from Longmire) and the ranger patrol cabin at Indian Henrys (6 miles from Longmire). Continue north on the Wonderland Trail for ³⁄₁₀ mile past the patrol cabin and turn right (north) on the Mirror Lake Trail.

For the **approach from the Kautz Creek trailhead** and picnic area 3.5 miles inside the Nisqually Entrance, take the Kautz Creek Trail north 5.7 miles to Indian Henrys Hunting Ground and ranger patrol cabin. There, the trail intersects with the Wonderland Trail. Turn left and continue north on the Wonderland Trail three-tenths mile to the Mirror Lake Trail, where this time you'll turn right (north), and follow the trail.

Point Success

Success Glacier

Success Cleaver

Pyramid Peak

1. Kautz Cleaver
2. Success Couloirs
3. Success Cleaver

To reach this Mirror Lake Trail junction via the **approach from the Westside Road,** begin on the road at its closure at Fish Creek (2,880 feet). Hike for 1 mile along the closed road, paralleling Tahoma Creek through the washout to the first sharp left-hand bend in the road. From this sharp turn, rather than continuing uphill on the road toward Round Pass, look for a newly established section of trail on the right-hand side. (The old Tahoma Creek Trail was washed out with the road.) Get on the new section, which soon rejoins the old Tahoma Creek Trail, hiking for 2.2 miles from the Westside Road to the trail's T intersection with the Wonderland Trail near the Tahoma Creek suspension bridge. (The old Tahoma Creek Trail is no longer indicated on many maps, even though it is still accessible and in good traveling shape.) Turn right on the Wonderland Trail, cross the suspension bridge, and continue toward Indian Henrys Hunting Ground. Look for the intersection with the Mirror Lake Trail at 1.2 miles from the bridge, and turn north (left) onto that trail.

All approaches bring you to the Mirror Lake Trail, which ascends through subalpine meadows to the base of Pyramid Peak. The terrain becomes alpine as you skirt the northwest shoulder of Pyramid Peak (at an elevation of 5,600 feet) and continue up the broad slopes of lower Success Cleaver. Pyramid Peak makes a great side trip with excellent views, but don't attempt to downclimb the north side back to lower Success Cleaver; it's steep, with loose rocks.

Climb Success Cleaver to between 7,500 and 8,500 feet. Climbers planning to ascend the Success Couloirs route should then head northeast onto the Pyramid and Success Glaciers. If you intend to climb the Success Cleaver route, continue up the cleaver. For the South Tahoma Headwall route, head north onto the South Tahoma Glacier.

Success Couloirs

Eastern, Central, and Western (Fickle Finger of Success)

These moderately steep snow couloirs rise from Success Glacier to the upper Kautz and Success Cleavers. There are three major couloirs—the eastern of which saw the first ascent—all of similar grade and challenge. These routes see little climbing activity. The couloirs are most enjoyably climbed when there is sufficient snow to cover the loose rock and pumice that constitute the underlying terrain.

Snowboarders and skiers have descended the climbing lines, some from Point Success. The headwall's southern aspect makes great corn snow on warm, sunny days, and the lack of crevasse difficulties makes the ride easier to navigate. The routes are steep, up to 45 degrees or more, and are prime avalanche terrain, so the descent is for accomplished snowboarders and skiers only.

Point Success

Success Glacier

1. Success Couloir Eastern
2. Success Couloir Central
3. Fickle Finger of Success
4. Success Cleaver

ELEVATION GAIN • About 11,400 feet from either Longmire or the Westside Road to Point Success.

WHAT TO EXPECT • Glacier travel; 30- to 50-degree slopes. Grade II.

TIME • 2 to 4 days; 8 to 10 hours from high camp to summit, 3 to 4 hours for descent to high camp.

SEASON • April through July.

FIRST ASCENT • Eastern Couloir—George Senner and Dick Walstrom; July 17, 1960. Central Couloir—James Couch, Ken Lyons, and party; 1987. Fickle Finger of Success—Alex Van Steen, Richard Alpert, David Branton, Mark Kelly, Steve Northern, and Pete Laird; July 25, 1997.

HIGH CAMP • From the approach at 7,500 to 8,000 feet on lower Success Cleaver, cross north on Pyramid Glacier. Camp on the small ridge separating the Pyramid and Success Glaciers, 8,500 feet, or continue farther and bivy on the Success Glacier itself, 9,800 feet. Do not camp too close to the couloirs, because avalanches from the headwall can bury camps.

Ascend north on the Success Glacier toward the base of the headwall. For the eastern couloir, cross the bergschrund near 10,000 feet and ascend the 30- to 40-degree snow slopes to the upper Kautz Cleaver, a rather straightforward climb. For the central couloir, cross the bergschrund near 10,400 feet and ascend similar grade slopes to the apex of the couloir. Depending on the yearly snowfall, there may be a short rock band to negotiate. Climb right (east) near the apex and ascend through the narrow rock band to gain the upper eastern couloir and Kautz Cleaver near 12,000 feet.

For the western couloir, or Fickle Finger of Success, ascend the Success Glacier to 10,000 feet and cross the bergschrund. The couloir climbs 40-degree snow slopes to gain the upper Success Cleaver route near 11,600 feet. Depending on the yearly snowfall, there may be a short rock band to cross or steep bulge in the snow slope, perhaps 50 degrees to gain upper Success Cleaver. From there, ascend and traverse similar grade snow and ice slopes on the eastern aspect of the cleaver crest to join the upper Kautz Cleaver route near 12,000 feet.

Above there, near 13,900 feet, the climb becomes steep, 40- to 50-degrees, for a pitch or two. The Kautz Headwall falls 3,500 feet precipitously below, so teams may elect to use pickets. Finish on easier snow slopes to Point Success.

Descent: Descend the route back to high camp.

Success
Cleaver

Touted as one of the longest climbs on Mount Rainier, Success Cleaver is one of the few routes on which climbers can ascend to the summit without setting foot on a glacier. The cleaver begins at Pyramid Peak, rising upon broad, gentle alpine slopes. The cleaver becomes steeper and narrower as it climbs more than 7,000 feet in elevation to Point Success.

Bivouac sites along the cleaver are dramatic. Slopes fall nearly a thousand feet on either side to Success and South Tahoma Glaciers. The climbing is not too difficult, though the final pitches to Point Success are steep, and exposure is great. Success Cleaver is alpine climbing drama.

ELEVATION GAIN • About 11,400 feet from either Longmire or the
Westside Road to Point Success.
WHAT TO EXPECT • Rockfall hazard; 30- to 45-degree slopes. Grade II.
TIME • 2 to 4 days; 8 to 10 hours from high camp to summit,
3 to 4 hours for descent to high camp.
SEASON • April through July.
FIRST ASCENT • Ernest Dudley and John Glascock; July 24, 1905.
HIGH CAMP • Tent platforms can be dug in the snow along the
cleaver's crest up to 10,500 feet. At 9,500 feet is a site
with room for a few tents.

Climber ascending Success Cleaver, near 9,000 feet

1. Success Cleaver
2. South Tahoma Headwall

Point Success

From the 7,000-foot elevation on the lower slopes of Success Cleaver beyond Pyramid Peak, ascend northeast toward the mountain over rolling, snowy terrain. Stay on the crest or immediately to the right (east) and ascend the gradually narrowing slope. The climbing isn't too steep—35 degrees—but the route crosses atop many steep chutes that fall precipitously to Success Glacier.

Above 10,500 feet, the route leaves the cleaver's crest, heading east as it traverses and climbs onto the headwall above Success Glacier. Continue climbing 30- to 40-degree slopes to the merging of the Kautz and Success Cleavers at 12,000 feet. Again the route swings onto the southeast side of the crest, along the upper Kautz Headwall, and climbs to Point Success. The final rock bands are climbed through steep snow gullies, sometimes at 45 degrees, with incredible exposure to the Kautz Glacier 3,500 feet below.

Since the route does not require any glacier travel, rope use is recommended only for parties that intend to belay pitches or fix protection. If a roped climber fell without a belay or fixed protection, it is unlikely that other team members could self-arrest to stop the fall, and they could be pulled off also.

Descent: Descend the route back to high camp. This is a long descent. Be extra careful because there is minimal room for mistakes, and the moderately steep slopes are unforgiving in an accident.

South Tahoma
Headwall

Possibly the longest of the headwall routes on Mount Rainier, the South Tahoma Headwall sees little climbing activity. On December 10, 1946, a Marine Corps transport plane crashed into the South Tahoma Glacier, killing all thirty-two people aboard. The route was closed for a few years because of the crash; rumors of its continued closure are inaccurate, and climbers are allowed to ascend the glacier and headwall. The headwall is nearly 4,000 feet high. Rising from the bergschrund at 10,300 feet on the South Tahoma Glacier, the route ascends steep snowfields and chutes as it climbs through terraced rock bands to Point Success. This climb has big air.

ELEVATION GAIN • About 11,400 feet from either Longmire or the Westside Road to Point Success.

WHAT TO EXPECT • Rockfall hazard; 30- to 55-degree slopes. Grade III.

TIME • 2 to 4 days; 8 to 10 hours from high camp to summit, 3 to 4 hours for descent to high camp.

SEASON • May through July.

FIRST ASCENT • Steve Marts and Fred Beckey; July 12, 1963.

HIGH CAMP • Camp between 8,000 and 8,300 feet on lower Success Cleaver or as high as 10,000 feet on the cleaver, depending on the route you take to get onto the headwall.

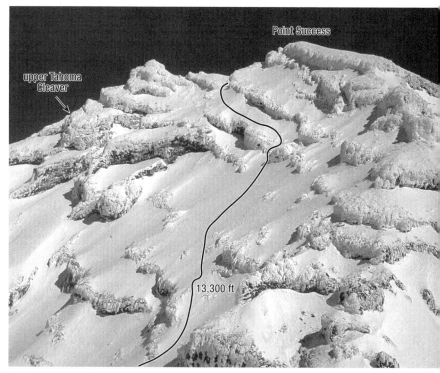

Close-up of upper South Tahoma Headwall

From the 8,300-foot elevation of Success Cleaver, ascend north across the South Tahoma Glacier toward the headwall. The glacier becomes severely broken in July and August. Navigate crevasse fields to the bergschrund at the base of the headwall at about 10,300 feet.

The headwall route climbs the central face up 40- to 55-degree snow or ice slopes. Stay right of the large couloir that falls from the northwest side (left) of the headwall and the upper Tahoma Cleaver. This gully dumps substantial debris from the upper mountain and Tahoma Cleaver.

Conditions on the headwall may be hard and icy, with 30- to 50-foot sections of steep ice that bypass rock bands. The route navigates through terraced ledges, at times jogging right, then left, high onto the upper ledges of the headwall. There are multiple route possibilities, and climbers should determine their line depending on current conditions. Above 13,800 feet, continue left, gaining the upper Tahoma Cleaver on the second of the highest headwall ledges. Continue around the cleaver and ascend the glaciated slopes to Point Success.

Approach Variation: If the glacier is too broken for navigation, you can ascend Success Cleaver to 10,000 feet and traverse onto the headwall through an exposed ledge system. This approach avoids the glacier and is not steep or technical, but there is no room for error as the route traverses 30- to 45-degree slopes. Teams that choose to rope up should place fixed protection, because it's unlikely that climbers could use self-arrest successfully to stop the fall of a ropemate on such steep, hard terrain.

Descent: Because of the consistently steep nature of this route, it is best to avoid descending the South Tahoma Headwall. Instead, descend Success Cleaver, keeping in mind that there is minimal room for mistakes on its moderately steep slopes.

TAHOMA CLEAVER ROUTE

A single major climbing route ascends from the Tahoma Cleaver approach, and that is the cleaver itself. The route is hard, classic Cascades volcano mountaineering.

Getting to Tahoma Cleaver and high camp: From the Westside Road at Fish Creek (2,880 feet), take the Tahoma Creek Trail 2.2 miles to the Wonderland Trail. Head left (north) on the Wonderland Trail, ascending Emerald Ridge. The trail leaves the forest and opens to the east, exposing the vast moraines of the Tahoma Glacier. Near 5,200 feet elevation, descend east off the trail. Begin crossing the lateral moraines, heading east directly toward the large gully that divides Glacier Island, the peak that anchors the base of Tahoma Cleaver.

Along the way toward Glacier Island, Tahoma Creek must be forded below the terminus of Tahoma Glacier; keep away from the terminus to avoid rockfall danger. If the creek's current is too deep or fast, ascend onto the lower glacier and cross it to Glacier Island. Watch your footing, as occasional patches of slick, black ice are hidden under loose rocks. The lower glacier and the moraines are steep, angle-of-repose slopes filled with loose rocks, boulders, mud, pumice, and other debris. Consider wearing a helmet and avoid climbing directly above other climbers.

A small creek drains the gully that splits Glacier Island and offers the last reliably running water along the route. Ascend the 30-degree snow gully to a large exposed rock at about 7,800 feet. Keep right of the rock as the slope exceeds 50 degrees and requires crossing a small crevasse near the top. The angle decreases considerably as the snow actually becomes the very tip of the South Tahoma Glacier. Continue on the glacial lobe for about 200 yards as the approach now climbs Tahoma Cleaver northeast toward the mountain.

From here, Mount Rainier rises unchallenged from a sea of glaciers. The view is stupendous: Success Cleaver and the South Tahoma Headwall loom to the east and northeast, while the Tahoma Glacier and Sunset Amphitheater fill the northern landscape. Turning around on a clear day reveals Mount

1. Tahoma Cleaver

upper
gendarme

Red
Gendarme

South
Tahoma
Glacier

1

St. Helens, seemingly a stone's throw away. The place is wild.

Now ascend snow hills that roll upward toward the impressive Red Gendarme (or Red Tower), a prominent composite rock feature at 10,000 feet, where tent platforms can be dug on the uphill side at 10,500 feet. The site holds two to five tents. If you want to camp higher, small bivy platforms can be dug around 11,300 feet, just below an upper gendarme (rock pillar) on the cleaver.

Tahoma
Cleaver

Standing alone on Mount Rainier's southwest flank, Tahoma Cleaver provides one of the longest and hardest climbing routes on the mountain. The cleaver, or ridge, begins at 8,500 feet and climbs steeply to a large buttress at 12,000 feet. Above the 400- to 500-foot-high buttress, a precipitous ridge continues to Point Success. The Tahoma Cleaver separates the South Tahoma and Tahoma Glaciers.

This climb sees few ascents. The strenuous approach, rock climbing difficulties, and inherently high commitment level dissuade most mountaineers. The rock on the route is quite rotten. The climb, like all rock routes on Rainier, requires speed, competent skills, a helmet, and good, cold conditions with plenty of snow.

ELEVATION GAIN • 11,400 feet from the Westside Road to Point Success.

WHAT TO EXPECT • Rockfall hazard; 30- to 45-degree slopes; fourth-class rock climbing. Grade III or IV.

TIME • 2 to 3 days; 7 to 10 hours from high camp to summit, carry over, and descend the Tahoma Glacier.

SEASON • April through July.

FIRST ASCENT • Klindt Vielbig, Anthony Hovey, Don Keller, Paul Bellamy, and Herb Steiner; June 7, 1959. Ledge variation—Dan Davis, Gene Prater, Tom Stewart, and Steve Marts; June 16, 1968. Lower buttress variation—E. Dawes Eddy, late June 1996.

HIGH CAMP • Bivy platform in the snow on the cleaver at 10,500 feet (just above the giant Red Gendarme) or between 11,300 and 11,700 feet (below the upper gendarme).

From 11,700 feet, drop off the right (south) side of the crest about 200 feet below the upper gendarme. Climb and traverse the steep and exposed snow slopes, below several gendarmes, to regain the crest of the cleaver about 100 yards from the large buttress at 12,000 feet. Follow the cleaver to the base of the buttress, which blocks the crest. From the base, traverse and angle up the left (north) side of the cleaver on a steep ledge (ramp).

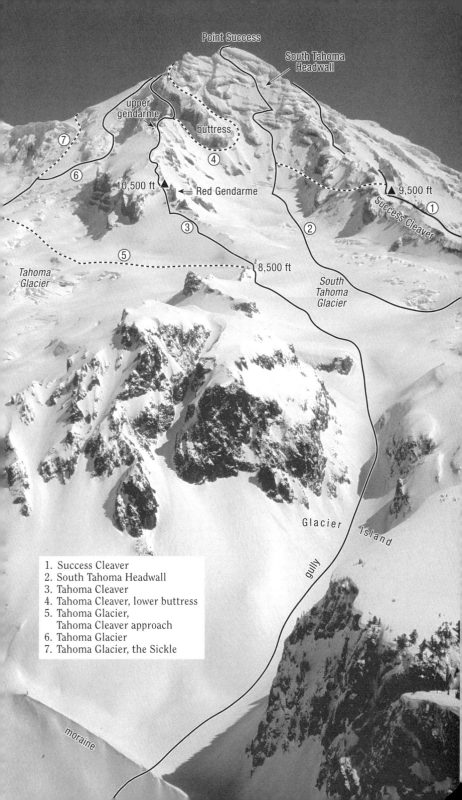

Point Success

South Tahoma
Headwall

upper
gendarme

buttress

④

⑦

⑥

10,500 ft ▲ ← Red Gendarme

▲ 9,500 ft

Success Cleaver

①

③

②

⑤

8,500 ft

Tahoma
Glacier

South
Tahoma
Glacier

Glacier Island

gully

1. Success Cleaver
2. South Tahoma Headwall
3. Tahoma Cleaver
4. Tahoma Cleaver, lower buttress
5. Tahoma Glacier,
   Tahoma Cleaver approach
6. Tahoma Glacier
7. Tahoma Glacier, the Sickle

moraine

fourth class
rock pitches

③

②

①

Tahoma Cleaver
buttress

12,000 ft

crest of cleaver

1. Tahoma Cleaver, lower buttress
2. Tahoma Cleaver, approximate original ascent
3. Tahoma Cleaver, ledge variation

The first-ascent party climbed 40 feet along this ledge to where a 25-foot solid rock step was climbed to access the rounded snow slope above the buttress. That section of rock was later reported to have fallen away.

The ledge variation continues along this steep ledge, or ramp, below a 150- to 200-foot rock cliff. The ledge is exposed and, depending on the season, may have loose rock or ice. Continue along the ledge for half a mile until it peters out below the cliffs. Ascend two pitches of fourth-class rock—not difficult but committing, steep, airy, and loose. The pitches give access to the upper Tahoma Cleaver.

For the lower buttress variation, stay on the right (south) side of the cleaver's crest above 11,700 feet. Instead of regaining the crest just below the buttress at 12,000 feet, continue to descend for 200 feet on the steep snow slope to the southern base of the buttress. Turn the corner and climb left up a broad, moderately steep snow slope, which gains the crest of Tahoma Cleaver above the rock buttress.

The crest of the upper cleaver is a steep, narrow snow ramp. Continue up, climbing the left-hand side of the crest to an easy 10-foot rock scramble that accesses the snow bowl below Point Success. The remaining few hundred feet are easily climbed to Point Success.

Descent: It is recommended that teams carry over on this route and descend the Tahoma Glacier.

▼▼▼

PUYALLUP CLEAVER ROUTES

These routes derive their classification from their proximity to the Puyallup Cleaver, the long, rocky ridge that separates the Puyallup and Tahoma Glaciers. The Puyallup Cleaver, ending at 11,300 feet, does not actually gain the upper reaches of Mount Rainier. It does, however, provide access to the **Tahoma Glacier route** and to the route up the ice flow known as **the Sickle,** and also to the **Sunset Amphitheater and Sunset Ridge routes.** The cleaver has great vistas and offers good, well-protected camps.

Getting to the Puyallup Cleaver and high camps: The principal approach to high camp is from the Westside Road at Fish Creek, where flood damage has resulted in long-term closure to vehicles 3 miles from the start of the road. (Before the closure, climbers also had approach options via the St. Andrews Creek and South Puyallup River Trails. The trails provide direct access to the west side, but the trailheads are a long way up the closed road. Some teams choose to ride bicycles up the road, with their packs, to gain access to these trails.)

From the Westside Road closure at 2,880 feet, hike (or bicycle) 3.5 miles north

Close-up of upper Tahoma Cleaver

Columbia Crest

South Tahoma Glacier

Glacier Island

Tahoma Glacier

Liberty Cap

Puyallup Cleaver

Emerald Ridge

Puyallup Glacier

1. Tahoma Cleaver
2. Early Season Variations
3. Tahoma Glacier
4. Tahoma Sickle
5. Sunset Amphitheater Routes
6. Sunset Ridge

to Round Pass. From Round Pass (bike rack available) take the South Puyallup River shortcut trail 0.6 mile (4.1 miles from trailhead) to the South Puyallup River trailhead. From there, head east up the South Puyallup River Trail 1.6 miles (5.7 miles from trailhead) to the South Puyallup River Camp and Wonderland Trail. Once there, cross the river and head north on the Wonderland Trail, climbing to St. Andrews Park 2.5 miles above (8.2 miles from the car). There, leave the trail near 6,000 feet and climb northeast through alpine meadows up the Puyallup Cleaver, passing Tokaloo Spire at 7,684 feet. Ascend the gentle snow and rock slopes of the cleaver. Excellent, well-protected bivy sites can be found along the way.

If approaching in the winter or early spring and snow is still covering the road, hike 1 mile along the Westside Road, paralleling Tahoma Creek through the washout to the first sharp left-hand bend in the road. From this sharp turn, look for a newly established section of trail on the right-hand side rather than continuing uphill on the road toward Round Pass. (The old Tahoma Creek trail was washed out with the road.) Hike on the new section, which soon rejoins the old Tahoma Creek trail, for 2.2 miles from the Westside Road to the trail's T intersection with the Wonderland Trail near the Tahoma Creek suspension bridge. During years when there is significant snowfall, it is possible to climb

Climbers making their way along the Puyallup Cleaver, near Tokaloo Spire

up a snow-filled Tahoma Creek from the road closure, avoiding the trail altogether except to bypass the narrow ravine near the suspension bridge. (The Tahoma Creek Trail is no longer indicated on many maps, even though it is still accessible and in good traveling shape.)

From the T, head left (north) on the Wonderland Trail ascending Emerald Ridge to approximately 5,600 feet. As the trail opens into subalpine meadows, the Tahoma Glacier comes into view. Before turning west and descending to South Puyallup River, head north and ascend the glacier. In the early season it may be possible to climb the entire Tahoma Glacier from this point, otherwise, make a traverse and climb across to the Puyallup Cleaver. Gain it between 7,000 and 8,000 feet.

Climbers attempting Sunset Ridge should leave the cleaver at 8,500 feet and traverse north across the Puyallup and South Mowich Glaciers. Those headed to the Tahoma Glacier or Sunset Amphitheater routes can continue up the cleaver toward St. Andrews Rock. A great high camp can be dug at 9,200 feet below lower St. Andrews Rock.

Tahoma Glacier
and the Sickle

Tahoma Glacier is the largest on Mount Rainier's west side. Spilling from the summit ice cap, the flow drains through the hourglass created between upper Tahoma Cleaver and Sunset Amphitheater. The grade decreases below 11,500 feet, where the glacier broadens and becomes a series of icefalls and crevasse fields.

One of Rainier's classic glacier climbs, the Tahoma can become very broken in late summer and a veritable oven on sunny days. The route is long by comparison with the other glacier routes. It provides excellent opportunities to practice the skills of glacier navigation, camp craft, and rescue. The glacier offers a standard route and one major variation.

ELEVATION GAIN • 11,500 feet from the Westside Road to Columbia Crest.
WHAT TO EXPECT • Glacier travel; 30- to 45-degree slopes. Grade II.
TIME • 2 to 4 days; 6 to 10 hours from high camp to summit, 3 to 5 hours for descent to high camp.
SEASON • April through early August.
FIRST ASCENT • Philemon Beecher Van Trump, Alfred Drewry, and Dr. Warren Riley; August 11, 1891. The Sickle—Leroy Ritchie, Larry Heggerness, Edward Drues, Bob Walton, Allan Van Buskirk, and Monte and Mark Haun; June 8, 1958.
HIGH CAMP • There is a nice camp at 9,200 feet on the Puyallup Cleaver, but other suitable sites can be chosen along much of the route.

1. Tahoma Glacier
2. Tahoma Sickle
3. Sunset Amphitheater Routes

Sunset Ridge

Sunset Amphitheater

Upper St. Andrews Rock

Lower St. Andrews Rock

From the 9,200-foot camp, ascend the Puyallup Cleaver's snow and rock slopes toward lower St. Andrews Rock.

For the **standard Tahoma Glacier route:** Between 9,500 and 10,000 feet, descend the open slope on the south for 200 feet to access the Tahoma Glacier. If the glacier is heavily crevassed below lower St. Andrews Rock, continue along the Puyallup Cleaver.

Once on the glacier, negotiate crevasses and icefalls to the hourglass constriction between Tahoma Cleaver and Sunset Amphitheater. The hourglass—between 11,500 and 13,000 feet—is steep, in some places 45 degrees, and it's common for teams to place pickets for protection. In general the glacier is most easily ascended on the north (left) side, though crevasses and glacier movement will dictate the route from year to year. The glacier may be tough to navigate, and good routefinding skills are necessary to complete the route.

Since the Tahoma Glacier can change dramatically throughout the year, several variations are possible. For the **Tahoma Cleaver approach,** start at 8,500 feet on Tahoma Cleaver, directly above Glacier Island, and traverse and climb north onto the Tahoma Glacier. The glacier can then be ascended, depending on icefalls and crevasses. This variation is best done early in the year.

For the **Emerald Ridge approach,** early season, ascend the Tahoma Glacier directly from Emerald Ridge (Emerald Ridge can be accessed via the Wonderland Trail, north of the Tahoma Creek suspension bridge). The Tahoma Cleaver is clearly visible to the north of Emerald Ridge. This direct approach is generally melted out by May.

For the Sickle route: From the top of the Puyallup Cleaver above upper St. Andrews Rock at 11,300 feet, head east onto the Tahoma Glacier and ascend the north (left) edge of the glacier up the ice flow known as the Sickle. This variation is sometimes said to remain in good shape throughout the summer, but this is not always the case. The Sickle, too, is subject to climatic changes and sometimes becomes quite broken.

Descent: Descend the Tahoma Glacier to high camp.

Sunset Amphitheater:
The Ice Cap and Headwall Couloir

The Sunset Amphitheater and Headwall is a large open cirque and accumulation zone for the South Mowich Glacier. The 1,500-foot south- and west-facing walls provide a dramatic backdrop to sunsets, providing the amphitheater's romantic name. These routes are best climbed during the spring and early summer, because the South Mowich Glacier is heavily crevassed and has numerous icefalls that make the approach difficult. Also, the routes become extremely hazardous when the winter snow and ice holding the predominantly rotten rock together melts; it's best to climb when temperatures are cold. These routes rarely see activity, despite their reasonable level of challenge and beautiful location.

Ice Cap
Headwall Couloir

Liberty Cap

Sunset Ridge

headwall

couloir

Sunset
Amphitheater
Ice Cap

bergschrund

bergschrund

②

①

Sunset Amphitheater

South Mowich Glacier

approx. 11,600 ft

ELEVATION GAIN • 11,400 feet from the Westside Road to Liberty Cap.

WHAT TO EXPECT • Rockfall hazard; glacier travel; 50-degree to vertical slopes. Grade III.

TIME • 2 to 4 days; 5 to 8 hours from high camp to summit, 4 to 7 hours for descent to high camp.

SEASON • April through June.

FIRST ASCENT • Sunset Amphitheater Ice Cap—J. Wendell Trosper and Fred Thieme; July 13, 1937. Headwall Couloir—Paul Charlton, Mike Gauthier, David Gottlieb, Glenn Kessler, Dee Patterson, and Jeremy Shank; May 25, 2000.

HIGH CAMP • There are excellent sites at 9,200 feet on the Puyallup Cleaver. Other possible bivouacs exist for teams wishing to camp closer to upper and lower St. Andrews Rocks.

From the 9,200-foot camp on Puyallup Cleaver, ascend snow and rock slopes toward lower St. Andrews Rock. If the South Mowich Glacier isn't too crevassed, ascend the left (north) side to upper St. Andrews Rock at 11,300 feet. If the glacier is broken, which is likely, remain on the cleaver's crest. Climb both lower and upper St. Andrews Rocks to the top of the cleaver, where the upper Tahoma and South Mowich Glaciers separate. The cleaver is composed of loose, rotten rock but is easy to climb.

For the **Sunset Amphitheater Ice Cap route,** ascend northeast into the Sunset Amphitheater cirque toward the lowest point in the amphitheater wall where

To Liberty Cap

Sunset Ridge

Sunset Amphitheater
Headwall

the summit ice-cap glacier pours down a steep icefall. Find the best location to cross the bergschrund at 12,500 feet and ascend the 30- to 50-degree snow and ice slopes through a glacier hourglass to the upper ice cap. The icefall can be vertical at some locations and good glacier ice-climbing skills may be necessary. The climbing is not as hard as it may appear, but since the difficulties are high and remote, the route is committing. Once on the summit plateau, climb north on gentle glacier slopes to Liberty Cap.

The **Sunset Amphitheater Headwall Couloir route** is a steep line from the upper South Mowich Glacier to upper Sunset Ridge. From upper St. Andrews Rock, climb north into the amphitheater toward the large couloir above a glacier-draped rock buttress. Cross the bergschrund above the buttress and ascend 400 feet of couloir, then turn right to ascend and traverse another 400 feet. The steep ramp leads to some small rock bands before exiting to upper Sunset Ridge. The climb is steep, sometimes 50 degrees, and tops out at 13,800 feet on Sunset Ridge. Continue upward to the northeast and Liberty Cap.

Descent: Descend the Tahoma Glacier or Tahoma Sickle back to St. Andrews Rock and high camp.

Sunset
Ridge

Separating the Sunset Amphitheater and Mowich Face, Sunset Ridge rises from a triangular base at 8,500 feet up the western corner of Mount Rainier. It is named in honor of the stellar sunsets it enjoys—weather permitting. Most of the climb itself is not a true ridge climb. Broad at its base, the route ascends a series of snowfields and gullies to gain the upper ridge near 12,000 feet.

The route alternates between the upper Mowich Face and upper Sunset Ridge to gain Liberty Cap Glacier and Liberty Cap. Climbers enjoy incredible views of the Sunset Amphitheater and Tahoma Glacier, which drops precipitously to the south. This is an excellent route with plenty of steep ice and exciting exposure.

ELEVATION GAIN • 11,400 feet from the Westside Road to Liberty Cap.

WHAT TO EXPECT • Rockfall hazard; glacier travel; 55-degree slopes. Grade III.

TIME • 2 to 4 days; 5 to 8 hours from high camp to summit, carry over and descend the Tahoma Glacier.

SEASON • April through July.

FIRST ASCENT • Lyman Boyer, Arnie Campbell, and Don Woods; August 27, 1938.

HIGH CAMP • Small platforms can be dug above 9,200 feet on the ridge, a larger more protected site exists at 9,200 feet on the divide between the South Mowich and Edmunds Glaciers.

Close-up of Sunset Amphitheater Headwall Couloir

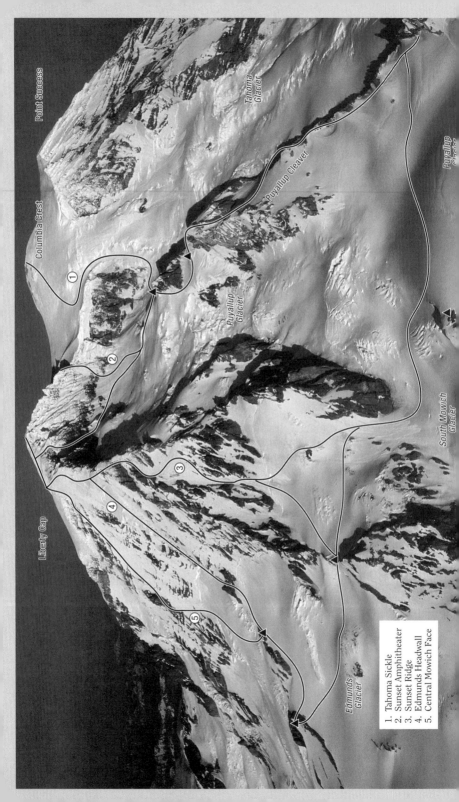

Point Success

Tahoma Glacier

Columbia Crest

Puyallup Cleaver

Puyallup Glacier

Puyallup Glacier

① ②

③

Liberty Cap

South Mowich Glacier

④

⑤

Edmunds Glacier

1. Tahoma Sickle
2. Sunset Amphitheater
3. Sunset Ridge
4. Edmunds Headwall
5. Central Mowich Face

From 8,500 feet on the Puyallup Cleaver, traverse north, crossing the Puyallup and South Mowich Glaciers. The South Mowich can be heavily crevassed. Skirt the lower rock buttress that forms the base of Sunset Ridge and ascend right (westerly) up the 30- to 40-degree snow gully to a small bergschrund below the rock bands at 9,600 feet.

Climbers can go left or right to bypass the large rock cliff above the bergschrund. The difficulties of either direction are similar as the slope angle increases slightly to a solid 45 degrees. There is a sensational tiny bivy ledge on the left-hand route at 10,200 feet, directly above a large gendarme. This pillar, composed of volcanic rock and mud, seems to defy gravity. The remains of a weather balloon can be spotted directly above the thin bivy ledge. Small bivy platforms can be dug if you elect to go right of the rock cliffs.

The route becomes steep and icy above 10,200 feet, with angles of 50 to 55 degrees, as it ascends a series of gullies and open faces to nearly 12,000 feet and tops out along the ridge. There are small sections of rock, but it is best to avoid these areas by staying on snow and ice slopes. The slope angle decreases for the next few hundred feet as the route climbs the ridge to 12,800 feet.

At this point, the ridge forces climbers out onto the upper Mowich Face. Traverse onto the face—a steep 50 to 55 degrees—and continue climbing to 13,200 feet, where the route regains the ridge. The slope angle continues to decrease as the route alternates along the ridge top and glacier to Liberty Cap. There may be crevasses above 13,600 feet on Liberty Cap Glacier.

Descent: This climb usually requires a carry-over unless teams elect to camp on the Puyallup Cleaver at 8,500 feet. Descend via the Tahoma Glacier or Tahoma Sickle.

MOWICH LAKE AND
CARBON RIVER APPROACHES

Six routes and several variations exist on Mount Rainier's northwest face and are most easily accessed from Mowich Lake.

These climbs are categorized by proximity to Ptarmigan Ridge or to the Mowich Face.

Mowich Face routes
Edmunds Headwall
Central Mowich Face
North Mowich Headwall
North Mowich Icefall

Ptarmigan Ridge routes
Ptarmigan Ridge
Ptarmigan Ice Cliff

Mowich Lake at nearly 5,000 feet in elevation is the largest lake in the park. It has become a popular destination because of its short yet scenic trails to Tolmie Peak Lookout and Spray Park. There is a ranger cabin on the south side and a free walk-in-only campground. The road to Mowich Lake usually doesn't open until late June, and frequently not until early July. Climbers should get their permits at the Park Service ranger station in Wilkeson; none are available at Mowich Lake.

The routes in this section top out on Liberty Cap (14,112 feet). To reach the true summit at Columbia Crest, climbers must travel nearly a mile, descending to the col at 13,600 feet before regaining the gentle slopes to 14,410 feet.

Carbon River approach: In this same general area, the Carbon River road goes to Ipsut Creek Campground, which offers climbers a way to approach routes on Liberty Wall, Liberty Ridge, Willis Wall, and Curtis Ridge. However, because it's often more practical to take on these routes from White River Campground, they are covered in the next section, on White River approaches. The Carbon River/Ipsut Creek approach provides quicker access to the routes, but the descent and return to the Ipsut Creek trailhead is unusually long. Some teams opt to approach from Ipsut Creek Campground and descend the Emmons/Winthrop Glaciers route to White River Campground. Climbers who want to start and end at the same trailhead prefer the White River Campground approach.

Edmunds Glacier

North Mowich Glacier

1. Edmunds Headwall
2. Central Mowich Face
3. North Mowich Icefall
4. Ptarmigan Ridge

To Mowich Lake

For the Carbon River approach to the Liberty/Willis/Curtis routes, take the 7.5-mile trail from Ipsut Creek Campground (2,300 feet) to Mystic Pass. Along the way, pass Carbon River Camp (2.9 miles from Ipsut Creek) and Dick Creek Camp (4 miles from Ipsut Creek). At Mystic Pass, just before the drop into Mystic Lake, ascend south along the climber's path through subalpine meadows up lower Curtis Ridge. Continue up the ridge to 7,200 feet, where the Carbon Glacier is best accessed. (For route details from this point, see the section on White River approaches.)

MOWICH FACE ROUTES

The Mowich Face possesses some of Mount Rainier's most dramatic alpine climbing. The face is shaped like a large triangle, 2 miles wide at the base and more than 4,000 feet high. With the apex at 13,600 feet, Sunset Ridge forms the southern side of the triangle, while Ptarmigan Ridge forms the northern side.

Climbing on the face can be characterized as long pitches of moderately steep snow and ice with some vertical rock bands. Climbers should be comfortable with constant exposure and short sections of steep ice and rock. Strong calves help. Belays and ice protection are called for, as any fall could prove catastrophic.

The best time to climb is in the early summer, when the approaches are direct, or in late fall, when the face turns icy and hard, making the climbing more challenging but the surface more stable. Mowich Face sees little climbing activity. Although the approach is long, the climbing is well worth it.

Getting to the Mowich Face and high camps: The approaches for these routes begin at Mowich Lake. From the lake, take the 3-mile trail to Spray Park, which slowly climbs through forest, past Eagles Roost Camp and Spray Falls, into the subalpine and alpine park. At the high point along the meadow trail, before the trail begins its descent toward the Carbon River, detour right and begin climbing the lower slopes of Ptarmigan Ridge.

Ascend gentle, open meadows to the small and stagnant Flett Glaciers. Continue up the ridge on snow or rock, passing between Echo Rock and Observation Rock. After passing Observation Rock, leave Ptarmigan Ridge at 8,300 feet and descend south for an elevation loss of 1,000 feet on 30- to 40-degree talus slopes to the North Mowich Glacier.

From 7,300 feet on the North Mowich Glacier, climb southwest on the glacier, negotiating icefalls and crevasses to the nunatak (rock protrusion in the glacier) at 9,200 feet, below the North Mowich Headwall. Here is a good bivy site for the North Mowich Headwall and North Mowich Icefall routes.

Climbers planning to ascend the Edmunds Headwall route or the Central Mowich Face route should continue traversing south on the North Mowich Glacier to another nunatak at 9,600 feet, below the central face.

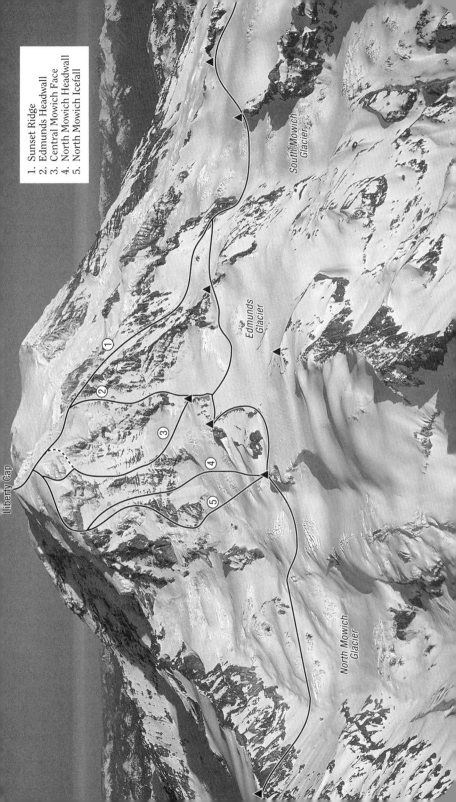

Liberty Cap

1. Sunset Ridge
2. Edmunds Headwall
3. Central Mowich Face
4. North Mowich Headwall
5. North Mowich Icefall

South Mowich
Glacier

Edmunds
Glacier

North Mowich
Glacier

Icy pitches high on Central Mowich Face

FIRST ASCENT OF THE CENTRAL MOWICH FACE

Dee Molenaar's professional career at Mount Rainier was relatively brief: three summers as a climbing guide, three more as a seasonal park ranger and slightly more than two years as a full-time ranger. But his skills as an artist and author—most prominently displayed in *The Challenge of Rainier,* a comprehensive chronicle of ascents on the peak—reveal Molenaar's deep historical knowledge of Northwest mountaineering. It is a history Molenaar helped shape by leading the first ascent up the Central Mowich Face.

The idea for the climb came to Molenaar in 1948 as he spent a night near Sunset Park in a fire lookout with a direct view of the tantalizingly untouched route.

It wasn't until 1966, when the forty-eight-year-old Molenaar was a geologist for the state of Washington that he attempted to climb the Central Mowich Face. On July 23, Molenaar left Klapatche Park with Jim Wickwire, Gene Prater, and Dick Pargeter. The men trekked across the Puyallup Glacier and set up a four-man tent on a rock island about 9,500 feet up the mountain. That afternoon, an enormous avalanche roared down the upper right side of the 45-degree face. Safely out of the avalanche's path, the four watched as huge blocks of ice careened downslope amid a billowing white cloud.

The men hoped to begin their climb at midnight, but a storm blowing across the upper mountain forced them to linger inside their sleeping bags. "Unfortunately, it was clearer in the morning, so we had to go up," Molenaar recalled. They headed across the freshly churned avalanche debris and moved rapidly up the broad Mowich Face. Four hours later, they reached the icy approach to a steep short rock cliff, the crux of the route at 12,700 feet. Molenaar led as they scrambled up the pitch.

Molenaar said snow and ice lingering at the base of the cliff created an approach route that made climbing the rock relatively easy. "That year the rock band was only 12 to 15 feet high, but in later years it was probably 50 feet," he said.

At Molenaar's urging, the climbers went left, toward an unexplored ice chute, and established a completely new route that did not join with the final steps of a known path up the nearby Edmunds Headwall. The four picked their way up the chute in the late-morning sun and arrived atop 14,112-foot Liberty Cap at 12:30 P.M. The men skipped the half-mile trip to the true summit at Columbia Crest and instead descended via the Tahoma Sickle back through Klapatche Park and back to their cars on the Westside Road.

All four of the climbers were skilled mountaineers who developed impressive backcountry resumes both on and off Northwest peaks. Wickwire would be among the first Americans to reach the summit of K2. Pargeter would become one of the Northwest's most innovative alpine mapmakers. Prater, tinkering in his shop, would create innovations that led to modern snowshoes. But Molenaar is modest about the team's climbing abilities in 1966. "We were just recreational climbers," he said.

S.C.

Edmunds
Headwall

The first of the Mowich Face routes to be climbed, the Edmunds Headwall is also considered the easiest and least hazardous route on the face. It ascends steep snow and ice slopes, never steeper than 55 degrees, to gain upper Sunset Ridge near 12,600 feet. Like the other headwall routes on Rainier, this climb is fun, airy, and direct. Before the Westside Road washed out, this route was best accessed from the St. Andrews Creek trailhead. With the road closure at

Fish Creek, the Westside Road is no longer a faster approach, and climbers should approach from Mowich Lake.

ELEVATION GAIN • 9,200 feet from Mowich Lake to Liberty Cap.

WHAT TO EXPECT • Rockfall hazard; 40- to 55-degree snow and ice slopes. Grade III.

TIME • 2 to 3 days; 6 to 8 hours from high camp to Liberty Cap. Carry over.

SEASON • May, June, July, and October.

FIRST ASCENT • John Rupley, Don Claunch, Fred Beckey, Tom Hornbein, and Herb Staley; June 23, 1957.

HIGH CAMP • Between 8,800 and 10,000 feet near the base of the face. Look for protection from rock and ice that may fall from the face.

Ascend to the base of the wall on the Edmunds Glacier. Find the best location to cross the bergschrund somewhere around 9,600 feet, usually on the left side of the main Edmunds Headwall snow gullies. Begin climbing 30- to 40-degree snow or firn slopes. Climb directly up the face, bypassing rock bands through wide snow gullies. Virtually every major chute provides access to the snow and ice slopes above.

Across the Edmunds Glacier bergschrund, a climber begins the ascent of Mowich Face via the Edmunds Headwall.

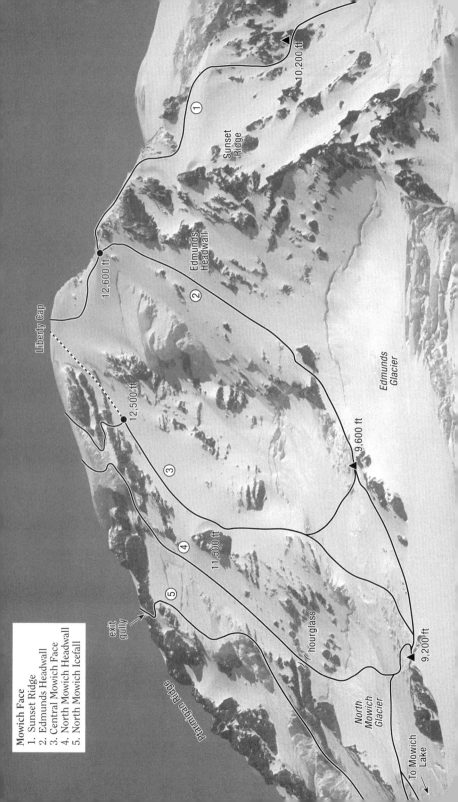

Mowich Face
1. Sunset Ridge
2. Edmunds Headwall
3. Central Mowich Face
4. North Mowich Headwall
5. North Mowich Icefall

10,200 ft

Sunset Ridge

Edmunds Headwall

12,600 ft

Liberty Cap

12,500 ft

Edmunds Glacier

9,600 ft

① 1

② 2

③ 3

④ 4

⑤ 5

11,500 ft

exit gully

hourglass

9,200 ft

Ptarmigan Ridge

North Mowich Glacier

To Mowich Lake

At times, slope angle increases to 55 degrees and short patches of ice may be found.

Near 12,600 feet, the route connects with upper Sunset Ridge. There the angle decreases for the next few hundred feet as it continues along to 12,800 feet, where the ridge forces a leftward traverse onto the upper Mowich Face. Traverse steep ice, 50- to 55-degrees, and climb until the angle decreases above the Mowich Face apex at 13,500 feet. From there the angle continues to decrease as the route alternates along the ridge top and Liberty Cap Glacier to Liberty Cap. There may be crevasses above 13,600 feet on the Liberty Cap Glacier.

Descent: Teams should carry over and descend the Emmons/Winthrop Glaciers route (exiting at White River Campground) or descend the Tahoma Glacier and return to camp.

Descending the Tahoma Glacier makes for a long trip that may require significant routefinding. Descend the Tahoma to 8,500 feet on the Puyallup Cleaver and traverse north to the base of Sunset Ridge. Then climb to the 9,200-foot rock divide below the left arm of Sunset Ridge and traverse the upper Edmunds Glacier back to high camp, 6 to 10 hours.

Central Mowich
Face

The second Mowich Face route to be climbed, the Central Mowich Face is a little longer and more committing than the Edmunds Headwall. This is another long and steep alpine classic, ascending the center of the Mowich Face triangle above the North Mowich Glacier. The route also offers a significant variation.

Expect moderately steep ice and snow, with the possibility of water ice and short sections of fourth-class rock. Although the pitches are not harder than what is found on the Edmunds Headwall, the route is precipitous and airy, with fewer areas to take breaks. Additionally, the lower portion is exposed to the hanging glacier on the Mowich Face. Speed and confidence on steep terrain are necessary.

ELEVATION GAIN • 9,200 feet from Mowich Lake to Liberty Cap.

WHAT TO EXPECT • Rockfall and icefall hazards; 40- to 55-degree snow and ice slopes. Grade III or IV.

TIME • 2 to 4 days; 6 to 9 hours from high camp to Liberty Cap. Carry over.

SEASON • May, June, July, and October.

FIRST ASCENT • Dee Molenaar, Gene Prater, Jim Wickwire, and Dick Pargeter; July 24, 1966. Upper variation—Bill Cockerham, Ed Marquart, Bill Sumner, and Del Young; July 4, 1967.

HIGH CAMP • A good bivy site can be found on the nunatak at 9,600 feet on the North Mowich Glacier. Avoid camping near the face because of avalanche hazard.

1. Central Mowich Face, exit variation
2. Central Mowich Face
3. North Mowich Headwall

upper Ptarmigan Ridge

12,700 ft

12,500 ft

upper North Mowich Headwall

12,000 ft

upper Central Mowich Face

Ascend the upper edge of the North Mowich Glacier toward the center of the Mowich Face. Carry a few ice screws and pickets along. Cross the bergschrund near 10,400 feet and begin climbing hard snow and ice slopes directly up the face. This lower section of the route is exposed to significant ice and rock avalanches from the hanging glacier on Mowich Face; move quickly.

Angle left, climbing on 35- to 45-degree snow and ice slopes toward a prominent rock outcropping on the face near 11,500 feet. Staying left helps to avoid the hazards from the hanging glacier. From the rock outcropping, begin angling right on 45- to 55-degree ice slopes toward the rock bands above. Climb below and parallel to the three rock bands to 12,700 feet, where a short pitch of ice and rock (12 to 40 feet, depending on the year) gains access to the first snow ledge above the rock.

Continue left (north) along the narrow ledge as it drops slightly and turns an exposed corner to access an ice chute that climbs to upper Ptarmigan Ridge. The 45- to 55-degree ice chute climbs to the top of a glacier bulge over three pitches of steep ice. There is a rock band on the right. The grade decreases above the chute as the route climbs onto the broad crest of upper Ptarmigan Ridge. Ascend the glacier to Liberty Cap.

The route offers a Grade IV **upper variation.** From the rock band at 12,500 feet, continue ascending up and right, paralleling the rock band on your left. Bypass the rock bands on your left and ascend directly up the steep face to the apex of the Mowich Face. The angle is steep above the hanging glacier—50- to 60-degree ice slopes that relax where the Sunset and Ptarmigan Ridge routes meet at 13,500 feet. Bring ice screws; this variation is harder than the standard Mowich Face route. Finish by climbing Liberty Cap Glacier to Liberty Cap; watch for crevasses.

Descent: Teams should carry over and descend the Emmons/Winthrop Glaciers route (exiting at White River Campground) or descend the Tahoma Glacier and return to camp.

Descending the Tahoma Glacier makes for a long trip that may require significant routefinding. Descend the Tahoma to 8,500 feet on the Puyallup Cleaver and traverse north to the base of Sunset Ridge. Then climb to the 9,200-foot rock divide below the left arm of Sunset Ridge and traverse the upper Edmunds Glacier back to high camp, 6 to 10 hours.

North Mowich
Headwall

Climbing the left side of the Mowich Face, the North Mowich Headwall ascends a hard line up the major northern ice slope to gain the crest of Ptarmigan Ridge. The climb has many technical sections that include vertical rock and ice, both on the lower face and higher just below the crest of Ptarmigan Ridge. Bring ice screws and pickets for the route.

At the time of its first ascent, the route was considered one of Rainier's hardest. Dan Davis, a member of the first-ascent team and a veteran of twenty-four routes on Rainier, considers this the best climb the mountain has to offer. The technical climbing and aesthetic values are high.

ELEVATION GAIN • 9,200 feet from Mowich Lake to Liberty Cap.

WHAT TO EXPECT • Rockfall and icefall hazards; 40- to 55-degree snow and ice slopes; fifth-class rock or easy aid. Grade IV.

TIME • 2 to 4 days; 6 to 10 hours from high camp to Liberty Cap. Carry over.

SEASON • May, June, July, and October.

FIRST ASCENT • Dan Davis, Mike Heath, Mead Hargis, and Bill Cockerham; July 22, 1968.

HIGH CAMP • A good bivy site can be found at 9,200 feet on the nunatak that divides the Edmunds and North Mowich Glaciers. Avoid camping near the headwall because of avalanche hazard.

Traverse and climb the North Mowich Glacier to the base of the Mowich Face, below the northern series of major snow and ice slopes. Cross the bergschrund near 10,000 feet and climb directly up snow to an hourglass in the first rock band. Climb through the short and difficult constriction on ice or rock; ice screws and a belay may be necessary.

Above the hourglass, ascend 40- to 45-degree snow or ice directly up the face to the rock bands below the ice cliff at 12,000 feet. Traverse up and right on the ledges to the narrowest rock band below the ice cliff and steep glacier.

1. Central Mowich Face
2. North Mowich Headwall
3. North Mowich Icefall
4. Ptarmigan Ridge

Liberty Cap

Ptarmigan Ridge

exit gully

③

②

①

④

12,500 ft

Mowich Face

North

Mowich

hourglass

rock
step

Icefall

bergschrund

North Mowich Glacier

Climb through hard fifth-class rock (or A1 aid climbing) for 50 feet, gaining the top of the rock band. There a steep ice slope leads right, above the ice cliff. Ascend the 60-degree slope to gain upper Ptarmigan Ridge.

The angle now decreases, and the route finishes on the broad glacial crest of upper Ptarmigan Ridge and Liberty Cap Glacier to Liberty Cap; watch for crevasses.

Descent: Teams should carry over and descend the Emmons/Winthrop Glaciers route (exiting at White River Campground).

North Mowich
Icefall

Climbing the far left edge of the Mowich Face, the North Mowich Icefall route actually parallels the icefall, ascending the extreme left of the Mowich Face to finish on upper Ptarmigan Ridge. Steep ice and short pitches of fifth-class rock are found, similar to the North Mowich Headwall; however, more rockfall has been noted, as much of this route lies below the cliffs of upper Ptarmigan Ridge. Bring ice screws and pickets for the route. Prolific climber Jim Wickwire, a member of the first-ascent team, confided that this route may be his personal favorite on Mount Rainier.

ELEVATION GAIN • 9,200 feet from Mowich Lake to Liberty Cap.

WHAT TO EXPECT • Rockfall and icefall hazard; 40- to 50-degree snow and ice slopes. Grade IV.

TIME • 2 to 4 days; 6 to 9 hours from high camp to Liberty Cap. Carry over.

SEASON • May, June, July, and October.

FIRST ASCENT • Jim Wickwire and Rob Schaller; June 26, 1970.

HIGH CAMP • A good bivy site can be found at 9,200 feet on the nunatak that divides the Edmunds and North Mowich Glaciers. Avoid camping near the headwall because of avalanche hazard.

Climb southeast around a rocky rib to the head of the North Mowich Glacier below the right side of the North Mowich Icefall. Traverse and stay above the bergschrund (near 9,000 feet) on steep 45-degree ice (possibly hard) and climb the snow gully that parallels the lowest section of the icefall. Rockfall and icefall is possible here, from the cliff bands and ice above.

Continue climbing up and right for several pitches to a 40-foot rock band. Climb on solid rock, fourth class, to gain another short snowfield. Climb it to another rock pitch that gains access to another broad snow slope. Continue upward and right, exiting the last snow slope below the icefall, 200 feet above the hourglass on the North Mowich Headwall route.

Continue up the extreme left side of the open snow face, paralleling the headwall route for 300 feet. Once the highest section of icefall is passed, diagonal left up the glacier to the narrowest exit gully in the cliff bands above. There may be a bergschrund at the top of the hanging glacier; expect hard snow or ice, 45 degrees.

At the exit gully, a vertical step in a narrow draw gains the upper Ptarmigan Ridge route. The gully is 5 to 15 feet long depending on the year, with solid rock; it may be verglassed. Climb through the gully onto Liberty Cap Glacier. There the slope angle decreases, with the route finishing along the broad glacial crest of upper Ptarmigan Ridge to Liberty Cap; watch for crevasses.

Descent: Teams should carry over and descend the Emmons/Winthrop Glaciers route (exiting at White River Campground).

PTARMIGAN RIDGE ROUTES

Principal climbing routes on Ptarmigan Ridge are the standard route with its two variations and the Ptarmigan Ice Cliff route. The ridge is consistently exciting and challenging, providing good climbing from start to finish.

Getting to Ptarmigan Ridge and high camp: From Mowich Lake, take the 3-mile trail to Spray Park. At the high point along the meadow trail through the park, before the trail begins descending toward the Carbon River, detour right and begin climbing the lower slopes of Ptarmigan Ridge. Ascend gentle, open meadows to the small and stagnant Flett Glaciers. Continue up the ridge on snow or rock, passing between Echo Rock and Observation Rock. After passing Observation Rock, continue along the upper edge of the Russell Glacier, which gently falls to the left (east) while steep scree slopes fall to the North Mowich Glacier south of the Ptarmigan Ridge crest. The ridge narrows beyond 9,600 feet and crests near 10,300 feet, where there is an excellent bivy site.

Ptarmigan Ridge
and Ice Cliff

Ptarmigan Ridge forms the impressive northwest flank of Mount Rainier. Adorned with tumbling glaciers and ice cliffs, the ridge is massive and broad, lacking the crested definition of other ridges. The climbs ascend moderate to steep snow and ice, with short sections of rock throughout. Bring ice screws and pickets. Above 10,300 feet, climbers take either the standard route (with a choice of two variations farther up) or the Ice Cliff route.

Many Pacific Northwest climbers consider Ptarmigan Ridge to be one of Mount Rainier's classics, rivaling even Liberty Ridge. Alex Bertulis, an accomplished Northwest climber with numerous Rainier ascents, calls it Washington State's preeminent alpine route.

1. Ptarmigan Ridge
   a. 2nd Variation
   b. 1st Variation
2. Ptarmigan Icecliff

Liberty Cap

Liberty Cap Glacier

North Mowich

Close Up of Ptarmigan Ridge
1. 2nd Variation
2. 1st Variation

① ② ①

exit gulley

11,500 ft

ELEVATION GAIN • 9,200 feet from Mowich Lake to Liberty Cap.

WHAT TO EXPECT • Rockfall and icefall hazard; 40- to 55-degree snow and ice slopes; short sections of fifth-class climbing. Grade IV.

TIME • 2 to 4 days; 6 to 9 hours from high camp to Liberty Cap. Carry over.

SEASON • Spring through July.

FIRST ASCENT • Wolf Bauer and Jack Hossack; September 8, 1935. Second variation—Arnold Bloomer, Glenn Kelsey, Harold Pinsch, and Paul Williams; July 24, 1966. Ice Cliff—Fred Beckey, John Rupley, and Herb Staley; August 5, 1956.

HIGH CAMP • A great bivy site exists at 10,300 feet on the ridge crest, before climbers drop to the 10,200-foot notch on the ridge.

For the **standard Ptarmigan Ridge route,** begin at the low notch on the ridge at 10,200 feet, then descend and traverse west for ¼-mile onto the upper North Mowich Glacier. Move quickly; this area is subjected to significant icefall from the ice cliff above. Stay left as you descend until the lower rock buttress on Ptarmigan Ridge is cleared around 9,800 feet. Then turn left and cross the bergschrund to access a long diagonal snow slope that climbs up to the left. Ascend this 40-degree snow slope leftward toward the rock cliffs above. Before reaching the cliffs, traverse left below the rock to access a steep 50-degree snow chute that leads straight up to the base of an upper rock buttress at around 11,500 feet.

From here, there are two popular variations. In the **first variation,** the first-ascent team turned left at the base of the upper buttress and traversed and climbed the steep 45- to 55-degree frozen snow and ice onto the Liberty Cap Glacier; take ice screws. Once on the glacier via this variation, continue up a steep ice chute between the icefall on the left and rock buttress on the right to gain the upper glacier dome. Find the best route through the seracs and crevasses on this section.

The **second variation** climbs to the right from the base of the upper buttress over fourth-class rock, icy and verglassed, to a chute between two rock bands. The chute continues over moderately steep terrain, 40- to 50- degrees, for two pitches until the right band gives way to the upper North Mowich Icefall. Shortly after, look for the exit gully on the left that provides access to upper Ptarmigan Ridge. The exit gully is a vertical step in a narrow draw, 5- to 15-feet long, depending on the year. The rock is solid, but may be verglassed. After exiting the gully, regain the original line.

With either of these two variations, finish by ascending the broad glacial

1. Ptarmigan Ice Cliff
2. Liberty Wall Ice Cap

snow ramp

Liberty Cap Glacier

10,300 bivy

crest of upper Ptarmigan Ridge to Liberty Cap. Watch for crevasses on Liberty Cap Glacier.

For the **Ptarmigan Ice Cliff route,** begin at the Ptarmigan Ridge notch at 10,200 feet and climb to the base of the ice cliff on the east (left) side of the crest. Traverse and climb left on a sloping narrow ledge of black ice and glazed rock for 200 feet directly below the ice cliff. Move quickly because of severe icefall hazard. The ledge begins to broaden near the end of the ice cliff, where a steep snow/ice ramp cuts right and gains the Liberty Cap Glacier. Cut right and climb the ramp through the ice cliff to the heavily crevassed glacier above. Continue up the glacier, negotiating crevasses to reach Liberty Cap.

Descent: Carry over and descend the Emmons/Winthrop Glaciers or the Ingraham Direct/Disappointment Cleaver routes.

WHITE RIVER APPROACHES

Eleven routes and several variations cover much of Mount Rainier's north and northeast flank.

These climbs are categorized by proximity to lower Curtis Ridge or to Camp Schurman.

Lower Curtis Ridge routes

Liberty Wall Ice Cap
Liberty Wall Direct
Liberty Ridge
Willis Wall: Thermogenesis
Willis Wall: West Rib
Willis Wall: Central Rib
Willis Wall: East Rib
Willis Wall: East Willis Wall
Curtis Ridge

Camp Schurman routes

Winthrop Glacier and Russell Cliffs
Emmons/Winthrop Glaciers

The two Camp Schurman routes are best approached from White River Campground. The campground is 5 miles beyond the White River Ranger Station, where climbers get permits.

The nine routes accessed via lower Curtis Ridge are approached from White River Campground, too, and thus are included in this section. But they can also be approached from Ipsut Creek Campground at the end of the Carbon River road.

It is also possible to approach the lower Curtis Ridge routes from Sunrise, up the road from White River Ranger Station. Sunrise has a visitor center, ranger station, gift shop, and snack grill. Although Sunrise appears to offer a 2,000-foot elevation advantage over the White River Campground, this is actually lost when time and energy are spent routefinding and traveling cross-country to make the most of the feet gained.

Many of the eleven routes in this section top out on Liberty Cap (14,112 feet). To reach the true summit at Columbia Crest, climbers must travel nearly a mile, descending to the col at 13,600 feet before regaining the gentle slopes to 14,410 feet.

Ptarmigan Ridge

Carbon Glacier

Liberty Cap

① 1

② 2

③ 3

④ 4

⑤ 5

Winthrop Glacier

Emmons Glacier

⑤ 5

To White River

1. Liberty Wall*
2. Liberty Ridge
3. Willis Wall Routes*
4. Curtis Ridge*
5. Emmons/Winthrop Glaciers
* see other maps for close ups

LOWER CURTIS RIDGE ROUTES

The routes accessed from lower Curtis Ridge make up much of Mount Rainier's northern face. Many of them are considered Mount Rainier's hardest and most dangerous climbs. Lower Curtis Ridge is broad and sweeping, with gentle alpine slopes. Using the ridge, climbers can ascend to 7,200 feet and access the Carbon Glacier without the difficulties of negotiating the lower Carbon.

The entire north face, including **Liberty Wall, Liberty Ridge, Willis Wall,** and **Curtis Ridge,** is in full panoramic view from lower Curtis Ridge. Avalanches, waterfalls, and the jumbled Carbon Glacier are a few of the attractions. To the north lie Mount Baker and Glacier Peak and the city lights of Tacoma and Seattle spread out on the western horizon. The views are without doubt some of the most dramatic and spectacular on Mount Rainier.

Getting to lower Curtis Ridge: From White River Campground at 4,400 feet, follow the Glacier Basin trail 3.3 miles to Glacier Basin Camp at 6,000 feet. This trail is sometimes snow-covered until mid-June, but the path is wide and easy to follow. Glacier Basin is a popular and frequently filled camp for teams who elect to acclimatize and break the long day to Camp Schurman by stopping here first. Climbers headed to lower Curtis Ridge should attempt to cover more distance before setting up an intermediate camp.

From Glacier Basin, follow the climbers' path up the moraine toward the snout of the Inter Glacier, which lies in the southwest corner of the Inter Creek and Glacier Basin. The trail is not maintained, but a good social trail does exist. At approximately 6,600 feet, turn west (right) and ascend scree slopes to St. Elmo Pass (7,400 feet) and a possible bivy. From the pass, drop down to the Winthrop Glacier at 7,200 feet and traverse to lower Curtis Ridge. Most teams take 6 to 8 hours to reach lower Curtis Ridge from the White River parking lot. Traverse west on the broad ridge to 7,200 feet.

For the alternative **Carbon River approach** to lower Curtis Ridge, begin at Ipsut Creek Campground at the end of the Carbon River road in the northwest corner of the park. The Carbon River/Ipsut Creek approach provides quicker access to the routes, but the descent and return to the Ipsut Creek trailhead is unusually long. Some teams opt to approach from Ipsut Creek and descend the Emmons/Winthrop Glaciers route to the White River Campground. From Ipsut Creek Campground (2,300 feet), take the 7.5-mile trail to Mystic Pass. Along the way, pass Carbon River Camp (2.9 miles from Ipsut Creek) and Dick Creek Camp (4 miles from Ipsut Creek). At Mystic Pass, just before the drop into Mystic Lake, ascend south along the climber's path through subalpine meadows up lower Curtis Ridge. Continue up the ridge to 7,200 feet.

From 7,200 feet on Curtis Ridge, climbers headed for Liberty Wall, Liberty Ridge, or Willis Wall descend a snow and scree slope to access the Carbon

Russell
Glacier

1. Liberty Wall Ice Cap
2. Liberty Wall Direct
3. Liberty Ridge
4. Willis Wall: Thermogenesis
5. Willis Wall West Rib
6. Willis Wall Central Rib
7. Willis Wall East Rib
8. East Willis Wall
9. Curtis Ridge

Carbon
Glacier

7,200 ft
bivy

Mount Adams

Winthrop
Glacier

Glacier. Getting to the Carbon from Curtis Ridge above 7,200 feet is difficult due to a very large cliff. Once on the Carbon Glacier, negotiate the crevasse systems and ascend the glacier to the intended route. The glacier becomes heavily crevassed and very circuitous by mid-July. Climbers attempting Curtis Ridge simply stay on the ridge and start climbing upward.

These routes all share the same recommended descent: the Emmons/Winthrop Glaciers route. Descend to Camp Schurman at 9,460 feet. From Camp Schurman, you can either climb over Steamboat Prow (fourth-class, loose rock) to the top of the Inter Glacier or descend the Emmons Glacier to Camp Curtis (9,000 feet), carrying over the ridge to the Inter Glacier. Descend the Inter Glacier to Glacier Basin and hike out the Glacier Basin Trail. Climbers usually take 5 to 10 hours from summit to trailhead. Teams climbing Liberty or Willis Wall may prefer to descend Liberty Ridge.

Liberty Wall:
The Ice Cap and Direct

Liberty Wall lies between Liberty and Ptarmigan Ridges. The wall is reminiscent of Willis Wall—moderately steep and terribly dangerous; in fact, the Liberty Wall routes may be the most dangerous on Mount Rainier. Rockfall and icefall are common from the Liberty Cap Glacier and the rock cliffs above. Overall, the two principal routes on Liberty Wall—the Ice Cap route and the Direct route—are similar to Willis Wall, with hard ice prevalent because of the numerous avalanches that clean the face. The routes are characterized by 40- to 55-degree ice slopes and gullies. The Liberty Wall Direct requires climbers to surmount the ice cliff, which may require near-vertical ice climbing for one pitch. The climbing would be great, if the ice cliff weren't so active. These routes are for fast, slightly crazy, and ambitious climbers.

ELEVATION GAIN • 9,700 feet from White River Campground to Liberty Cap (or 11,800 feet from Ipsut Creek Campground to Liberty Cap).

WHAT TO EXPECT • Rockfall and icefall hazards; 40- to 50-degree snow and ice, a vertical pitch on the direct route. Grade IV or V.

TIME • 2 to 5 days; 8 to 10 hours from high camp to Liberty Cap. Carry over.

SEASON • May, June, and October.

FIRST ASCENT • Ice Cap—Paul Myhre, Don Jones, and Roger Oborn; June 30, 1968. Direct—Dusan Jagersky and Gary Isaacs; September 20, 1971.

HIGH CAMP • On the Carbon Glacier between Liberty and Ptarmigan Ridges at 8,500 feet, away from the wall. The site provides great access to the route and allows climbers to scope the wall prior to the ascent.

Liberty Cap

Liberty Cap
Glacier

Black
Pyramid

2

3

Liberty
Wall

Ice Cliff

Thumb
Rock
10,760 ft

Ptarmigan Ridge

1

1. Liberty Wall Ice Cap
2. Liberty Wall Direct
3. Liberty Ridge

Carbon
Glacier

1. Ptarmigan Ice Cliff
2. Liberty Wall Ice Cap
3. Liberty Wall Direct
4. Liberty Ridge
5. Thermogenesis
6. Willis Wall West Rib

Mowich Face

Liberty Cap Glacier

Liberty Cap

Black Pyramid

Willis Wall

Thumb Rock

Liberty Wall Ice Cap: Ascend the Carbon Glacier to the headwall between Ptarmigan and Liberty Ridges. Cross the bergschrund and climb a 40-degree snow slope (ice in late season) up and to the right. Head to the snow gullies that access a second snow/ice slope, below the ice cliff. Ascend these gullies (45 degrees) and climb the second snow/ice slope toward the rock bands below the exit ramp in the ice cliff. (For a variation from the standard route, it is possible to cut right, above these gullies, and finish via the Ptarmigan Ice Cliff route.) Mixed climbing ascends the rock bands and gains the exit ramp. Climb the ramp onto Liberty Cap Glacier. Continue up the glacier, negotiating crevasses to reach Liberty Cap.

Liberty Wall Direct: Ascend the Carbon Glacier to the headwall between Ptarmigan and Liberty Ridges. Cross the bergschrund and climb a 45-degree snow slope (ice in late season) up and to the left. Continue up through a series of small rock bands and snow chutes to the base of the ice cliff. Climb the ice cliff. It changes from year to year, but teams can expect a difficult ice-climbing lead with belays to gain Liberty Cap Glacier above. (The first-ascent party used ten ice screws.) Once above the ice cliff, negotiate crevasses and continue to Liberty Cap.

Descent: Carry over and descend the Emmons/Winthrop Glaciers route to Camp Schurman.

LIBERTY RIDGE SURVIVAL STORY

David Quillen and Angela Morgan had spent 2½ days climbing to Thumb Rock on Liberty Ridge. The pair from Alabama felt ready for the upper ridge, having climbed much of the Emmons route before, and other mountains around the northwest.

Very carefully, the pair climbed exposed icy terrain using running belays while "simul" climbing and occasionally belaying pitches. It took them most of the day to reach the Liberty Cap. Fatigued, they pitched camp and enjoyed the lights of the Puget Sound. By 4:00 A.M., however, the temper of the mountain had changed. Visibility decreased, while wind speed and precipitation increased dramatically, leading to whiteout conditions. A significant storm had blown in.

Quillen and Morgan broke camp and attempted to find a route over to the Emmons/Winthrop Glacier but quickly recognized how futile it is to attempt moving on a glacier in whiteout conditions and high winds. Finding no suitable place to take cover, they decided to bivouac deep in a crevasse near the summit col at 13,700 feet.

While fighting the storm, the pair searched until they found a small crevasse slot. There, they fixed an anchor of two ice screws and rappelled 50 feet into a cold, dark hole to wait out the weather.

On a shelf in the crevasse, the pair huddled inside sleeping bags, wrapping themselves in their tent. The temperature hovered between 20–25 degrees and little food other than Gorp remained. With no fuel to run the stove, they were forced to melt water by collecting spindrift in plastic bottles and placing the bottles in their sleeping bags. Twice each day, one climber ascended the fixed rope to the surface to check weather conditions and reset the emergency signal marker, a red piece of fabric attached to a metal tent pole, which they had stuck in the ice on the large summit plateau.

Despite their increasingly desperate situation, the team remained calm and stayed together. They considered descending, but the storm, the winds, and the avalanche conditions were too fierce to take on, given their deteriorated condition. The Park Service was aware that the two were overdue and probably stranded but could do nothing because the weather was too severe for both flying and climbing on the upper mountain. Not until 3 days later would periods of clear skies make flying and searching possible.

Finally, a small hole in the ice near the summit col was spotted by a U.S. Army Chinook helicopter sent to search for the pair. Next to it stood a tent pole with a red marker. The ship hovered over the hole for some time, but saw no activity. With sunset approaching, climbing rangers David Gottlieb, Jeremy Shank, and Stoney Richards were dropped off to perform a ground search. They soon found the two climbers. Both were alive, but hypothermic, dehydrated, hungry, and in desperate need of better shelter. They had spent 3 days and 2 nights in the summit crevasse.

Although this story has a happy ending—Quillen and Morgan used commendable survival techniques to stay alive in a location and under conditions that have killed others—it illustrates how easily climbers can find themselves in trouble.

Every year, teams overestimate their skill and ability when measuring up to Liberty Ridge. The route is committing, longer, and more strenuous than it appears. A 2- to 3-day trip can easily turn into a 4- to 7-day ordeal when the weather kicks up its heels. Add a little altitude sickness and general fatigue and your team suddenly moves at a snail's pace above 13,000 feet. If you want to climb Liberty Ridge and not spend a week doing it, make sure you're in the best shape possible and are comfortable moving with a pack on exposed big-mountain terrain.

M.G.

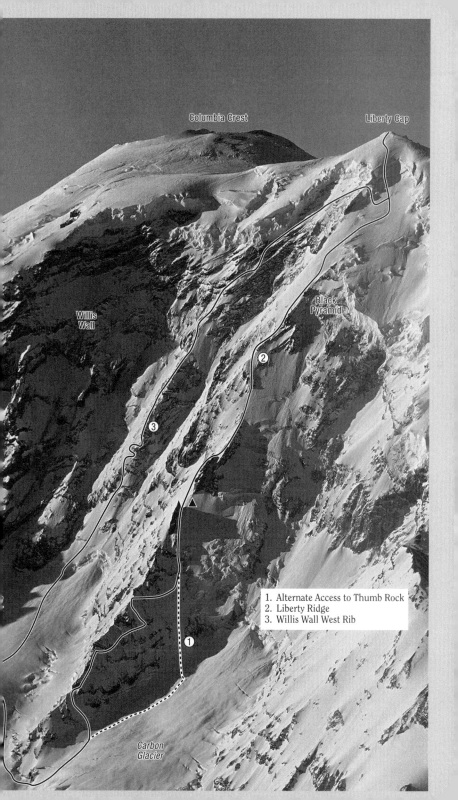

Columbia Crest

Liberty Cap

Willis
Wall

Black
Pyramid

② 2

③ 3

① 1

1. Alternate Access to Thumb Rock
2. Liberty Ridge
3. Willis Wall West Rib

Carbon
Glacier

Liberty
Ridge

Featured in *Fifty Classic Climbs of North America* (by Steve Roper and Allen Steck, Sierra Club, 1996), Liberty Ridge is truly the celebrated mountaineering classic of Rainier. The 5,500-foot ridge splits the steep north faces of Willis Wall and Liberty Wall, providing moderately difficult and protected climbing to the summit. This committing climb can only be accessed by crossing the jumbled ice and crevasses of the 900-foot-deep Carbon Glacier.

The exposed ridge challenges climbers with moderate to steep ice climbing and a perched bivy at Thumb Rock. Willis and Liberty Walls are the backdrops that provide a constant showcase of ice avalanches and rockfall from the summit ice cap. Since the climb is so long and committing, climbers must plan their trip well, usually needing to carry their gear to the summit and descend another route.

ELEVATION GAIN • 9,700 feet from White River Campground to Liberty Cap (or 11,800 feet from Ipsut Creek Campground to Liberty Cap).

WHAT TO EXPECT • Rockfall and icefall hazard; 55-degree ice slopes; glacier travel. Grade III or IV.

TIME • 2 to 4 days; most parties need 2 days to reach the Thumb Rock high camp (10,760); 5 to 10 hours from high camp to Liberty Cap. Carry over.

SEASON • May to mid-July.

FIRST ASCENT • Ome Daiber, Arnie Campbell, and Jim Borrow; September 30, 1935.

INTERMEDIATE CAMP • Lower Winthrop Glacier (7,200 feet), lower Curtis Ridge (7,200 feet), or Carbon Glacier (7,200 to 8,500 feet).

HIGH CAMP • Thumb Rock (10,760 feet).

Liberty Ridge can be gained on the Willis Wall side (east) or the Liberty Wall side (west). Then climb the west side of the ridge crest, ascending moderate snow and scree slopes (30 to 40 degrees) to Thumb Rock (10,760 feet), a large gendarme composed of questionable rock. The saddle just on the uphill side of this prominent rock formation provides an excellent high camp. The area is small, however, and can be crowded on busy weekends. Also note that falling rock from Thumb Rock is possible.

From Thumb Rock, choose one of three short variations to gain the ridge above the rock face behind camp. The east face variation on the Willis Wall side is a moderate snow slope staying close to the rock. It gains the ridge 400 feet above camp and is exposed. The right-center gully is the steepest variation, having a 15-foot ice pitch (70 to 80 degrees) in a narrow gully that runs out

Above Thumb Rock, climbers on Liberty Ridge

onto the ridge directly above the rock. The west face variation on the Liberty Wall side is also a moderate snow slope with exposure.

Once the ridge crest is regained, ascend 40- to 50-degree snow and ice slopes to the base of the Black Pyramid at 12,400 feet. Then traverse toward Willis Wall and climb the open face. This is the steepest part of the climb, sometimes 55 degrees. It runs for three or four rope lengths and can be hard and icy, particularly near the top of the Black Pyramid. Climb to the crest of the ridge above the Black Pyramid, where the slope angle decreases and the route joins Liberty Cap Glacier at 13,000 feet.

From there, ascend moderately steep glaciated slopes toward the bergschrund directly above. Depending on the year and season, the bergschrund may require a short section (10 to 40 feet) of vertical ice climbing to surmount, or it may simply involve end-running the obstacle. Above the bergschrund, the route continues on the glacier for the last few hundred feet of elevation gain to Liberty Cap.

Descent: Carry over and descend the Emmons/Winthrop Glaciers route to Camp Schurman.

Routes on the Willis Wall

If Mount Rainier has one noted and feared place, it is the Willis Wall on the northern face. The massive wall begins at 9,600 feet and rises steeply 4,000 feet over

1. Thermogenesis
2. Willis Wall West Rib
3. Willis Wall Central Rib
4. Willis Wall East Rib
5. East Willis Wall
6. Curtis Ridge

Liberty Cap

Columbia Crest

Winthrop Glacier

snow, ice, rock, and frozen volcanic mud and ash to the summit ice cap. The wall has three ribs or incipient ridges—the west, central, and east ribs—and they offer the least hazardous lines up the main wall by avoiding avalanche/ice chutes. Although the climbing is not any steeper than on many of Rainier's other hard routes, this wall shouts danger. Climbers considering these routes should begin with a good assessment of the dangers and be prepared for hardship, fear, physical strain, and constant objective hazards.

The primary consideration is speed. Towering above much of the wall is a 200- to 300-foot ice cliff that randomly releases avalanches of ice and rock that sweep the face. A good portion of the wall can be swept by a large avalanche at any time without notice. Other hazards include small slides of snow and rock that frequent the gullies. Willis Wall is committing once on route. The only possible escapes require a long and exposed traverse to Liberty Ridge or Curtis Ridge. Couple these considerations with the fact that climbers can't see incoming weather from the south, and the Willis Wall proves to be some of Mount Rainier's most hazardous terrain.

Willis Wall's allure faded among climbers soon after the major routes were climbed. In 2004, park officials estimated no one had climbed the wall in at least a dozen years.

Consider climbing Willis Wall only under ideal conditions that include a few days of cold weather with no precipitation preceding the climb. The cold days should help rocks and snow adhere to the wall. Assessing the wall prior to the climb is of great benefit, too. Consider this an opportunity to check the activity of the summit ice cliff and to get an overall sense for what's going on. Some teams ascend the wall unroped in the interests of faster progress. The ability to move fast, and a familiarity with moderate ice and rocky terrain with intense exposure, is mandatory. If roping up, bring a few pickets, ice screws, and some pitons for protection.

Of the Willis Wall climbers I interviewed, not one mentioned the views, aesthetic values, or quality climbing features of the routes. Their predominant concerns and comments revolved around the ominous ice cliff, frozen rock slab ledges, and frequency of small debris avalanches in the gullies.

Getting to Willis Wall: From 7,200 feet on Curtis Ridge, descend a snow and scree slope to the Carbon Glacier. (Avoid going too high onto Curtis Ridge, because it quickly becomes a large cliff and denies access to the Carbon.) Once on the glacier, negotiate the crevasse systems and ascend toward Willis Wall. The glacier is heavily crevassed and very circuitous by mid-July. Select only a campsite that is well away from the wall and from the possibility of being destroyed by an avalanche. Large avalanches may travel as much as a mile or more out from the base.

THE PERSONALITIES OF THE WILLIS WALL

Willis Wall took its name from Bailey Willis, a turn-of-the-century geologist who spent years charting the north side of what he called Mount Tacoma. As he watched what seemed like constant avalanches of ice and rock rain down the face's sheer slopes, Willis was convinced no climber who attempted the wall would ever live to tell about it.

For nearly six decades, National Park Service rangers shared Willis's view and prohibited climbing on Willis Wall. But as the rules relaxed in the late 1950s, some of the Northwest's top mountaineers began to look for potential routes up the wall's east, west, and central ribs.

An East Coast climber named Charlie Bell claimed an unauthorized solo ascent of the West Rib in June 1961. Ed Cooper and Mike Swayne climbed the east edge of the wall in 1962. Finally, in 1963, after studying the wall for six years, Dave Mahre led a route up the East Rib with Jim Wickwire, Fred Dunham, and Don Anderson. Their 21-hour climb marked the first time anyone climbed directly up Willis Wall's face without veering to one side to avoid an overhanging ice cliff at the top.

The first winter ascent of the wall took place in 1970. Wickwire and Alex Bertulis worked their way up the Carbon Glacier along the wall's West Rib over 5 days in February. Bertulis believed frigid temperatures would keep rocks frozen in place. "I wouldn't be caught dead on it during the summer, because the rock is so loose on that wall," Bertulis said in a 2001 interview with *The News Tribune* of Tacoma. "It's not very hard climbing. It's just dangerous climbing during warm weather."

Bertulis had observed the wall for more than a month before his winter ascent. He twice flew over the summit to inspect a 150-foot serac leaning like the Tower of Pisa above their route. Convinced winter's frigid temperatures would lock the tottering ice in place, Bertulis and Wickwire went ahead with their climb. As the pair came within 100 feet of the leaning serac, "we heard this big crunch," Bertulis said, "and we both realized that the serac was about to go." The pair hurried past the base of the ice tower. When they were about 50 feet beyond it, "the whole serac gave way," Bertulis said. "Months of calculations, and it goes right when you're there," he said.

S.C.

Willis Wall:
Thermogenesis

This long couloir on the west side of Willis Wall separates the wall from Liberty Ridge. The first-ascent party climbed the couloir by mistake while searching for the

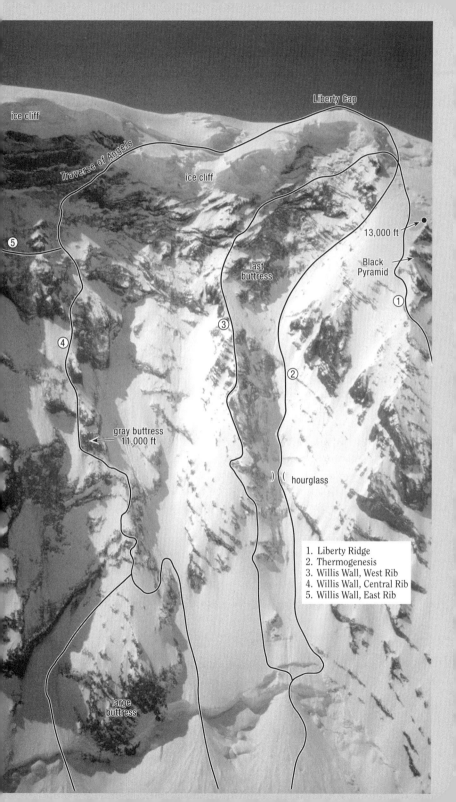

ice cliff

Liberty Cap

Traverse of Angels

ice cliff

⑤

last
buttress

13,000 ft

Black
Pyramid

①

③

②

④

gray buttress
11,000 ft

hourglass

1. Liberty Ridge
2. Thermogenesis
3. Willis Wall, West Rib
4. Willis Wall, Central Rib
5. Willis Wall, East Rib

large
buttress

West Rib in the dark. After ascending the couloir for a bit, they noticed their mistake and quickly completed the climb. They reported occasional small slides of loose, pebbly debris, and the entire route was swept twice the following day by avalanches.

The route is actually an ice chute that is frequently dumped upon by the ice cliff above. The route tops out at about 13,500 feet, where it joins the upper Liberty Ridge route. Of all the routes on Willis Wall, Thermogenesis is the most hazardous.

ELEVATION GAIN • 9,700 feet from White River Campground to Liberty Cap (or 11,800 feet from Ipsut Creek Campground to Liberty Cap).

WHAT TO EXPECT • Serious rockfall and icefall hazard; sustained 35- to 55-degree snow and ice slopes, with one short 60-degree section. Grade III-IV.

TIME • 3 to 5 days; 5 to 7 hours from high camp to the upper Black Pyramid on Liberty Ridge. Liberty Ridge descent to high camp, 5 hours from Liberty Cap; or carry over.

SEASON • Winter through May.

FIRST ASCENT • Steve Doty, Jerome Eberharter, and Jon Olson; May 20, 1978.

HIGH CAMP • The Carbon Glacier, away from the wall, below 8,500 to 9,000 feet.

Climb the Carbon Glacier to 9,800 feet toward the far western couloir of the Willis Wall. Cross the bergschrund on the large debris cone of snow and ice and climb the 30- to 50-degree firn snow and ice slopes. The steepest section is in the hourglass one third of the way up the couloir, where a short section of 60-degree ice is found. Near 12,500 feet and directly below the giant ice cliff, the couloir diagonals right to gain upper Liberty Ridge.

Some reprieve from the danger is offered once climbers reach the steep Black Pyramid pitch on Liberty Ridge (see route description for Liberty Ridge). The slope angle decreases above the Black Pyramid, on the crest of Liberty Ridge as the route joins Liberty Cap Glacier. In some years, the bergschrund requires a short, vertical ice climb to access the glacier above. Continue to Liberty Cap.

Descent: Descend Liberty Ridge, or carry over and descend the Emmons/Winthrop Glaciers route to Camp Schurman.

Willis Wall:
West Rib

This rib is a protrusion, broad and snowy at its base, crested and somewhat protected in the middle, and broad with exposed rocky cliff bands for the last 500 feet below the ice cliff. Any protection offered is actually just a token, because large rib-sweeping avalanches and slides are possible.

The most hazardous sections are at the points where climbers access and exit the crested rib. The exit requires traversing onto a broad face of narrow terraced ledges below the ice cliff. Climber Alex Bertulis said that less than 5 minutes after he and Jim Wickwire crossed under the ice cliff, a large serac broke free and swept part of the route.

ELEVATION GAIN • 9,700 feet from White River Campground to Liberty Cap (or 11,800 feet from Ipsut Creek Campground to Liberty Cap).

WHAT TO EXPECT • Serious rockfall and icefall hazard; 35- to 55-degree rock, snow, and ice slopes with traversing. Grade IV or V.

TIME • 3 to 5 days; 6 to 8 hours from high camp to upper Liberty Ridge. Liberty Ridge descent to high camp, 5 hours from Liberty Cap; or carry over.

SEASON • Winter and spring.

FIRST ASCENT • Charlie Bell; June 12, 1961. First winter ascent—Alex Bertulis and Jim Wickwire; February 11, 1970.

HIGH CAMP • The Carbon Glacier, away from the wall, below 8,500 feet.

Ascend the Carbon Glacier toward the base of the Willis Wall's far western couloir (start of the Thermogenesis route) and a possible location to cross the bergschrund, 9,800 feet. Once across, climb and traverse left out of the gully and onto the broad lower cleaver.

Continue up a frozen snowfield toward the narrowing crest (an easy 30 to 35 degrees). A 60-foot section of rock requires fourth-class climbing to gain snow ramps that lead to the crest of the rib. Ascend the rib, bypassing any rock bands below and to the left, through moderate snow ramps that regain the crest.

Climb the rib crest to the last buttress. Bypass that buttress on the left over short snow and rock bands to gain an upper terraced ledge below the ice cliff. Climb that ledge up and right to the corner below the ice cliff. Climbing the icy ledge and rounding the corner is considered the most difficult. After the corner (with the ice cliff still above), traverse onto the steep, open face that leads to upper Liberty Ridge. A short rappel may be needed to get on Liberty Ridge. Climb onto the Liberty Cap Glacier, crossing the bergschrund near 13,700 feet. Continue to Liberty Cap.

Descent: Descend Liberty Ridge, or carry over and descend the Emmons/Winthrop Glaciers route to Camp Schurman.

Willis Wall:
Central Rib

Heavily buttressed, the Central Rib ascends terrain similar to the West Rib. However, it requires more traversing to avoid rock bands that block the rib crest.

The rib is more of a face and gully climb than a climb of a crested rib, and this proves circuitous and time-consuming.

The story of a tough Central Rib ascent in May 1971 gives a flavor of the possible hazards of a Willis Wall route. Climbing in hard, icy conditions, Eddie Boulton and Jim Wickwire were forced to bivouac on the wall near 13,000 feet in a storm. They sought shelter in a protected moat/cave as avalanches swept its entrance throughout the night. When the weather did not relent the next day, they forced their way through deep snow to Liberty Cap, where they endured another desperate snow-cave bivouac. Eventually, 7 days after leaving the trailhead at Ipsut Creek, they made it down to the highway near the White River Ranger Station. Wickwire says the experience of those bivouacs and others like them on Rainier were critical to his later survival near the summit of K2.

ELEVATION GAIN • 9,700 feet from White River Campground to Liberty Cap (or 11,800 feet from Ipsut Creek Campground to Liberty Cap).

WHAT TO EXPECT • Serious rockfall and icefall hazard; 35- to 55-degree rock, snow, and ice slopes with traversing. Grade IV or V.

TIME • 3 to 5 days; 7 to 10 hours from high camp to Liberty Cap. Liberty Ridge descent to high camp, 5 hours from Liberty Cap; or carry over.

SEASON • Winter through June.

FIRST ASCENT • Paul Dix and Dean Caldwell; June 20, 1965.

HIGH CAMP • The Carbon Glacier, away from the wall, below 8,500 feet.

The Central Rib begins against the Carbon Glacier as a large buttress that blocks direct access. Gain the wall by crossing the bergschrund on large snow-deposition cones to the left or right of the buttress, 9,800 feet. Ascend frozen snow or ice to terraced ledges that give access to the rib crest. Climbers have reported a barrage of hail-size rock and ice until the rib crest was gained. Then ascend the rib, bypassing four archlike rock bands by moving below and to the left on steep snow traverses and gullies.

After the fourth arch, climb snow slopes right of the crest for a few hundred feet to a crumbly gray buttress overhead. Traverse left when feasible and gain the top of the gray buttress via an open snow slope. Above this buttress, ascend left toward a short, narrow snow or ice chute that leads to a rightward traverse on slab rock or verglas. Ascend the slab rock to a steep snow and rock cliff—a "frosty cliff"—where a 40-foot traverse on difficult rock provides access to an easy 20-foot vertical cliff that tops out on the rib crest. Continue scrambling up moderate snow slopes, joining the original East Rib route, and proceed about three rope lengths to the steep rock that forms the base of the ice cliffs.

A climber traverses steep, icy snow from the top of the East Rib to the Central Rib of the Willis Wall. Note ice cliffs above. © Jim Wickwire

The ice cliffs rest on three terraced rock bands. Climb steep, frozen conglomerate consisting of rock and mud for 150 feet (fourth-class climbing) to a ledge. Traverse right on the short, exposed ledge for 15 feet to a short fifth-class step that gains the second of the terraced ledges. From the second ledge, traverse and climb 40 feet to a narrow, exposed ledge and blind corner. Turn the corner (possible verglas or snow) and climb 20 feet to easier snow slopes that reach the exit ramp between the ice cliffs. This traverse—the Traverse of Angels—is airy; belays and protection are difficult to place. Once the summit plateau is reached above the ice cliff, climb west on gentle glacier slopes to Liberty Cap.

Descent: Descend Liberty Ridge, or carry over and descend the Emmons/Winthrop Glaciers route to Camp Schurman.

Willis Wall:
East Rib

The East Rib was the first of the Willis Wall ribs to be climbed. The rib is actually a series of buttresses—less defined on the lower third of the wall, prominent on the second third, then nonexistent as the rib flattens for the last third to exit between the ice cliffs. The route follows the rock buttresses for two-thirds of the way up the wall. Although a longer and less direct route than the other two Willis Wall ribs, the crest of the East Rib offers some protection from the ice cliff and rockfall hazards above. Higher on the buttressed rib, however, climbers must commit to a long rightward traverse below the ice cliff—or else exit left to upper Curtis Ridge, a much safer option.

ELEVATION GAIN • 9,700 feet from White River Campground to Liberty Cap (or 11,800 feet from Ipsut Creek Campground to Liberty Cap).

WHAT TO EXPECT • Serious rockfall and icefall hazard; 35- to 55-degree rock, snow, and ice slopes with traversing. Grade IV or V.

TIME • 3 to 5 days; 7 to 10 hours from high camp to Liberty Cap. Liberty Ridge descent to high camp, 5 hours from Liberty Cap; or carry over.

SEASON • Winter through June.

FIRST ASCENT • Dave Mahre, Fred Dunham, Jim Wickwire, and Don Anderson; June 8, 1963.

HIGH CAMP • The Carbon Glacier, away from the wall, below 8,500 feet.

Climb the Carbon Glacier to the eastern edge of the wall, left of the small lower East Rib rock outcroppings. Cross the bergschrund on a deposition cone and climb snow slopes to the crest of the first main rock buttress on the rib. Rockfall from upper Curtis Ridge is likely here; protection is offered once on the crest.

Climb the rib and arc right to the crest of a second buttress; then continue toward the final and largest buttress, which lies 1,500 to 1,700 feet above the Carbon Glacier. A 75-foot section of loose and very steep rock must be climbed to gain the crest of the largest buttress, or eastern rib. From the crest of the largest buttress, climb on snow and rock to the head of the rib crest, at about 12,200 feet. (An exit variation is possible from this point; see below.) A prominent terraced snow ledge to the right must be traversed. The long traverse on the snow ledge is exposed to the ice cliffs and therefore hard and icy. Traverse the ledge to where the East Rib and Central Rib routes join. Now proceed about three rope lengths to the steep rock that forms the base of the ice cliffs.

The ice cliffs rest on three terraced rock bands. Climb steep, frozen conglomerate consisting of rock and mud for 150 feet (fourth-class climbing) to a ledge. Traverse right on the short, exposed ledge for 15 feet to a short fifth-class step that gains the second of the terraced ledges. From the second ledge, traverse and climb 40 feet to a narrow, exposed ledge and blind corner. Turn the corner (possible verglas or snow) and climb 20 feet to easier snow slopes that reach the exit ramp between the ice cliffs. This traverse—the Traverse of Angels—is

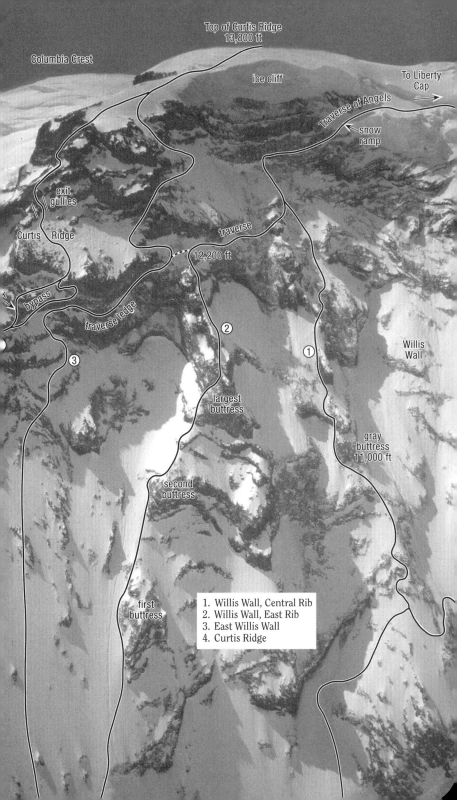

Columbia Crest

Top of Curtis Ridge
13,800 ft

ice cliff

To Liberty
Cap

Traverse of Angels

snow
ramp

exit
gullies

Curtis Ridge

traverse

12,200 ft

bypass

traverse ledge

②

①

Willis
Wall

③

largest
buttress

gray
buttress
11,000 ft

second
buttress

first
buttress

1. Willis Wall, Central Rib
2. Willis Wall, East Rib
3. East Willis Wall
4. Curtis Ridge

airy; belays and protection are difficult to place. Once the summit plateau is reached above the ice cliff, climb west on gentle glacier slopes to Liberty Cap.

Exit variation: From the head of the rib crest where the snow ledge leads to a rightward traverse, climb to the left instead. You can then ascend moderate snow, ice, and rock to finish the climb on the upper East Willis Wall route (class 4) to exit on upper Curtis Ridge.

Descent: Descend Liberty Ridge, or carry over and descend the Emmons/Winthrop Glaciers route to Camp Schurman.

Willis Wall:
East Willis Wall

The least hazardous of the Willis Wall routes, this climb stays east of the three major ribs and avoids much of the exposure to the ice cliff above. Skirting along the eastern flank of Willis Wall, the route ascends a series of snowfields, chutes, ledges, and short rock bands to finish through the exit gullies of upper Curtis Ridge. Although the ice cliff is not as threatening, the route still exposes climbers to extensive rockfall from upper Curtis Ridge. The first-ascent party chose this route after a number of ice-cliff avalanches swept the route they had intended to ascend on the wall.

ELEVATION GAIN • 9,700 feet from White River Campground to Liberty Cap (or 11,800 feet from Ipsut Creek Campground to Liberty Cap).

WHAT TO EXPECT • Rockfall and icefall hazards; 35- to 55-degree rock, snow, and ice slopes with traversing. Grade IV.

TIME • 3 to 5 days; 7 to 10 hours from high camp to Liberty Cap. Liberty Ridge descent to high camp, 5 hours from Liberty Cap; or carry over.

SEASON • Winter through June.

FIRST ASCENT • Ed Cooper and Mike Swayne; June 26, 1962.

HIGH CAMP • The Carbon Glacier, away from the wall, below 8,500 feet.

Climb to the head of the Carbon Glacier, left of the Willis Wall, East Rib. Cross the bergschrund and climb the western flank of Curtis Ridge via uneventful 30- to 45-degree snow slopes through rock bands that require scrambling. A series of snow ledges and ramps climb to the base of a major rock cliff above (near 11,000 feet). There, another key snow/ice ledge leads right on a long traverse to bypass the major rock cliff. That ledge ends in a broken rock band. Ascend the rock band, actually a steep fourth-class boulder field with very loose rocks, to the snow slopes above. Climb carefully; significant rockfall is possible.

From the top of the boulder field, climb a series of moderate snow and rock ramps—first to the right, then to the left—to the final snow tongue from upper Curtis Ridge, at 13,300 feet. Continue along the snow crest to the top of Curtis Ridge at 13,800 feet. From here, you can either cross the broad summit col south to the crater rim and Columbia Crest, or traverse gentle glacier slopes west to Liberty Cap.

Descent: Descend Liberty Ridge, or carry over and descend the Emmons/Winthrop Glaciers route to Camp Schurman.

Curtis
Ridge

Curtis Ridge is the largest and most prominent of Mount Rainier's northern ridges, dividing the Willis Wall and Carbon Glacier on the west from the Winthrop Glacier on the east. The lower ridge is broad at the base, narrowing as it ascends to an apex at 10,300 feet, where the technical climbing begins.

Years of unsuccessful attempts and a fatality in 1969 led many climbers to regard this route as a rockfall death trap. Climbers in later years reported the route to be less dangerous than originally perceived and called the rock quite solid by Mount Rainier standards. In any case, an early start with fast climbing means a safer ascent. Curtis Ridge is a hard classic that demands good skills in routefinding, rock climbing, and snow climbing.

ELEVATION GAIN • 9,700 feet from White River Campground to Liberty Cap (or 11,800 feet from Ipsut Creek Campground to Liberty Cap).

WHAT TO EXPECT • Rockfall and icefall hazard; 35- to 55-degree snow and ice slopes with traversing; fifth-class rock and A2 aid climbing. Grade IV.

TIME • 3 to 5 days; 6 to 8 hours from high camp to the top of Curtis Ridge at 13,800 feet. Carry over.

SEASON • Winter through June.

FIRST ASCENT • Gene Prater and Marcel Schuster; July 21, 1957.

HIGH CAMP • There is an excellent bivy ledge on the east side of the Curtis Ridge crest, 200 feet before a prominent rock gendarme at 10,200 feet. You can also bivy at the base of the gendarme.

From 7,200 feet on Curtis Ridge, climb on gradually steeper and more avalanche-prone snow slopes to the apex of the ridge at 10,300 feet. At this point, traverse the crest until you reach a 200-foot-deep notch in the ridge. Here, descend the west side of the ridge approximately 100 feet on loose rock or snow to a rappel station. Rappel 70 feet to the snow or loose rock ledge, below and west of the notch and ridge crest.

Columbia Crest

13,800 ft

Traverse of Angels

①

rock
▲gendarme

②

③

1. Willis Wall East Rib
2. East Willis Wall
3. Curtis Ridge

Photo taken from the bivy site at 10,200 feet © Sanderson/Steiger Collection

Continue along for roughly 300 yards, staying on the crest of the ridge when possible. Vertical steps along the ridge crest can be bypassed on either side without major difficulty. There is an excellent site for high camp on the east side of the ridge crest at 10,200 feet, about 200 feet before the prominent rock gendarme, where another small bivy site exists. Pass the gendarme on the left (east), then traverse to the Willis Wall side of the crest and climb to the first major rock band.

From here, there are a couple of options to gain the snowfield above the first rock band. The first option is an open-book, 75-foot A2 crack that lies straight ahead west of the ridge crest and provides direct access to the snowfield above. Negotiating this obstacle is time-consuming.

The other option is to climb and traverse to the right, below the rock band, on a series of snow steps that lead to a small snow slope. Continue climbing up, looking for a snow ledge that traverses downward and to the left. Traverse to the end of this ledge, where 10 to 15 feet of easy third-class climbing provides access to the snowfield above the first rock band. Take small chocks (half-inch to 1.5 inches) and pickets for rock or snow protection along both the right and left traverses.

At the snowfield, climb up and leftward on firn snow to a small rock band, passing by it to get to the second major rock band. Bypass this second major band by traversing a snow/ice slope to the right, where a 20- to 30-foot section of third-class rock gains access to the second firn snowfield. From here, traverse up and leftward to the exit gullies.

The gullies are straightforward. Several small rock bands must be passed in the gullies, and they require either fifth-class climbing or mixed climbing depending on conditions. Above the rock bands, gain the Curtis Ridge snow dome. Continue along the easy snow crest to the top of Curtis Ridge at 13,800 feet. From here, you can either cross the broad summit col south to the crater rim and Columbia Crest, or traverse gentle glacier slopes west to Liberty Cap.

Descent: Carry over and descend the Emmons/Winthrop Glaciers route to Camp Schurman.

CAMP SCHURMAN ROUTES

Camp Schurman high camp provides the best access for the Winthrop Glacier/Russell Cliffs route and for the Emmons/Winthrop Glaciers route. Camp Schurman sits at the base of Steamboat Prow—where two ridges merge from below into a triangle that divides the largest glaciers on Rainier, the Emmons and Winthrop. The Inter Glacier fills the recess between the ridges on the backside of Steamboat Prow.

At 9,460 feet, Camp Schurman is Rainier's second-most popular high camp, after Camp Muir. Camp Schurman has a ranger hut and outhouse. Located on the northeast side of Rainier, the camp enjoys great sunrises of pink and gold. Little Tahoma—at 11,138 feet, Washington's third-highest peak—lies to the southeast of the camp, while the urban glow of the Puget Sound region illuminates the northwestern horizon after sunset.

Climbers spending the night will probably camp on the snowy edge of the Winthrop Glacier. Build sturdy camps and anchor everything well; Camp Schurman is noted for fierce, tent-destroying winds. Since glaciers flank the camp, excellent opportunities to practice crevasse rescue or ice climbing are a stone's throw away.

To White River Campground

To lower Curtis Ridge Routes

St. Elmo Pass

Glacier Basin

Inter Glacier

Camp Schurman

Emmons Flats

Camp Curtis

The Corridor

①

Emmons Glacier

②

Disappointment Cleaver

Fryingpan Glacier

③

1. Emmons/Winthrop Glaciers
2. Disappointment Cleaver
3. Little Tahoma via Fryingpan Glacier

Getting to high camp: Begin from White River Campground at 4,400 feet, taking the Glacier Basin trail 3.3 miles to Glacier Basin Camp at 6,000 feet. Follow the climbers' path from the basin up the right side of the creek to the snout of the Inter Glacier at 6,800 feet, in the southwest corner of the valley. The Inter Glacier serves as a great training ground for inexperienced climbers.

Ascend the Inter Glacier, negotiating crevasses as needed to Camp Curtis (9,000 feet). This camp on the south side of Ruth Ridge can accommodate teams of four or fewer climbers. From Camp Curtis, traverse and descend 150 feet to the Emmons Glacier on a climbers' path of loose rock and clay. Rope up and ascend the glacier, paralleling the edge of Ruth Ridge to the base of Steamboat Prow and Camp Schurman (9,460 feet).

Another camp, Emmons Flats (9,800 feet), sits above Camp Schurman. Emmons Flats is entirely on the glacier, and those spending the night must use the blue-bag waste disposal system.

Winthrop Glacier/ Russell Cliffs

The Winthrop Glacier/Russell Cliffs route is rarely climbed. The Winthrop Glacier offers the same climbing terrain as the Emmons/Winthrop route: crevasses, icefalls, seracs, and snow bridges. It attracts teams who prefer routefinding and want to avoid the Emmons boot track.

Continuing the adventure, teams traverse into the large cirque above Russell Cliffs, with access to the steep gullies, faces, and buttresses of upper Curtis Ridge. Although the Russell Cliffs variations are not hard, they are exposed and intimidating. This is a route for teams looking for something unusual and wild in a summit climb from Camp Schurman.

ELEVATION GAIN • 10,000 feet from White River Campground to Columbia Crest.

WHAT TO EXPECT • Rockfall and icefall hazard; 45- to 50-degree snow and ice slopes; short rock steps on the central route; glacier travel. Grade II or III.

TIME • 2 to 3 days; 6 to 9 hours from Camp Schurman to the summit, 3 to 4 hours for descent to Camp Schurman.

SEASON • Spring through July.

FIRST ASCENT • Don Jones, Jim Kurtz, Dave Mahre, and Gene Prater; July 1960. Central bowl—Dean Bentley, Jim Springer, and John L. Thompson; July 8, 1973. Upper headwall— Chris Mahre, Dave Mahre, and Gene Prater; 1974.

HIGH CAMP • Camp Schurman (9,460 feet) or Emmons Flats (9,800 feet).

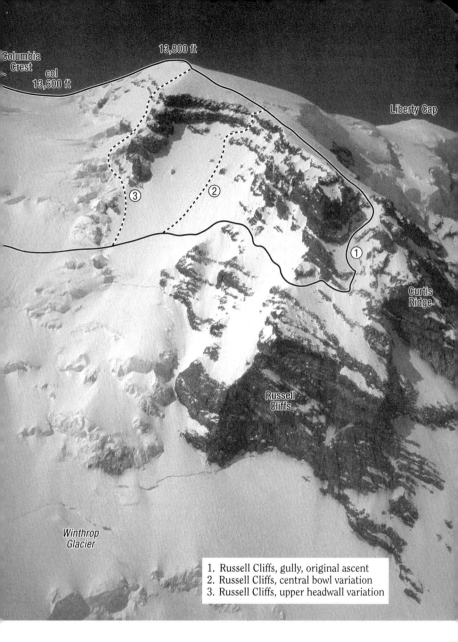

Columbia
Crest
col
13,600 ft
13,800 ft

Liberty Cap

③

②

①

Curtis
Ridge

Russell
Cliffs

Winthrop
Glacier

1. Russell Cliffs, gully, original ascent
2. Russell Cliffs, central bowl variation
3. Russell Cliffs, upper headwall variation

From Emmons Flats, head west onto the Winthrop Glacier. Traverse and climb through the cirque between the shoulders of the Emmons and Winthrop Glaciers. There are many large crevasses here, and teams should waste little time; an active icefall heads the cirque. Negotiate the crevasses and ascend the raised shoulder of the Winthrop; depending on the year, you may encounter a short section of 60-degree ice.

Once on the shoulder, ascend moderate glacier slopes to between 12,000 and 12,500 feet. Find the best access into the large, open-face cirque above Russell Cliffs. From here, climbers have three options in ascending to upper Curtis Ridge.

The **far-right gully** is the original route and involves a long traverse. The cliffs below intensify the exposure in the 45-degree gully. Depending on the season, there may be a short rocky or verglassed section near the top before the gully exits to upper Curtis Ridge.

The **central bowl variation** is not as steep as the gully, but climbers must negotiate a small vertical rock band to exit the cirque onto upper Curtis Ridge. This may involve a short step of ice or fifth-class rock.

The **upper headwall variation** climbs the long, steep snowface left of the large buttressed rock. This route crosses a crevasse or bergschrund before climbing the 50-degree face. Small rock bands near the top are easy to climb in reaching upper Curtis Ridge.

From 13,800 feet on the top of Curtis Ridge, cross the broad summit col south to the crater rim and Columbia Crest.

Descent: Descend the Emmons/Winthrop Glaciers route to Camp Schurman.

DELMAR FADDEN'S FATAL CLIMB

Delmar Fadden was a twenty-two-year-old adventure seeker who in 1936 made the first successful midwinter ascent of Mount Rainier via the Emmons Glacier. His mysterious death on his descent and his passion for life in the years before his fatal climb have helped make Fadden one of the most enigmatic characters in the mountain's history.

Fadden grew up in the Seahurst area of King County and took to the wilderness at an early age. In 1932, he embarked on a 30-day solo trek across the Olympic Mountains, joyously destroying his compass and burning his map days after his parents dropped him off near Lake Quinault. By the time he was picked up on August 29, the teenager had shed 30 pounds from his lean frame and confessed he had survived the last few days on plant bulbs, frogs, and several grouse that he killed with rocks.

Fadden made several failed attempts to climb Mount Rainier. Finally, in September 1932, he completed a solo ascent to the summit via the Emmons Glacier. When the film from his climb came back blank, Fadden returned to Rainier the following weekend and repeated the feat, racing from Sunrise to Columbia Crest in just 10 hours.

The idea of a winter ascent seemed to consume Fadden, even though weather often turned against him during his attempts and his Depression-era equipment seemed to regularly fail. Despite breaking his snowshoes at the start of a solo Rainier trip in late December 1934, Fadden pressed on through deep snow to Steamboat Prow. "It seemed hopeless to continue," he wrote, "yet to turn back before I had actually begun was ugly to me."

Fadden returned alone to Mount Rainier in January 1936, ostensibly to spend a week skiing, snowshoeing, and sketching in Glacier Basin but secretly hoping to reach the summit. When Fadden's twin brother reported him overdue, park rangers began a search. They tracked his footprints around Glacier Basin and Inter Glacier, and on January 23 found wands marking a route above Steamboat Prow. Experienced climbers arrived from Seattle to help in the search, expanding an operation that by then had gained national attention.

On January 29, a small search plane spotted a body on the frozen snow about 13,000 feet up the Emmons Glacier. Two days later, a team of five braved temperatures estimated at minus 25 degrees Fahrenheit to climb up to Fadden's frozen corpse, which lay face down on the snow. He wore no gloves, held no ice ax, and was missing the left crampon on his soft-soled mukluks. Searchers guessed Fadden had fallen, been knocked unconscious, and likely froze to death before he awoke. His body was carried out on a toboggan and reached the White River Ranger Station on February 2.

Photos from Fadden's camera revealed images from the summit, and comparisons to recorded weather patterns placed him there around January 17. The following summer, climbers followed Fadden's trail markers to the crater rim, located his camp, and found enough empty cans to suggest he had spent several days on the summit.

The volunteer efforts in Fadden's well-publicized recovery pushed ranger Ome Daiber to draw up a list of climbers that he could call in an emergency, an informal group that led to the creation of Seattle Mountain Rescue. Fadden's legacy also survives in his soul-baring poems, which generally appeared as a few lines scribbled in scrapbooks. Among the most quoted is, "If a dream / Meant anything to me / Would it seem / A bold reality? / If I knew / My hand of fate, / Would I do — / Or hesitate?"

S.C.

Emmons/
Winthrop Glaciers

The Emmons/Winthrop Glaciers route is Mount Rainier's least technical and second-most popular climb. The climb is longer and more physically demanding than the most popular track, the Ingraham Direct/Disappointment Cleaver. The Emmons/Winthrop route ascends the upper mountain within the broad area where the streams of the two glaciers flow side by side.

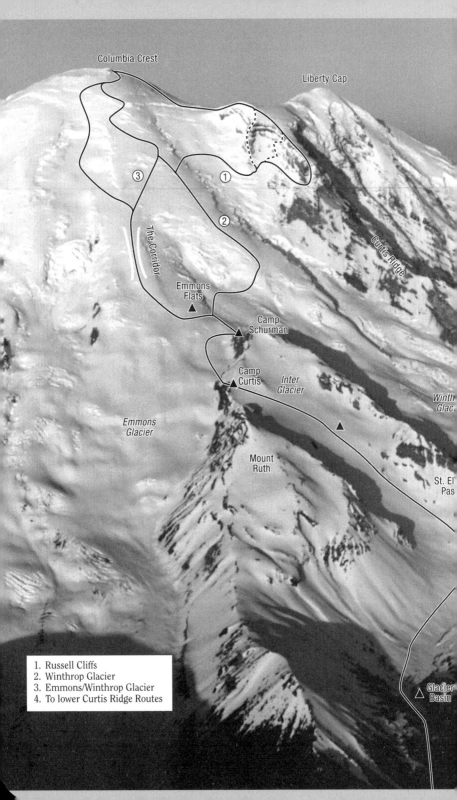

Columbia Crest

Liberty Cap

③

①

②

Curtis Ridge

The Corridor

Emmons Flats ▲

Camp Schurman ▲

Camp Curtis ▲

Inter Glacier

Winth Glac.

Emmons Glacier

▲

Mount Ruth

St. El Pas

Glacier Basin △

1. Russell Cliffs
2. Winthrop Glacier
3. Emmons/Winthrop Glacier
4. To lower Curtis Ridge Routes

Climbers enjoy the approach through old-growth forest and subalpine and alpine terrain. Once on the mountain, the climb requires good glacier navigation skills as teams weave in and around immense crevasses. Opaque blue glacial ice, towering seracs, cavernous crevasses, and suspect snow bridges dot the route. The Emmons/Winthrop route makes for excellent, exciting glacier mountaineering.

ELEVATION GAIN • 10,000 feet from White River Campground to Columbia Crest.

WHAT TO EXPECT • Glacier travel; 30- to 40-degree snow and ice slopes. Grade II.

TIME • 2 to 3 days; 7 to 9 hours from Camp Schurman to the summit, 3 to 4 hours for descent to Camp Schurman.

SEASON • Mid-May through September.

FIRST ASCENT • Unknown; railroad surveyors may have climbed the route in 1855.

HIGH CAMP • Camp Schurman (9,460 feet) or Emmons Flats (9,800 feet).

Since this route is completely on glacier snow, it changes from year to year and season to season, depending on the snowfall, crevasses, and icefalls that determine access to the summit. From Emmons Flats, ascend southerly to the Corridor, a prominent snow slope with fewer crevasses and gentle slopes that rises higher than the rest of the Emmons Glacier. Enter the Corridor between 10,000 and 10,300 feet and ascend to 11,200 feet, where the route becomes steeper (30 to 35 degrees).

From 11,200 feet, the route may take a variety of directions. Ascend glacier slopes through crevasses and seracs, sometimes traversing onto the Winthrop Glacier. The Winthrop frequently has a smooth shoulder above 12,200 feet, with few crevasses and icefalls. This slope can also be icy and is frequently quite hard; carry pickets for use as running protection.

Between 13,500 and 13,700 feet, a bergschrund usually forms at the top of both the Emmons and Winthrop Glaciers. This always creates some fuss, and challenges climbers every year. At any time of the year, it may require downclimbing, steep and icy climbing, exposed traversing, and belays to access the final slopes and the crater rim at 14,250 feet. From the rim, it's a 15-minute walk to Columbia Crest.

Descent: Descend via the same route.

LITTLE TAHOMA

At 11,138 feet, Little Tahoma (commonly referred to as "Little T") weighs in as Washington State's third-highest summit. Its significance, however, is often

Little Tahoma, 11,138, and the Emmons Glacier as seen from Camp Schurman

dwarfed because it has such a popular neighbor, Mount Rainier. From Mount Rainier, Little T stands as an impressive sentinel of rock that divides the glaciers of Emmons and Ingraham. Climbers ascending one of Rainier's two most popular routes, the Disappointment Cleaver or Emmons/Winthrop Glacier, enjoy dramatic views of Little Tahoma's jagged west ridge and steep north face. Its silhouette has graced many beautiful sunrise pictures.

Getting There

In the winter or for early season climbs, the standard route is best reached from Paradise. See the introduction to Camp Muir routes, for directions on how to reach the Muir Snowfield. Later in the season, once the White River entrance to the national park is open, the route can also be approached from Fryingpan Creek. From the White River entrance, drive 2 miles to the park-

ing lot just beyond the Fryingpan Creek bridge at 3,800 feet. The trail begins across the highway.

Standard
Route

An ascent up Little Tahoma's standard route is relatively straightforward in clear weather. Climbers should be warned, however, that its rock should be viewed with distrust. Little Tahoma is actually the remains of a once-larger Mount Rainier. Eruptions, mudflows, and years of glaciation have eroded Rainier's original mass, leaving Little Tahoma a satellite peak. Therefore, its rock, like Rainier's, is volcanic, loose, and crumbly.

Despite these warnings, the climb is aesthetically pleasing and provides outstanding views of Rainier's east face. It's an excellent mountain to climb, when the weather is fierce up high. It is also a great ski descent in the early season.

Emmons Glacier

Ingraham Flats

Fryingpan Glacier

Camp Muir △

Anvil Rock

Whitman Glacier

Whitman Crest

① ② ②

ELEVATION GAIN • 7,400 feet from Fryingpan Creek to the summit; roughly 6,000 feet from Paradise to the summit.

WHAT TO EXPECT • Glacier travel; 30- to 40-degree snow and ice slopes, rockfall hazards. Grade II.

TIME • 2 to 3 days; 3 to 5 hours from Meany Crest to the summit, 2 to 3 hours for descent.

SEASON • Winter or early season via Paradise, early season through July via White River.

FIRST ASCENT • J.B. Flett, Henry H. Garrison; August 29, 1894 (via East Shoulder); first ski ascent by Paul Gilbreath and J. Wendell Trosper; April 1933.

HIGH CAMP • A variety are possible, Meany Crest (7,573 feet), Whitman Crest (9,300 feet), Ingraham/Whitman Glacier divide (8,800 feet) and Camp Muir (10,080 feet).

White River/FryingPan Creek approach: For the first 2 miles, the trail ascends gradually through old-growth forest to a point overlooking Fryingpan Creek, and at 3 miles passes a large avalanche debris zone. The last mile to Summerland (5,998 feet) follows a steep switchback through meadows that in season are rife with flowers. In early season, it's possible to ascend Meany Crest directly from Summerland. Later, it's better to continue above Summerland on the Wonderland trail for approximately one-third mile, leaving the trail near 6,100 feet to head uphill in a southwesterly direction. Skirt rocky cliffs on the right (northwest), while climbing south to Meany Crest (lots of nice campsites, with the possibility of running water), and then ascend southwesterly onto the eastern edge of Fryingpan Glacier near the high point of Meany Crest at 7,573 feet.

Ascend the Fryingpan Glacier in a southwesterly direction to a saddle just west of a high point on Whitman Crest. This marks the divide between the Fryingpan and the Whitman Glaciers. There is camping at the pass, or on the flats just west of the notch. This area can be icy late in the season.

Once through the notch (9,300 feet), head west and ascend the Whitman Glacier toward the summit of Little Tahoma. The slope angle gradually increases as you climb to the head of the glacier at approximately 10,300 feet. The final 800 feet of route, depending on the snow cover that year, ascends class 2-3 rock that is notoriously loose. Though the climbing is nontechnical, use caution, as nothing is trustworthy.

Paradise approach: From 8,600 feet on the Muir Snowfield, below Moon and Anvil Rocks, traverse northeast below Anvil Rock onto the upper Paradise Glacier. Once you've rounded Anvil Rock, continue to head northeast and traverse across the Cowlitz Glacier toward Cathedral Rocks, avoiding the crevasse fields below 8,400 feet. Cross Cathedral Rocks, a rock cleaver that divides

1. Route from Paradise to Little Tahoma

Ascending the final rock gullies towards Little Tahoma's summit

the Cowlitz Glacier from the Ingraham Glacier, at a gap near 8,450 feet. Once on the Ingraham, continue north and east across the glacier, as crevasses allow, toward a prominent notch near 8,800 feet, a few great camping sites exist there. Crossing through that notch leads one to the Whitman Glacier. Continue up the Whitman Glacier towards Little Tahoma's summit via the standard route.

Descent: Descend via the climbing route.

GLOSSARY

Alpine start. An early departure from camp. Climbers get up before dawn and try to complete the ascent before the heat of the day warms snow and ice and increases hazards.

Aspect. The exposure or direction a slope faces. The Emmons Glacier has a northeastern aspect, the Tahoma Glacier a southwestern.

Bergschrund. The uppermost crevasse at the top of a glacier. The bergschrund marks the point at which snow and ice break away from the snowcap and begin moving down the mountain. A bergschrund can pose a serious challenge as climbers try to cross over, through, or around it.

Bollard. A solid mound of snow fashioned by mountaineers to serve as an anchor for the rope.

Buttress. A broad, steep wall, usually below the end of a ridge.

Carry over. To carry all gear to the summit and then descend another route, with no intention of returning to high camp.

Cleaver. A prominent earthy or rocky ridge that divides (cleaves) two glaciers.

Col. A high pass between two summits. On Rainier, the word col generally refers to the low points between the mountain's three highest peaks: Columbia Crest, Liberty Cap, and Point Success.

Cornice. Wind-drifted snow piled on a ridge top and often overhanging; a cornice can break off and avalanche.

Couloir. A steep, deep chute usually filled with snow.

Crevasse. A crack or fracture in a glacier, sometimes hundreds of feet deep. Crevasses can be hidden by snow, making them a treacherous hazard. They change shape as the glacier flows down the slope.

Firn, or **névé.** Old glacial snow.

Fumarole. A vent or hole where hot volcanic gases escape, common along Rainier's summit crater rim.

Gendarme. A rock pinnacle; these features get their name from the French police known for standing straight, like pillars.

Glissading. Sliding on one's rear or feet on snow for a rapid descent; it is not recommended on glaciers.

Headwall. The beginning, or "head," of a cirque or basin. Generally a steep wall.

High camp. A high-altitude alpine site where climbers camp before moving on to the summit.

Silhouetted climber, Steamboat Prow

Icefall. A turbulent, broken section of a glacier, composed of crevasses, seracs, and other ever-changing snow features. An icefall typically forms where glaciers move down steep slopes. Icefall also can refer to falling ice, just as rockfall refers to falling rock.

Lenticular cloud. The lens-shaped cloud cap that frequents the summit of Mount Rainier. Formed by condensing moisture as it cools when rising over the summit, these clouds often precede bad weather.

Moat. The gap that is melted between a rock face and an adjoining snowfield or glacier. Moats can be deep, and difficult to cross.

Moraine. The rocky ridge at the base (terminal moraine) and sides (lateral moraine) of a glacier. Moraines, made of an unstable mix of rock and sand deposited by the glacier, mark the glacier's previous terminus.

Nunatak. A terrestrial "island" surrounded by a glacier.

Rime ice. Freezing, wind-blown moisture that collects against objects (rocks, gear, and clothing) and forms opaque ice crystals that extend into the windward side.

Rock band. A continuous rock formation, usually long and narrow. On Rainier, they frequently have snow slopes above and below.

Scree. Loose, rocky debris, usually below cliffs; scree makes for tough walking.

Serac. A large tower of ice and snow on a glacier. Seracs are usually found around or in icefalls. They make for great ice climbing, but they occasionally fall over, sometimes tumbling for thousands of feet down the glacier.

Short-rope. To tie a climber into the rope close behind a lead climber.

Spindrift. Loose, powdery snow that is easily windblown. Accumulated spindrift can be a substantial avalanche hazard.

Suncups. Melted depressions in the snow, appearing as large, cuplike waves; caused by wind and sun.

Talus. Loose, rocky debris, usually below cliffs; similar to scree, but larger.

Verglas. Rock covered with thin ice.

Wands. Markers used by climbers to indicate a route or cache of gear. These are typically 3-foot-long bamboo garden sticks with highly visible tape on the top.

Whiteout. A condition of limited visibility and flat, deceptive lighting caused by fog, clouds, or storms, preventing safe or accurate navigation and orientation.

SUGGESTED READING AND OTHER SOURCES OF INFORMATION

Barcott, Bruce. *The Measure of a Mountain: Beauty and Terror on Mount Rainier.* Seattle: Sasquatch Books, 1997.

Beckey, Fred. *Cascade Alpine Guide 1: Columbia River to Stevens Pass.* 3rd ed. Seattle: Mountaineers Books, 2000.

Cox, Steven M. and Kris Fulsaas editors. *Mountaineering: The Freedom of the Hills.* 7th ed. Seattle: Mountaineers Books, 2003.

McClung, David and Peter Schaerer. *The Avalanche Handbook.* 2nd ed. Seattle: Mountaineers Books, 1993.

Molenaar, Dee. *The Challenge of Rainier.* Seattle: The Mountaineers, 1979.

Selters, Andy. *Glacier Travel and Crevasse Rescue.* 2nd ed. Seattle: The Mountaineers Books. 1999.

Wilkerson, James. *Medicine for Mountaineering.* 5th ed. Seattle: The Mountaineers Books, 2001.

INFORMATION SOURCES

Mount Rainier National Park
Tahoma Woods
Star Route
Ashford, WA 98304-9751
360-569-2211
e-mail: *morainfo@nps.gov*
Climbing web site: *www.nps.gov/mora/climb/climb.htm*

HIGH-CAMP RESERVATIONS

360-569-4453
fax: 360-569-3131
e-mail: *mora_wilderness@nps.gov*

CAMPGROUND RESERVATIONS
(Cougar Rock and Ohanapecosh; July 1–Labor Day)

1-800-365-CAMP

HOTELS IN MOUNT RAINIER NATIONAL PARK
(Paradise Inn And National Park Inn)

Mount Rainier Guest Services
P.O. Box 108
Ashford, WA 98304
360-569-2275
www.guestservices.com/rainier

MOUNT RAINIER GUIDE SERVICES

Alpine Ascents International: 206-378-1927, *www.alpineascents.com*
American Alpine Institute: 360-671-1505, *www.mtnguide.com*
Cascade Alpine Guides: 800-981-0381, *www.cascadealpineguides.com*
Mount Rainier Alpine Guides: 360-569-2604, *www.rainierguides.com*
Rainier Mountaineering, Inc.: 360-569-2227, *www.rmiguides.com*

NORTHWEST WEATHER AND AVALANCHE CENTER

206-526-6677
www.nwac.noaa.gov

ABOUT THE UIAA

The UIAA is the international federation for climbing and mountaineering and is recognised by and works closely with the Olympic Movement, United Nations, and World Conservation Union. The UIAA promotes access for the freedom to enjoy mountaineering in a responsible way with minimum impact on the environment. Through a network of experts in 98 member associations in 68 different countries, the UIAA helps to protect mountain areas and climbing sites and encourages development for local communities. The UIAA has a Summit Charter and a dossier of proposals to promote cooperation and peace, protection of the environment, and sporting excellence. For further information visit *www.uiaa.ch*.

The UIAA encourages the inclusion of information in guidebooks that helps visitors from overseas to understand the most important information about local access, grades, and emergency procedures. The UIAA also encourages climbers and mountaineers to share knowledge and views on issues such as safety, ethics, and good practice in mountain sports. The UIAA is not responsible for, and accepts no liability for, the technical content or accuracy of the information in this guidebook. Climbing, hill walking, and mountaineering are activities with a danger of personal injury and death. Participants should be aware of, understand and accept these risks, and be responsible for their own actions and involvement.

INTERNATIONAL GRADE COMPARISON CHART

UIAA	USA	GB	F	D	AUS
V-	5.5	4a	5a	V	13
V	5.6	4b	5b	VI	14
V+	5.7	4c	5c	VI	14
VI-	5.8	4c	5c	VIIa	15
VI	5.9	5a	6a	VIIb	15
VI+	5.10a	5a	6a+	VIIc	16
VII-	5.10b	5b	6b	VIIIa	17
VII	5.10c	5b	6b+	VIIIb	18
VII+	5.10d	5c	6c	VIIIc	19
VIII-	5.11a	6a	6c+	IXa	20
	5.11b	6a	6c+	IXa	21
VIII	5.11c	6b	7a	IXb	22
	5.11d	6b	7a	IXb	23
VIII+	5.12a	6b	7a+	IXc	24
IX-	5.12b	6c	7b	Xa	25
	5.12c	6c	7b+	Xa	26
IX	5.12d	7a	7c	Xb	27
IX+	5.13a	7a	7c+	Xc	28
X-	5.13b	7b	8a	XIa	29
	5.13c	7b	8a+	XIa	30
X	5.13d	7b	8b	XIb	31
X+	5.14a		8b+		32
XI-	5.14b		8c		33
	5.14c		8c+		34
XI	5.14d		9a		

INDEX

ABOUT THE AUTHOR

Mike Gauthier started backpacking in the Washington wilderness at age eleven. He began his career in the National Park Service as a volunteer backcountry ranger in Olympic National Park in 1985 and joined the climbing staff at Mount Rainier in 1990. Now, he is the supervisor and program manager of mountaineering and search and rescue operations. Mike has summited Mount Rainier over 170 times by twenty-nine different routes, during all seasons. He conducts workshops in mountain and rope rescue techniques, cold weather survival skills, backcountry snowboarding, avalanche awareness and wilderness leadership. In 1998 he was designated a Wilderness Rescue Hero by the American Red Cross and was publicly recognized as one of America's twenty-five toughest men. In addition to his activities at Mount Rainier, he has led eight expeditions to Alaska, including Mount McKinley. He is an avid snowboarder, rock climber, and photographer. His photographic artwork is on permanent display in the National Park Inn in Longmire, Washington, and on the web at *www.crevasse.com*. Mike lives in Mount Rainier National Park.

ABOUT THE CONTRIBUTORS

Writer **Skip Card** grew up in Tacoma and spent his early years exploring Mount Rainier's trails and foothills. A recreational mountaineer, Card has climbed Rainier and most other Northwest volcanoes. In 1999, while a reporter for *The News Tribune* of Tacoma, he helped produce eight special sections commemorating Mount Rainier National Park's 100-year anniversary. He became *The News Tribune's* outdoor recreation writer in 2000 and spent the next several years extensively covering the park. Card cowrote the trail guide *Best Rain Shadow Hikes: Western Washington*. He now lives in Manhattan with his wife, Jean Margaret.

Paul Kennard has been banging about the glaciers at Mount Rainier for over twenty-five years. After the catastrophic eruption of Mount St. Helens in 1980, Paul lead a team whose goal was to measure the glacier ice on the major Cascade volcanoes for purposes of volcanic hazard recognition. This project culminated in his being awarded a master's degree in glaciology (or geophysics) from the University of Washington in Seattle. Currently, Paul is a fluvial geomorphologist—or river specialist—at Mount Rainier National Park. By order of the park's superintendent, glaciers are considered "frozen rivers,"and Paul is pleased to have them as part of his professional interest. He continues to participate in glacier research, including projects tracking the changes in glacier size and dynamics in response to climate change.

Dr. Jim Litch has climbed and guided several 8,000-meter peaks including Mount Everest. He is a veteran of twenty-two expeditions worldwide and seventy-eight ascents of Mount Rainier. A former climbing ranger for Mount Rainier and Denali National Parks, Jim has worked rescues on five continents. Active as a lecturer, he has published articles on high-altitude medicine. Jim lived in the Himalaya for five years, two of them above 13,000 feet in the Mount Everest region, where he ran a hospital, clinics, and a community health program. Jim travels and practices high-altitude medicine while working on international health projects as a clinical assistant professor at the University of Washington.

Mark Moore became interested in snow and mountain weather as a professional ski patroller in the early 1970s. After obtaining a master's degree in atmospheric sciences, Mark helped found the Northwest Weather and Avalanche Center in Seattle and has been its director since 1988. He has been an instructor at the U.S. National Avalanche School, Northwest Avalanche Institute, American Avalanche Institute, and Alaska Avalanche School and has authored numerous articles on mountain weather and avalanches. An avid skier, snowboarder, and outdoor enthusiast, he likes to experience what he forecasts—right or wrong.

Eric Simonson has climbed Mount Rainier every year since 1970 and has nearly three hundred ascents to his credit. Over the years his job as a co-owner of International Mountain Guides has taken him on about one hundred expeditions worldwide; he led the Mallory and Irvine Research Expedition in 1999 and has climbed the Seven Summits. When he's not off doing an expedition or lecturing about leading expeditions, he enjoys teaching mountaineering skills to a new generation of guides and climbers. Eric lives in Ashford and Tacoma with his wife Erin and is looking forward to someday climbing Mount Rainier with his young daughter Audrey.

THE MOUNTAINEERS, founded in 1906, is a nonprofit outdoor activity and conservation club, whose mission is "to explore, study, preserve, and enjoy the natural beauty of the outdoors. . . . " Based in Seattle, Washington, the club is now the third-largest such organization in the United States, with seven branches throughout Washington State.

The Mountaineers sponsors both classes and year-round outdoor activities in the Pacific Northwest, which include hiking, mountain climbing, ski-touring, snowshoeing, bicycling, camping, kayaking and canoeing, nature study, sailing, and adventure travel. The club's conservation division supports environmental causes through educational activities, sponsoring legislation, and presenting informational programs.

All club activities are led by skilled, experienced instructors, who are dedicated to promoting safe and responsible enjoyment and preservation of the outdoors.

If you would like to participate in these organized outdoor activities or the club's programs, consider a membership in The Mountaineers. For information and an application, write or call The Mountaineers, Club Headquarters, 300 Third Avenue West, Seattle, WA 98119; 206-284-6310. You can also visit the club's website at *www.mountaineers.org* or contact The Mountaineers via email at *clubmail@mountaineers.org.*

The Mountaineers Books, an active, nonprofit publishing program of the club, produces guidebooks, instructional texts, historical works, natural history guides, and works on environmental conservation. All books produced by The Mountaineers Books fulfill the club's mission.

Send or call for our catalog of more than 500 outdoor titles:

The Mountaineers Books
1001 SW Klickitat Way, Suite 201
Seattle, WA 98134
800-553-4453
mbooks@mountaineersbooks.org
www.mountaineersbooks.org

The Mountaineers Books is proud to be a corporate sponsor of The Leave No Trace Center for Outdoor Ethics, whose mission is to promote and inspire responsible outdoor recreation through education, research, and partnerships. The Leave No Trace program is focused specifically on human-powered (nonmotorized) recreation.
Leave No Trace strives to educate visitors about the nature of their recreational impacts, as well as offer techniques to prevent and minimize such impacts. Leave No Trace is best understood as an educational and ethical program, not as a set of rules and regulations.
For more information, visit *www.LNT.org,* or call 800-332-4100.